the
cookie
cookbook

the

cool

cookbook

the cookie cookbook

by

deloris kitchel clem

Castle Books, New York

To

Mary Ann Leone Hummelman

acknowledgments

Words, spoken or printed, are inadequate to express my sincere thanks to the individuals, groups, and companies who have helped me in the lengthy (but pleasant) task of collecting cookie recipes, researching, and writing this cookie cookbook.

A very special "thank you" belongs to Mary Morgan, regional home economist for Lucky Stores, Inc., La Mesa, California, for her answers to so many questions pertaining to the food products that go into creating cookies and for permission to use some of her delightful recipes.

Also, a special "thank you" belongs to the staff of the Diamond Walnut Kitchen and the Diamond Walnut Growers, Inc., Stockton, California, for providing three exclusive recipes for this cookie cookbook. The recipes are Walnut Tea-Time Dainties, Walnut-Orange Refrigerator Cookies, and Candied Walnut Balls. I'm grateful to these people for permission to use other delightful recipes devel-

7

oped in their test kitchen and for being so helpful with research problems.

Another special "thank you" must be extended to Mrs. Joanne W. Hill, program director of the San Diego, California, office of the Dairy Council of California, and to the staffs of the National Dairy Council, the American Dairy Association, and the American Butter Institute, all of Chicago, Illinois, for their valuable assistance in researching information pertaining to butter, milk, cream, and other dairy products that are so necessary to cookies.

If I attempted to name each individual and company that has helped me during the past five years to develop my private collection of recipes into a cookie cookbook containing not only my favorite recipes, but those of many American housewives, it would become a trying task for the writer and the reader. For this reason, I'll confine my appreciation—as much as possible.

The staffs of Dudley-Anderson-Yutzy, New York, New York; Daniel J. Edelman and Associates, Inc., and Wheat Flour Institute, both of Chicago, Illinois; and the Western Beet Sugar Producers, Inc., Los Angeles, California, have supplied many of the interesting little-known facts about the history of cookies and the food products that go into making cookies that appear in this cookie book. I shall be personally indebted forever to these wonderful people, whom I have never met. Also, I shall be indebted always to the staffs of California Raisin Advisory Board, Fresno, California; Florida Citrus Commission, Fruit Orange, Florida; General Foods Kitchens and The Nestlé Company, Inc., both of White Plains, New York; Pan-American Coffee Bureau, New York, New York; The Pillsbury Company, Minneapolis, Minnesota; The ReaLemon Company, Chicago, Illinois; Robertshaw Controls Company, Youngwood, Pennsylvania; Sun-Maid Raisin Growers of California, Kingsburg, California; Swift and Company, Chicago, Illinois; and United Fruit Company, Boston, Massachusetts.

Other companies to whom I am grateful for the time and effort their staffs extended to supply information and recipes for this cookie book include: American Honey Institute, Madison, Wisconsin; The Borden Company, New York, New York; Corning Glass Works, Corning, New York; Dole Corporation, San Jose, California; General Electric Company, Louisville, Kentucky; Hiram Walker Incorporated, Detroit, Michigan; Master Newspaper Syndicate, Inc., New York, New York; Grocery Products Division, Abbott Laboratories, North Chicago, Illinois; The Quaker Oats Company, Chicago, Illinois; Tappan Company, Mansfield, Ohio; The Taylor Wine Company, Inc., Hammondsport, New York; and WearEver Aluminum, Inc., New Kensington, Pennsylvania.

Among the many individuals who have been so helpful and deserve much more than a simple word of thanks are: Mrs. Lennie (Mary) Hummelman, Chula Vista, California; Mrs. Jeannette Branin, San Diego, California; Mrs. R. A. (Agatha) Haring and Mrs. John McCarthy, both of Wichita, Kansas; Mrs. E. T. (Eleanor) Nelson, Augusta, Kansas; Mrs. Alma Long, Eureka, Kansas; Mrs. Mell (Vera) Buxton, Mrs. G. C. Cast, Mrs. E. A. (Elaine) Fetting, Mrs. Percy (Nettie S.) Fullinwider, Mrs. Mertin (Lucille) Jennerjohn, Mrs. Arnold Kahler, Mrs. Clyde J. Klemp, Mrs. Rose Korte, Mrs. T. (Mike) Leber, Mrs. H. Shelby Lee, Mrs. Pearl Mathews, Mrs. Percy C. (Doris K.) Menning, Mrs. Carl (Dorothy) Neidhold, Mrs. Herman (Bert) Schulze, and Mrs. W. H. (Edna) Wulk, all of Appleton, Wisconsin; and Mrs. John (Irehne) Budzien, Milwaukee, Wisconsin.

The thanks a writer extends to her typist and clerical

---

assistant is never sufficient, but must be expressed—this time to Miss Claire Harling and Mrs. William (Patricia) Clay, both of San Diego, California.

Most of all I wish to express my heartfelt thanks to Mrs. Grace Thrasher Kitchel Treat, my mother, and Mrs. Nancy Ode Thrasher, my maternal grandmother, both of Cotter, Arkansas, for teaching me how to bake cookies—even as a child.

Another big "thank you" must be extended to Billy Mack Clem, my husband, who has been so patient and understanding about all the notes and recipes cluttering our home.

DELORIS KITCHEL CLEM,
Santa Clara, California.

contents

12 THE COOKIE COOKBOOK

PART III: COOKIE RECIPES

introduction

In many children's books of verse there is a little poem about a cat singing praise and giving thanks to a milk pitcher for its delightful contents. This happy, contented cat has no idea that the cow in the field actually is responsible for the delectable fluid inside the milk pitcher. This is the way most children are about Mother's cookie jar.

The children come dashing home from school or play looking for something to satisfy their active appetites; so, they reach into the cookie jar with a comment or thought of praise—for the cookie jar. Seldom do they realize all the time and effort that Mother spends to fill that cookie jar for their delight.

Everything has a history, even cookies. However, the history of cookies is obscure. The most definite thing known in regard to the history of cookies is how the word itself evolved. It came from the Dutch word *"koekje,"* which was formed from the Dutch word *"koek"* (cake). Who made the first cookie and when it was served is unknown; however, it is believed by some historians that some of the first cookies to be baked were known as Simnel Cakes and were served in England during the Sixteenth Century. Many old cookbooks contain recipes for small cakes, which resemble our modern recipes for cookies. The old-fashioned recipes required many eggs, but this was due to the fact that eggs served as a leavening agent before the development of baking powder and soda.

Making cookies was much more difficult for the Colonial American "goodwife" than for today's homemaker. She was responsible for churning the cream to make the butter. She had to obtain the sugar by snipping it from hard ten-pound loaves. The equipment she used in preparing the ingredients was not ideal: she had to use cloth to sift the flour and small twigs to beat the eggs.

One of the favorite cookie recipes in Colonial America was for Butter Drop-Do (or Dough) Cookies. Since it took the early "goodwife" so much time and effort to prepare these and other cookies, it is no wonder that she developed the habit of sharing her baked cookies and recipes.

As America developed and the populace traveled more, the proprietors of roadside inns began offering cookies and other baked goodies as part of the regular fare. Approximately 20 years ago, the Toll House Inn in Whitman, Massachusetts, added pieces of chocolate chopped from a candy bar to the old colonial Butter Drop-Do Cookies; thus the all-time favorite Toll House Cookies were developed. There continue to be many variations made to this chocolate chip recipe by today's homemakers.

Although the history of cookies is sparse, through the centuries hundreds of cookie recipes have been developed from the old-fashioned small cakes. These recipes have been shared and passed from one family to another, one neighbor to another, and one generation to another. Each family, neighbor, and generation has changed the exchanged recipes until today there are dozens of variations for a certain cookie recipe, such as the sugar cookie. Today, the exchanging and varying of cookie recipes still continues.

Regardless of the thousands of cookie recipes, actually there are only three basic types:

1. Thin batter
2. Soft dough
3. Stiff dough

Thin-batter recipes are for bars and squares. This type of recipe is extremely simple and quick to prepare. Thin-batter recipes resemble cake batter, except the batter is poured into large square or rectangular pans, causing the batter to spread very thin over the surface of the baking pans. After baking, thin-batter recipes should be cut immediately, thus becoming tiny bars and squares that can be piled easily and conveniently into the cookie jar.

Soft-dough recipes are for drop cookies. These recipes are easy and usually quick to prepare. Once the soft dough has been mixed, the dough is dropped directly from a spoon, preferably a teaspoon, onto a glossy, sideless baking sheet. If thick, moist cookies are desired, the dough should not be pressed after it has been dropped onto the baking sheet. Instead, the dough should be dropped onto the baking sheet, and placed directly into a preheated oven. If slightly crisp cookies are desired, the soft dough should be dropped onto a shiny baking sheet, then flattened—with the bottom of a glass, or with the tines of a fork that have been dipped in flour. As soon as the soft dough has been flattened, the baking sheet should be placed directly into a preheated oven.

Stiff-dough recipes are for rolled, refrigerator, pressed, and formed cookies. These recipes are more difficult and time-consuming to prepare than thin-batter or soft-dough recipes. Nevertheless, the "eating" rewards of these various recipes are worth the extra effort—especially during the holidays or for special teas, parties, and dinners. Also, stiff-dough recipes can be varied many, many ways through the method of cutting, decorating, or frosting.

Rolled cookies are made by rolling the stiff dough on a dough board and cutting into desired shapes before placing on a bright, shiny baking sheet and baking in a preheated oven. Refrigerator cookies are made by forming stiff dough into rolls, wrapping in waxed paper, and chilling in the refrigerator until ready to slice and bake. Refrigerator cookies can be pressed into a butter carton, small loaf pan, refrigerator tray, or some container with a shape desired. The thinner the slice from chilled refrigerator cookie dough, the crisper the cookie.

Pressed cookies are made by placing stiff dough into a cookie press (the dough must not contain nuts or fruits); the dough is pressed from the cookie press onto a shiny baking sheet and placed in a preheated oven to bake. Formed cookies are made by molding small bits of the stiff dough between palms of the hands and placing on a shiny baking sheet. Formed cookies should be baked in a preheated oven.

The finished product of these three basic types of recipes (thin batter, soft dough, and stiff dough) have numerous advantages over cakes, pies, and other desserts. For one thing, cookies are usually much simpler to eat and not as messy as a "hunk" of cake or a "wedge" of pie. Cookies can be kept unrefrigerated over a much longer period of time than cakes or pies. Besides, when cookies dry out they can be popped into a warm oven for a few moments and they come out fresh as can be desired. Certain types of cookies, such as honey-molasses, are tastier after they have been baked, stored in air-tight containers a week or two, and then eaten.

Another great advantage of cookies over cakes, pies, and other desserts is the fact that cookie recipes can be varied at great lengths without causing a complete failure. This gives housewives a chance to be creative and individualistic in their baking. What unprofessional chef, with a limited food budget, dares to vary cakes and pastries?

Words cannot express the pleasure and satisfaction many housewives derive from baking and serving cookies to families and friends. A housewife doesn't have to be a "born baker" to make successful, tasty cookies. All she needs is a recipe, the necessary ingredients, and a desire to bake a batch of cookies. If she happens to get a little too much flour, sugar, shortening, raisins, or some other ingredient, the results will not be disastrous. A batch of edible cookies will be the reward for her efforts. The cookies may not be perfect, but that delightful taste that only cookies have will be produced.

No matter what the reason may be for baking cookies, any housewife should be sure to bake enough to fill the cookie jars in her kitchen. And, if there aren't any cookie jars in her kitchen, by all means she should get some immediately and let her family experience one of the great pleasures of life: reaching into the cookie jar in Mother's kitchen and wondering just what kind of cookies will be found today.

All housewives would be wise to take one precaution regarding cookies. That is: don't bake the same cookie recipes over and over again. This will create a dislike for cookies sooner than anything. For those housewives having only one or two favorite recipes, this collection of favorite recipes from many families, neighbors, and friends has been prepared. These recipes are for sharing; and the finished products are for sharing, too.

PART I

ingredients of cookies

1. flour

Flour is to a cookie what thread is to a garment. Flour "seams" all the ingredients in a cookie recipe together.

Flour, used in baking, is made from wheat, rye, rice, barley, oats, and maize. These grains have been growing since prehistoric times. Ancient civilizations in Europe and Asia Minor used wheat and barley in their diets, while the ancient Mayas and others in the New World used maize, often known as Indian corn.

WHEAT

With the passing of time and a continuously increasing population throughout the world, man learned to cultivate and mill the grains. Wheat has become one of the most important flour grains today, especially throughout the areas inhabited by the white race. The annual flour-milling capacity for the United States alone is over twenty-five billion pounds. In fact, wheat flour has been called the main-

21

stay of the American diet, just as rice has often been referred to as the mainstay of the Oriental diet.

Back when America was being colonized, wheat was already one of the staple grains in many European countries. However, the early colonists had to be content with maize, which the Indians taught them to cultivate, harvest, dry, and pound into a meal. This meal was the basic ingredient for their bread—journey-cake. Today these journey-cakes are called corn cakes or johnny-cakes.

The early settlers in America craved yeast bread like they had eaten in Europe; therefore, within a surprisingly short period of time, the settlers brought seeds of wheat and other grains to the colonies. They sowed, harvested, and milled the wheat in water mills that sprung up along the banks of rapid streams.

MILLING

During the early days of milling in America, the mills were called grist mills. The mills were within hauling distance of the farmland where the grains were harvested. Flour was made from the grains, mainly wheat, by being ground between large flat circular stones. These stones had ridges that aided in the grinding action and had to be recut when they wore smooth.

Invention of steam power resulted in better methods of milling, which is continued today in large milling companies. Heavy power machinery, operated by steam, mills wheat, corn, rye, buckwheat, and barley. Through the modern process of milling wheat, the grains are crushed again and again, sifted until the bran (the dark protective coating) and the embryo (the wheat germ) have been removed. Since bran is dark and coarse, the removal of it makes flour whiter and finer. The embryo is dark and oily; therefore, it has to be removed during the milling process, because it will cause flour to spoil.

The milling industry has learned, as a result of the great development and interest in nutrition during the 1930's, that milling wheat into a fine white flour results in the loss of many valuable minerals and vitamins. Through research, the milling industry has learned how to replace these minerals and vitamins—after the wheat has been milled and processed into a fine white flour. The replacement of these minerals and vitamins is called "flour enrichment."

FLOUR ENRICHMENT

The U.S. government has established standards for enriching ingredients in flour and has made it compulsory that flour used in commercially-baked products be enriched. More than half of the state governments in the U.S. have passed laws making it mandatory that all white flour sold commercially be enriched—to protect the health of its people.

The final stage of the milling process is very important. It is during this phase that flour is treated to improve its appearance, baking qualities, and nutritional value. For example, flour in its natural color has a yellow tinge; however, gases are used to bleach it to a clean, snowy white. The bleaching process can make the flour age sooner; but the milling industry, through standards set by the U.S. government, has found means of preventing aging.

In food value, wheat lags far behind many food items. The reason for this is that the amount of amino acids in wheat proteins is very small, compared to animal proteins. Only small quantities of Vitamin A and Vitamin B are to be found in flour. Whole wheat flour contains much energy value and vitamins; however, this type of flour spoils very easily. Consumer preference for white flour has limited the manufacturing of whole wheat flour.

The edible fats and oils, sugar, and other ingredients used in a cookie recipe contain the food value that flour lacks. This is one of the main reasons all these various ingredients combine so well into such tasty cookies.

The term flour actually means flower or best part. Although there are many kinds of flour (wheat flour, whole wheat flour, rye flour, buckwheat flours, etc.), the term has come to be understood as meaning wheat flour.

TYPES OF FLOUR

To make the world of cookery even more challenging, seven main groups of flours are milled and sold commercially. Each of these are milled for special uses in baking. These flours are: all-purpose flour, cake flour, self-rising flour, bread flour, pastry flour, macaroni flour, and the speciality flours.

All-purpose flour is the most popular in the average homemaker's kitchen. This flour is milled especially for use in preparation of cookies, bread, and cakes (except angel food cakes). During the milling process, this type of flour has been blended so that it will give satisfactory results in all general household recipes. No matter what recipe (requiring flour) is used, all other ingredients must be added when all-purpose flour is used.

When emergencies arise, all-purpose flour can be substituted for cake flour. Two tablespoons less all-purpose flour should be used than the amount of cake flour required in the recipe. *Caution:* cake flour should never be substituted for all-purpose flour, if satisfactory results are wanted. All-purpose flour is also called general-purpose or family flour by some milling companies.

Cake flour is the most fine-textured flour on the market. It is milled specially for making the lightest cakes. Although the protein content is low in cake flour, this flour is the preferred ingredient for cake baking. All other ingredients must be added to this flour. Cake flour is not recommended for use in the average cookie recipe.

Self-rising flour is milled specially for biscuit making. The main difference between this flour and the others is that salt and baking powder have been added to self-rising flour during the milling process. A recipe requiring self-rising flour should be followed exactly—the leavening ingredients have been pre-proportioned in the flour, so substitution by the average homemaker would be unwise.

Since the salt and baking powder have been blended into self-rising flour, a homemaker can save time by using this type of flour when making bar cookies. The right blend of leavening and flour has been accomplished; therefore, the homemaker can save measuring and blending time. If self-rising flour is substituted for all-purpose flour, caution should be taken to omit salt and baking powder required in the recipe.

Bread flour is milled primarily for bakeries. One great advantage of using this type of flour is that the protein content is fairly high. Bread flour is extremely good for the preparation of yeast breads.

Pastry flour is milled specially for pastry recipes. This particular flour is used chiefly in commercial baking. Pastry flour is milled almost as finely as cake flour, and it is low in protein.

Macaroni flour is milled specially for making macaroni, spaghetti, and noodles commercially. This type of flour is high in protein.

Speciality flours include such flours as whole wheat and

rye. These flours are used to obtain particular flavors and textures in a recipe. When a recipe requires one of the speciality flours, no other type of flour should be substituted. A speciality flour should *never, never* be substituted in a recipe requiring all-purpose flour, cake flour, or any of the other flours.

A speciality flour should never be used in a cookie recipe unless the recipe specifies it. A speciality flour does not require sifting before measuring. Whole wheat flour, which is one of the speciality flours, is also known as entire wheat and graham flour.

MEASUREMENT

Sifting and accurate measurement of flour is a must. The biggest reason, according to a staff member of a large flour company, is to make the recipe turn out right. Too much flour in a cookie recipe will cause the cookie dough to be hard to handle and shape, and the finished product to be dry and hard. Not enough flour in a cookie dough will cause the dough to spread during the baking process.

In order to get accurate measurements of flour, the flour *must be sifted just before measuring*. Sifting aerates the flour and makes it measure more; therefore, if a recipe requires one cup of sifted flour and one cup of unsifted flour is "dumped" into the mixing bowl, one cup plus a few tablespoons of flour is being used. Flour should never be sifted into the canister with the idea that it won't need sifting later when being used in a recipe. Why? Because flour sifted into the canister will pack during storage, just as it packs while being sacked and stored on the grocer's shelves.

After flour has been sifted, it should be measured into one of the standard measuring cups that has the one-cup marking at the rim. This will make accurate measurement easier to obtain; also, level measurement will be simpler to make. The sifted flour should be spooned lightly into the measuring cup up to the necessary measurement line. Caution should be taken not to pack or shake the cup. To get a level measurement without causing the sifted flour to pack, the flour should be leveled gently with a spatula or the straight edge of a knife.

The sifter is one key to success in correct measurement of flour for any cookie recipe. Thus, extreme care should be taken to keep the flour sifter clean. This can be done very easily by storing it properly. Each time the sifter is used, the excess flour should be dusted off with a clean dish towel; it should be placed in a clean paper sack or some other container and stored until ready for re-use. Cover the sifter before storing so it will not collect dust or grease.

To determine if a cookie recipe is requiring approximately the proper amount of flour, it helps to know exactly how much liquid is required per cup of flour to make a particular type of batter or dough. For example, to make a soft dough three cups of flour should be used with one cup of liquid. To make a stiff dough, four cups of flour should be used with one cup of liquid; pour batter, one cup of flour to one cup liquid; drop batter and sponge batter, two cups of flour to one cup of liquid.

Flour can be used in various ways to help expedite cookie baking. For example, a knife being used to cut refrigerator dough can be kept clean of any excess dough by being dipped in flour as necessary. Of course, the knife can be chilled in the refrigerator at the same time the refrigerator cookie dough is being chilled. Regardless of how the knife is prepared, it should be a thin, sharp, clean knife to get the best results.

Extra flour will tend to make cookies tough. For this

reason, care should be taken to use flour sparingly during the handling, rolling, and making of rolled cookie recipes.

Flour should be stored in a bin or a covered canister.

2. sugar

Sugar is one of the basic ingredients of any cookie recipe. There are several reasons why it is important enough to be one of the basic ingredients.

First, sugar is the ingredient that makes cookies taste sweet. Second, it aids in the browning of cookies. Third, it is important to the process which makes "crisp cookies crisp and chewy cookies chewy."

Not only is sugar important to the success of cookie recipes, it is of great value to man. In fact, sugar is that food item which provides man with heat and energy for his body. Besides, it is one of the tastiest foods eaten by man.

PRODUCT OF NATURE

Sugar is a product of nature. This food substance is manufactured by growing plants. Actually, it is manufactured in the green leaves of plants by a process known as photosynthesis.

This process begins with the roots of plants absorbing water from the soil in which they are growing. The water surges upward through the stem of the plant and out into the leaves. In the meantime, carbon dioxide enters the plant through the plant's pores. Through this action of absorbing water and carbon dioxide, the plant obtains three chemical ingredients of sugar: hydrogen, oxygen, and carbon.

Many plants produce sugar; however, the two most important sources of sugar today are sugar cane and sugar beet. A third important source of this fuel is the maple tree. Minor sources include grapes, corn, wood, date, and nipa palm.

Cane sugar supplies are furnished mainly by Cuba and India. Other sugar cane producing countries are Brazil, the Hawaiian Islands, and the Phillippines. A tropical climate is needed to grow sugar cane.

Beet sugar is produced in most European countries, in the Near East, Far East, and Americas. It is grown extensively in twenty-two states in the United States. The reason for the widespread production of beet sugar is that the sugar beet will grow in temperate zones, whereas sugar cane must be confined to tropical zones.

For years home economists have been testing sugar. Through hundreds of tests they have proven that sugar produced by the plants of cane and beet are equal in sweetness, purity, whiteness, and fineness. Each sugar gives the same results in all types of cookery and each is of equal value for table use.

HISTORY

The history of sugar is as ancient as the history of man. Also, its history is as involved as the history of man and man's world. The first men found their source of sugar energy in honey and plants containing sugar, which were the first known sources of concentrated sugar.

It is believed that sugar cane and its sugar product originated in India; however, the history of sugar is older than recorded history.

During the fourth century the process of crystallizing sugar was discovered in Europe. During that century the crystals served mainly for medical purposes. It was a thousand years before man discovered a refining process which produced the type of sugar used in modern cooking.

Since that time man has worked continually to improve sugar. It wasn't until the fifteenth century that man actually began producing sugar commercially. Today, great sugar plantations, processing plants, and distribution centers are to be found all over the world.

One of the first bills to be passed by the First Congress of the United States concerned sugar. This bill was a raw sugar tariff of one cent a pound and was enacted in 1789. Although the rates varied, this law remained in force until 1890.

Again in 1894 Congress enacted another sugar tariff, which was the only implement of national sugar policy until 1934. Between the two sugar tariffs, Congress required a bounty of two cents on each pound of domestically-produced sugar.

The period between 1894 and 1934 was an eventful one for the sugar industry. Mainly, it was a period of ups and downs. It was a chaotic period for the sugar traders and consumers alike. Prices changed constantly from stable to high to low to temporary stability and then to long periods of depression.

Problems of the sugar industry were solved through the enactment of the Jones-Costigan Act, which became an effective law of the United States on May 9, 1934. This act was amended in 1937 and the name was changed to the Sugar Act. Since 1937 this Sugar Act has been re-enacted and amended numerous times; nevertheless, the fundamental principles and techniques are the same: to provide an ample supply of sugar to Americans, and at reasonable prices; to encourage foreign sugar trade; and to maintain a healthy economic climate for the sugar industry.

NUTRITION

Carbohydrates are among food classes considered by food researchers as essential to the human body. The other classes, which have been divided according to their chemical composition, are proteins, fats, minerals, and vitamins.

Since sugar is a pure carbohydrate, it is therefore a concentrated energy food. Carbohydrates provide the human body with a source of energy. Sugar can supply energy faster than any other food. Within five minutes after sugar has been consumed by a human, the body begins to use it.

Research chemists are learning a lot of new things about sugar and its nutritional role. For one, sugar actually can be an aid to reducing. A three-year study made by Harvard's Department of Nutrition proved that overweight people who quit eating sugar completely lost no more weight than those who continued to eat sugar while dieting. In fact, it has been learned that dieting is effective only when a person cuts down on the total quantity of food—not by cutting any particular food out of his diet completely.

After years of extensive research, chemists have failed to support the belief that sugar is responsible for the decaying of teeth. Scientists have arrived at the conclusion that healthy teeth require a nutritionally balanced diet that will promote general health. Sugar's important role in nutrition is that it provides the human body with the required amount of energy. Besides, sugar tastes good and it counteracts unpleasant flavors of other foods, such as chocolate.

MEASUREMENT

Correct measurement is of utmost importance in the cookie making process. This is as true for the measurement of sugar as it is for flour or any other ingredient.

Sugar is measured proportionately to other ingredients in cookie recipes. Since the recipes have been developed by home economists in test kitchens throughout the United States, a wise homemaker will not tamper with the sugar measurement of recipes. Too much or too little sugar will change the sweetness, texture, tenderness, and grain of cookies.

When measuring sugar, it is best to use a standard measuring cup that can be purchased at department and hardware stores throughout the United States. The large measuring cups, such as those holding two-cup measures, will save time during the mixing process.

Sift granulated sugar before measuring if it happens to be lumpy. To measure sugar, spoon it lightly into a dry measuring cup. After spooning the sugar into the cup, level it off with a straight-edged knife. It is not necessary to knock or tap the cup to pack the sugar.

Measure confectioners' sugar by the same method; however, if confectioners' sugar is lumpy, press it through a sieve before measuring.

Brown sugar should be pressed through a sieve to remove any lumps before measuring. Also, lumps can be removed from brown sugar by heating the sugar (in the box) in a 250°F. oven about fifteen minutes and then pressing lumps with a rolling pin. To prevent brown sugar from becoming hard and lumpy, store in the refrigerator. When measuring brown sugar, pack it into a dry measuring cup; level off with a straight-edged knife.

3. edible fats and oils

Edible fats and oils consist of: lard, butter, margarine, shortening, salad and cooking oils. All of these are derived from animal fats or vegetable oils. These fats and oils are of the utmost importance to man's diet. Besides adding flavor and texture to food, these fats and oils give man one of the most concentrated sources of energy.

Lard and butter are animal fats. Lard is made from the fatty tissues of pork, while butter is made by the churning of cream.

Margarine, shortening, salad and cooking oils are vegetable oils. These vegetable oils come from seeds and seed coats of certain plants. Cotton seed and soybean oils are the main ones used in the preparation of cooking oils.

REFINING TECHNIQUES

Before refining techniques evolved, edible fats and oils were used by man just as rendered from animal tissues or pressed from seeds. Due to this factor, animal fats were used mainly by the inhabitants of northern climates, while vegetable oils were the main source of cooking oils for inhabitants of the world's tropical and semi-tropical regions.

Methods of refining have increased and improved as a result of consumer demand. Rendering is the process by which animal fats are separated from the fatty tissues of pork and beef. Three main methods of rendering animal fats are the wet or steam process, dry rendering, and the open kettle method.

During the wet or steam process of rendering, the fatty tissues are trimmed from pork (lard) or beef (suet) and heated under pressure; the cells rupture, thereby liberating the fat. In dry rendering, fatty tissues are trimmed from pork or beef, placed in jacketed drums which are under agitation, and heated until the fat erupts and drains from the tissues. In the open kettle method of rendering, which is the least used of the three rendering methods, fatty tissues of pork or beef are trimmed, placed in open steam-jacketed kettles, and heated until the fat escapes from the cells.

SEPARATING VEGETABLE OILS

Vegetable oils are derived from seeds and seed coats of plants through three methods: hydraulic pressing, screw pressing, or solvent extraction. Cells containing the vegetable oil must be ruptured by heat, mechanical methods, or both, before the oil can be separated from other materials within the seeds or seed coats.

In hydraulic pressing, oil is separated from other materials by placing the seeds or seed coats in mechanical or hydraulic presses and pressing. However, prior to this process, the seeds or seed coats must be cleaned of all lint, hulled, flaked through movement between rollers, and steam cooked.

During the screw pressing method, flakes or cracked meats of the seeds are heated and passed through screws in cages or barrels until the oil is pressed out. Through the solvent extraction method, solvents are used to extract oil from flaked meat of the seeds. In order to obtain oils through this method, petroleum hydrocarbons usually are boiled continuously between 140° to 160°F.

There is an extensive list of the various types of edible fats and oils that are used in modern kitchens. Nevertheless, those that are of the greatest value in the baking of cookies are butter, margarine, and shortening.

It is true that hydrogenated oils, oleomargarine, lard, chicken or goose fat can be substituted for butter or shortening in cookie recipes. If lard is used as a substitute, 1/5 less the quantity required in the recipe should be used. Lard is excellent for tart-type cookie recipes. Oleomargarine is one of the best substitutes for all types of cookie recipes. When substituting oleomargarine or any of the others mentioned above, except lard, the same quantity as required in the recipe should be measured.

BUTTER

Butter is a real favorite with cookie bakers, because it has a zestful, natural flavor, which is not lost during the baking process. The distinctive flavor butter imparts to freshly baked cookies matures as the cookies are stored. Along with the smooth flavor, butter gives a uniformly fine texture to cookies; also, butter provides cookies with a distinctive yellow color, which cannot be obtained through the use of any other edible fat or oil.

The keeping qualities of cookies baked with butter is much greater than cookies baked with other fats and oils. In fact, cookies prepared with butter (when stored properly

—kept cool in a covered jar, canister, or foil wrapping) will remain moist for weeks. For this reason alone, butter is the perfect choice of fat to use for baking large quantities of cookies for storing weeks prior to Christmas or other holidays.

The nutritive value of butter is extremely great. Almost 100 per cent of butterfat can be digested easily. Butter is a rich source of natural Vitamin A, and it contains the sunshine Vitamin D. Vitamin A helps man to grow, to have healthy eyes and skin, and to keep tissues healthy enough to resist infections.

Butter should be kept clean, cool, and covered. It should be kept in the coldest part of the refrigerator, and it should be left wrapped in the original package. No more than $\frac{1}{4}$ to $\frac{1}{2}$ pound of butter should be removed from the original package and placed in a covered butter dish. The remainder should be stored in the freezing compartment of the refrigerator until ready to be used. When not being used, the butter dish containing butter should be stored in the refrigerator.

In its original package, butter can be stored in the freezing compartment of the refrigerator for as long as one month. However, for a longer period of time it is desirable to wrap the butter in moistureproof, vaporproof freezer packaging material and to freeze it solid until ready for use. This helps protect the flavor and freshness of the butter.

The history of butter is believed to have begun more than 2000 years before the Christian era. A story has been told about a nomad riding across the desert of the Middle East with a goatskin of milk. At the end of the journey, he tried to take a sip of milk from the goatskin; however, to his dismay, he discovered the heat and jostling had churned the milk, causing a golden yellow product (known today as butter) to rise to the surface. Before butter became widely accepted as a food, it was regarded as a sign of wealth and was stored in the earth with trees planted above to mark the spot.

SHORTENING

Shortening is excellent for cookie recipes, because it makes cookies crisp and crunchy, or chewy—depending on the amount of shortening used in the recipe. Also, it makes cookies more tender. The outstanding qualities of shortening, each making it a perfect ingredient for cookie baking, are: it is white, odorless, and tasteless; it is easy to measure, cream, and beat; and it is workable over a wide range of temperatures.

Shortening is 100 per cent fat, or a combination of fats. It is one of the most digestible of all edible fats and oils—93 to 95 per cent. Since it is one of the best sources of energy for man, it is very nutritious.

One great advantage of shortening is that it will remain fresh and sweet without refrigeration. Usually, it is sold commercially in attractive one-pound and three-pound cans. These can be stored in the cupboard along with other baking ingredients, and there need be no fear of the shortening causing unwelcome odors or grease stains.

Shortening is favored for greasing cookie sheets prior to baking the cookies. However, it is unnecessary to grease cookie sheets unless the recipe suggests doing so. Caution should be taken when greasing cookie sheets. Too much shortening will cause the cookie dough to spread during the baking process. The sheets should be cool before being greased, even between bakings. It is the oven that should be preheated—not the pan.

GREASING BAKING SHEETS

One easy method of greasing cookie sheets is to blend ½ cup shortening and ¼ cup flour into a smooth paste. This shortening mixture should be spread very thinly on the cookie sheets. If desired, a supply of this shortening-flour mixture can be prepared and stored in a covered dish until needed.

Another easy method of greasing cookie sheets is to pour a small quantity of vegetable oil into a small slim jar, such as an olive jar. A pastry brush should be kept in the jar. Then, when cookie sheets need greasing, it is easy to brush with vegetable oil. When using this method take caution not to pour more vegetable oil into the jar than will be used, because vegetable oil should be stored in the refrigerator to maintain a fresh flavor.

When a cookie recipe requires melted shortening, one of the vegetable oils can be used. Such oils are odorless, yellow, tasteless, and contain 100 per cent fat. Vegetable oils can be stored in the cupboard until opened. After opening, vegetable oils will keep better in the refrigerator. Like solid shortening, vegetable oils are digestible and nutritious. But one of the most important things about vegetable oils is that they are so convenient to measure and combine with liquids.

Liquid vegetable oils can be used to coat measuring spoons and cups to eliminate sticking and inaccurate measuring of syrups, honey, peanut butter, and many other ingredients.

TRUE MEASUREMENTS

Getting the *exact* measurement of butter or shortening required in a recipe is the "key" to successful cookie baking. Too much butter or shortening will cause a batch of cookies to taste greasy, while not enough shortening will cause the cookies to be tough.

The first step in the correct measurement of butter or shortening is to select a standard measuring cup that has the one-cup measuring-line below the rim of the measuring cup. This prevents spillage or inaccurate measurement. Other types of measuring cups (standard cups with the one-cup mark at the very rim of the cup, or one of the nest of graduated measuring cups: $\frac{1}{4}$, $\frac{1}{3}$, $\frac{1}{2}$ or 1 cup measure) can be used, but not with as much ease and success.

Measurement of butter is comparatively easy, since butter is sold commercially in one pound prints. Each pound is usually divided into four $\frac{1}{4}$ pound sticks. Each $\frac{1}{4}$ pound stick is equal to $\frac{1}{2}$ cup of butter or 8 tablespoons. Half of each $\frac{1}{4}$ pound stick is equal to $\frac{1}{4}$ cup of butter or 4 tablespoons.

One of the most accurate methods of measuring less than one cup of shortening is to pour cold water into the measuring cup, then add shortening until the water level is at the one-cup mark. This is called the displacement method. How much water should be placed in the cup before beginning to place the shortening into the cup? The amount of water can be determined by subtracting the amount of shortening required in the recipe from one cup. For example, if the recipe required $\frac{1}{4}$ cup shortening, then $\frac{1}{4}$ should be subtracted from 1. This will leave $\frac{3}{4}$. Therefore, the amount of cold water should be $\frac{3}{4}$ cup. So, the cup should be filled $\frac{3}{4}$ full of cold water, then the shortening should be placed into the cup until water reaches the one-cup line of measurement.

At all times during the measuring of the shortening, the shortening should be kept under the water. When the displacement method of measuring is used, all water must be poured off the shortening before the shortening is added to the mixing bowl.

When shortening is soft (at room temperature) and easy to measure, it is simpler to scoop it directly from the can and pack it into the measuring cup. Shortening should be packed firmly into the measuring cup, then leveled with a spatula.

If a recipe calls for melted shortening, it can be measured before or after melting. Usually, it is much simpler to use one of the vegetable oils and pour it directly from the container into a measuring cup.

Butter or shortening can "make or break" a batch of cookies. So, a wise cookie baker will use only the fresh (and best) and measure carefully according to directions in the recipe.

4. liquids

Liquids are used in very limited amounts in the average cookie recipe. Liquids react to sugar, flour, and other ingredients in such a manner as to determine the degree of moistness or dryness of the baked cookies.

The way in which liquids react to the ingredients in a cookie recipe is: to act as a solvent for sugar and other ingredients, and to dissolve egg and flour proteins and starch in the ingredients.

Among the many types of liquids used in cookie recipes, milk and water are the two most popular ones. Milk makes a cookie richer, while water helps make a cookie more moist. Many milk products, such as sour cream, evaporated milk, and the newer nonfat dry milk, also are used frequently. Fruit juices, with orange and lemon juice being used most often, provide extra flavor as well as the degree of moistness or dryness of the finished product. Cold and hot coffee is used in some cookie recipes.

Actually, vanilla, almond, and other extracts, although used in small quantities, provide some moisture to cookie recipes; however, these extracts do not provide enough moisture to be considered of any value as liquids. The main role of extracts is as a flavoring. Other ingredients in a cookie recipe provide varying degrees of moisture. Among these ingredients are syrup, honey, molasses, coconut, pineapple, and applesauce.

HISTORY OF MILK

Milk has played an important role in the development of civilization; therefore, it should be no surprise to discover its value to cookie baking. Prehistoric drawings, found in the Sahara Desert and believed to be 8000 years old, tell picture-stories about cattle.

The word milk comes from the now extinct Sanskrit writings. The Sanskrit *"mrjati"* described the milking of an animal. It is from this Sanskrit word that the word milk was derived.

In 1611, the first dairy cows were brought to America's colonial town of Jamestown to prevent the starvation of its inhabitants. Although other cattle had been brought into the colonies before this time, it is believed that the year 1611 is the birth-date of dairying in America. Pioneers moving westward toward the Pacific took along a "food factory" (a cow). Since the movement of the early pioneers toward the west coast, dairy herds have changed considerably.

Along with the change in size and appearance of the dairy herd, an even greater change has occured in processing and distribution of the product—milk. Today, cows are milked by machines; the milk is pasteurized (sometimes homogenized and fortified with Vitamin D), poured into sanitary containers and sealed. The sealed containers of milk are taken to homes and markets across the entire United States.

MILK TERMINOLOGY

Within the dairy industry, milk is known by specific terms: fortified milk, homogenized milk, whole milk, skim milk, cultured buttermilk, or flavored milk. All of these milks, except the flavored milk, can be used successfully in any cookie recipe requiring milk.

Fortified milk usually contains extra amounts of the essential nutrients found in milk.

Homogenized milk is whole milk that has been processed mechanically to prevent separation of cream from the milk fluid. This type of milk contains additional Vitamin D.

Whole milk, which is usually pasteurized before being sold commercially, consists of approximately 10 per cent milk solids and almost four per cent butterfat. Skim milk contains small quantities of butterfat, because this butterfat has been skimmed from the milk.

Cultured buttermilk is skim milk that has been churned, and to which a special culture has been added. To accentuate the flavor of cultured buttermilk, salt is added sometimes.

Flavored milk is whole milk with the addition of a syrup or powder containing a flavor and sugar—such as chocolate. This milk is not recommended for use in cookie recipes.

Since dough for drop cookie recipes has to be so soft that it can be dropped from a teaspoon onto a cookie sheet, drop cookie recipes use more milk than other types of cookie recipes. The dough for bar cookies must be soft enough to be spread over the surface of a shallow pan; therefore, bar cookie recipes also require milk.

Rolled cookie recipes require a fairly firm dough, while refrigerator cookie recipes require a fairly soft dough. Both of these types of cookie recipes use milk; however, many of the rolled and refrigerator cookie recipes use other milk products (evaporated milk, sour cream, and nonfat dry milk), water, coffee, and fruit juices.

EVAPORATED MILK

Indirectly, Napoleon and his army are responsible for evaporated milk. Since hunger was as much an enemy of his army as his foes, the French Emperor offered a prize of money (12,000 francs) to anyone who could provide a means of preserving food that would prevent his army from starving to death or becoming too weak from hunger to fight. Eventually, Nicholas Appert, a Paris confectioner, discovered a means of keeping foods for long periods. Appert's method was to cook the food, seal it in an air-tight container, and re-cook it. In 1810, after fifteen years of experimenting, Appert was awarded the prize.

As a result of Appert's discoveries, other men began working with his theories. In 1885, a group of Swiss-born dairymen in Highland, Illinois, perfected machinery and techniques for processing evaporated milk.

Whole milk is pasteurized, concentrated to half its volume by evaporating a large percentage of the natural water in it. This concentrated milk is homogenized and fortified with Vitamin D. Next, it is poured into cans, sealed, and sterilized by heat. The result of this process is evaporated milk that will keep without refrigeration. This milk is very nutritious, since it contains protein, minerals, vitamins, lactose, and butterfat.

Evaporated milk is excellent to use in cookie recipes requiring cream. Also, it can be substituted in any cookie recipe requiring milk. However, when being substituted for milk, one precaution must be taken. Only one half the amount of milk required in the recipe should be used, the rest should be water. In other words, when evaporated milk is used in place of whole milk, equal amounts of evaporated milk and water should be substituted. For example, if a cookie recipe calls for one-half cup of milk, this can be substituted with one-fourth cup evaporated milk and one-fourth cup water.

CREAM—FRESH AND SOURED

When cream is used as a substitute for milk in a cookie recipe, the same amount as required in the recipe can be substituted. However, when cream is substituted the amount of fat (shortening or butter) used in the recipe should be reduced. Cream is butterfat that rises to the top of whole milk.

This same cream, when soured, is known as sour cream. Back in the seventeenth century, many European recipes used sour cream as a basic ingredient. Before pasteurization, sour cream actually was nothing more than cream that had soured. Today, it is altogether a different product. First, cream is pasteurized and homogenized. During the pasteurization process, bacteria that might cause the cream to sour are destroyed. After pasteurization and homogenization, selected cultures are added to the cream to create a sour cream with a tangy flavor and velvety texture.

Sour cream is used in very few cookie recipes. Most of these recipes are for some type of rolled cookie dough. Other types of cream that can be purchased commercially and used in the baking of cookies are light cream, table cream, half and half, light whipping cream, and heavy cream. All of these can be used in various cookie recipes. But recipes for the rich, holiday-type cookies require cream more than other types of cookie recipes.

NONFAT DRY MILK

Tartar warriors made a sun-dried skim milk product back in the thirteenth century. They carried this crude product along with them as nourishment during battle. Since that time, dairymen in many parts of the world have striven to develop a means of preserving nonfat milk solids. It wasn't until after the beginning of the twentieth century that nonfat milk became an important dairy food in the United States.

Nonfat dry milk is made from fresh liquid milk. All fat and water is removed from the liquid milk, and the nonfat dry milk remains. This product contains the protein, calcium, and carbohydrate values of whole milk.

The one advantage of using nonfat dry milk in baking is that it will cause the baked food to brown better and keep longer. Very few cookie recipes require dry milk. Nevertheless, it can be used in peanut butter cookies or brownies with the greatest success. In the future, dozens of cookie recipes probably will be developed using nonfat dry milk. In the meantime, homemakers can experiment with this dairy product in their cookie recipes. At the present time, commercial bakers use the largest amount of nonfat dry milk; because this type of milk improves flavor, nutrition, texture, and color of bread.

MEASUREMENT OF LIQUIDS

Regardless of the type of liquid required in a cookie recipe, for success the liquids must be measured accurately. And, in order to measure the liquids accurately, standard measuring cups and spoons should be used.

The standard measuring cup with the one-cup line below the rim of the cup is best for accurate measurements of liquids. The cup should be placed on the working table or cabinet top. After the required amount of liquid has been poured into the cup, the homemaker should stoop so that her eye is at a level with the line of measurement on the cup. Only by lowering the eyes to this measurement level can a homemaker be positive the correct amount of liquid has been poured into the cup.

Dozens of cookie recipes require a tablespoon of water, milk, or some type of fruit juice. A tablespoon, such as the ones used to spoon foods from bowls to plates at the dinner table, should never be used to measure liquids for recipes. Standard measuring spoons, which are sold commercially, must be used for accurate measurements. These measuring spoons are standard, while spoons in a set of silverware are not standard.

To measure a tablespoon (or less), the correct measuring spoon should be held steadily in the left hand. With the right hand, the liquid should be poured into the spoon until the spoon is full.

If some thick ingredient, such as molasses, is required in a cookie recipe, this can be measured in a spoon in the same manner that milk and other liquids are measured. However, after filling a spoon full of a heavy liquid, a spatula or knife should be used to level off the ingredient. Care should be taken to prevent heavy liquids from coating the outside section of the measuring spoon.

5. spices and herbs

Although there are approximately 55 spices and herbs known and used by homemakers throughout the world today, only nine of these spices and six herbs are popular ingredients in cookies.

The main role of these spices and herbs in cookie recipes is to add flavor. Most of them do not have any food value whatsoever. However, the addition of spices and herbs to cookie dough is very valuable: (1) in intensifying the natural flavors of the other ingredients, and (2) in giving variety to basic recipes. Thus, the lack of food value is relatively unimportant.

Since the flavors of spices and herbs are so strong, only small quantities can be used in any recipe. For the most part, only $\frac{1}{4}$ to 1 teaspoon can be used in the average cookie recipe.

Banana Oatmeal Cookies *(United Fruit Co.)*

Florida Orange Cookies and Fruit Nut Bars *(Dudley-Anderson-Yutzy)*

Orange Honey Cookies *(Dudley-Anderson-Yutzy)*

HISTORY

Who discovered spices and herbs? There is no definite answer for this question. In fact, it is unknown which spice was the first to be used by man. It is safe to assume that man accidently discovered spices and their value as a flavoring.

Which was discovered and used first? Again, there is no definite answer available. Some authorities believe cassia was the first. This belief is based upon historical records that reveal cassia was being used before 2700 B.C. Although few homemakers purchase and use cassia today, they do use many of the products made from it and the bark of the cassia tree. Much of the bark is marketed as cinnamon, which is extremely popular in cookie recipes. The unripe fruits of the cassia are gathered, dried, and sold as cassia buds; these buds are considered to be one of the most delightful of all the spices. Cassia oil is made from the bark and leaves of the tree.

Other ancient spices which are used today in cookie baking include cloves, ginger, and nutmeg. According to history, these spices originally grew in China, India, and tiny, remote islands. The Phoenicians, Egyptians, Chinese, and Arabs were responsible for trading these spices far and wide. At one time some of the spices were worth their weight in gold. In fact, they were so important to ancient man that battles were fought over spices and their trade routes.

VARIOUS ROLES

Not only were spices used in ancient times as a food flavoring, they also were used as preservatives, incense in temples and homes, medicine, and cosmetics. But, it was probably the mystery and glamour connected with the origin and trade routes which helped to create such a desirability and such high prices for spices and herbs.

Today, much of the glamour has been lost; thus, prices have fallen considerably. Nevertheless, the desire and need for spices in cooking remains. Since many of the spices and herbs are grown today in various parts of the world, this also has helped to create a cheaper market price for them.

FAVORITE FOR COOKIES

The spices and herbs needed to improve and enhance the flavors of certain ingredients in cookie recipes are: allspice, anise, caraway seeds, cardamon seed, cassia, cinnamon, cloves, coriander, fennel, ginger, mace, mince meat spice, nutmeg, poppy seed, and sesame.

Allspice. This spice comes in whole or ground form. It has a flavor resembling a mixture of cinnamon, nutmeg, and cloves. This is one of the spices discovered in more recent times. It actually is the dried berry of the pimento tree, which grows in the West Indies.

Anise. This spice is the fruit of a small plant that grows in India, Spain, and Mexico. This plant is an annual, and when the fruits dry they resemble seeds. Thus, from this comes anise or anise seed.

Caraway Seeds. This is an herb. It is sold commercially in whole or ground forms. It is the dried fruit of the biennial yellow-flowered aromatic herb *Carum carvi.* This herb is especially popular as a flavoring for certain holiday cookies.

Cardamon Seed. This is an herb and is seldom used, although it is very aromatic. It is the dried fruit of an East Indian herb, which belongs to the ginger family.

Cassia. This Chinese variety of the ancient spice known as cinnamon dates back to 2700 B.C. This spice is on the market in whole, ground, or even bud forms; however, ground cassia is the only form that is used in cookie recipes.

Cinnamon. This is one of the most popular spices in all American cookery, although it is used seldom in English or French cookery. Real cinnamon is the inner bark of a small evergreen tree that is native to Ceylon. This light-yellowish brown bark is very thin and smooth; the bark is extremely fragrant and tastes sweet, warm, and aromatic. This delightful spice was discovered growing wild in the forest of Ceylon and southern India centuries after Chinese cassia had been used. After being under the control of the Dutch and Portuguese, exporters finally managed to transplant some of the trees to Java, West Indies, Egypt, and Brazil; nevertheless, the Ceylon variety is still considered the best. Just as it was of tremendous value to traders in ancient times, today it is of great value to cookie recipes.

Cloves. This spice was once worth its weight in gold. Although this ancient spice is not so expensive today, it is still valuable. Having a powerfully fragrant odor, cloves are deep brown and have a hot acrid taste. They are marketed in whole or ground form; the ground form is used in cookie recipes. Cloves actually are the dried flower-buds of an evergreen in the myrtle family. These trees grow from thirty to forty feet high and are found in Madagascar, Ceylon, and Zanzibar. This tree is native to the Molucca Islands and was used by the Chinese centuries before the birth of Christ.

Coriander. This is an herb. Although it is not extremely popular, the aromatic seeds of this herb are very delightful in some cookie recipes. It is sold in whole (seed) or ground form; the whole form is preferred for cookie baking. This Old World herb belongs to the carrot family.

Fennel. This is a perennial European herb which belongs to the carrot family, as does the coriander. The aromatic seeds of this herb are wonderful in certain cookie recipes. The flavor of fennel is similar to that of anise.

Ginger. This ancient spice is believed to be native to Asia. It is the underground stem of a perennial plant that grows to approximately four feet in height. There are two types of ginger—black ginger (unscraped root stock) and white ginger (scraped and peeled). Both are sold commercially in root or ground form. The ground form is best for cookie recipes.

Mace. This spice is a product of the nutmeg tree, which has been known in Europe since the twelfth century. Mace is the material around the nutmeg kernel; and it is one of the most expensive, yet most delicate of spices. It is sold commercially in blades or ground. The ground form is used in a few cookie recipes and has an aroma resembling nutmeg.

Mince Meat Spice. This spice is very modern. It is a mixture of many spices (allspice, cinnamon, etc.) and is becoming more popular each year as an ingredient in cookie recipes.

Nutmeg. This is one of the most ancient and popular spices. *Noix muscade* (musk nut) is the original French name for nutmeg, while in Malaya it is called the *pala*. It grows on the Myristica tree in the little West Indian islands, where approximately 80 species of nutmeg trees grow and provide consumers with more than 400 kinds of oils. The nutmeg tree is noted for its beauty—symmetrical with dense green foliage. This tropical evergreen produces a fruit which opens and allows the seed (or nutmeg) to drop from it; thus, the nutmeg is the dried kernel of the tree's fruit, while mace is the husk of its fruit. This hard dry seed resembles an acorn in size and shape. It is so flavorful that only a very, very tiny amount is necessary for any cookie recipe. Nutmeg trees do not bear any fruit until they are eight years old, then they yield fruit for over 60 years. There are several superstitions in the Orient regarding the nutmeg. For example, it is believed that nutmeg trees will not live unless they are planted within hearing distance of the sea. This spice is sold whole or ground; the ground form is best for cookie recipes.

Poppy Seed. This is an herb. It is the seed of one variety of the poppy plant. For the most part, this herb is imported from central Europe. It is especially popular as an ingredient in holiday cookie recipes.

Sesame. This is an herb that grows in East India. The seeds of this herb are small and flat. These seeds are delightful in some cookie recipes because after baking they emit a flavor resembling toasted almonds. Sesame seeds are sold commercially in hulled or unhulled forms. The hulled forms are better and easier to use in baking.

If modern homemakers and economists continue experimenting, in the next decade it is possible that many other spices and herbs can be added to this list. Even though spices and herbs must be used in small quantities and with care, they must be used because it is their role to enhance the flavor of other ingredients and at the same time stimulate appetites.

MEASUREMENT

Accurate measurement of spices and herbs is of great importance. They should be measured in one of the standard measuring spoons, which range from $\frac{1}{4}$ to 1 teaspoon measure. A regular teaspoon should never be used in the measurement of spices and herbs; teaspoons belonging to silverware sets are usually larger than the standard measuring teaspoon and are not of a standard size. Besides, it probably would be difficult for a homemaker to accurately guess $\frac{1}{4}$ of a teaspoon in a regular dinner spoon.

After filling the correct measuring spoon with the particular spice or herb desired, the spoon should be leveled by gently raking a table knife across the top of the measuring spoon. This makes the measurement more accurate. The spices or herbs should be measured and added to the flour and other dry ingredients. These should be sifted once before blending into the shortening mixture because it is through sifting that the spices and herbs are distributed evenly throughout the batter.

Spices and herbs are sold at grocery markets all over the United States. These have been imported from various sections of the world. They are prepared and stored in small cans or glass jars before being marketed. They are packed in air-tight containers in order to preserve their fragrance and freshness.

Spices and herbs must never be exposed to air and light for very long, because they will loose their freshness. In fact, they even loose their flavor when merely standing over a long period of time. Thus, wise homemakers should be sure to keep all spices and herbs stored in air-tight containers, preferably glass jars that are labeled with the name of the product. Also, homemakers should discard the old spices and herbs periodically and replenish the spice cabinet; the cost is fairly small and the rewards great. Only nationally known brands of spices and herbs should be purchased, and then only in small quantities.

GROWING SPICES AND HERBS

Spice and herb gardens can be raised right in the backyard or in window pots. Several delightful gardening books have been published on this subject and will enable those interested to raise and dry their own spices and herbs—right at home in the kitchen.

6. extra flavors

It is those extra flavors combined with the basic ingredients that sometimes enable homemakers to create cookies filled with extremely delightful flavor and beauty. These extra flavors are derived through the proper use of fruits, nuts, extracts, condiments, and chocolate.

Since fresh fruits are so delectable, it is understandable that these could add a lot of flavor and texture to most cookies. All forms of fruit (fresh, dried, frozen, or canned) can be used in cookie baking. The ever-popular fruits can add as much variety as flavor to cookie recipes.

Among the fruits popular in cookie recipes are raisins, dates, figs, bananas, apples, peaches, apricots, pineapples, cherries, berries, oranges, lemons, limes, and citron. Coconut is not to be omitted! Some of these fruits, such as raisins or dates, can be chopped and blended into the cookie batter; some of them, such as oranges, can be peeled and the peel grated and blended into the batter, while some of the juice

57

is used as a liquid for extra flavor in the batter. Chopped or grated fruit is used when the fullest flavor of a particular fruit is desired. Wise homemakers should keep a large supply and variety of fruits in their kitchens.

DRIED FRUITS

Dried fruits are more popular as an ingredient for fillings in cookie and bar recipes. Apples, apricots, peaches, and prunes are among the favorite dried fruits for fillings and bars. During the colder winter season, a good supply of dried fruits should be kept handy, because filled and bar cookies are heartier and are preferred by many people during the fall and winter seasons. When dried fruits are to be used, the fruits should be soaked until soft. This prepares the fruits for easier chopping.

Raisins are one of the oldest fruits, with a history dating back over 2000 years. Their value was so great in 1000 B.C. that the Israelites paid their taxes to King David with raisins. In America, it was the unsuccessful prospectors in the gold fields of California during the great Gold Rush of 1849 who started the raisin industry. Some of these prospectors started farming grapes in California's San Joaquin Valley, where today more raisins are produced than anywhere in the world.

If dried fruits are purchased in bulk, these should be washed and dried before being used. However, if dried fruits are purchased in packages, these need not be washed. When dried fruits become too dry, they can be plumped by placing in a pan over boiling water.

CANNED FRUITS

American grocery markets sell a large variety of canned fruits. Many cookie recipes require a canned fruit instead of a fresh or frozen fruit. When this is the case, the fruit should be measured, with a standard measuring cup, very accurately.

According to Zenja Cary, home economist, it is difficult to suggest substitutions for cookie recipes that have been tested already. Such recipes have been developed scientifically and any change (like substituting fruit for sugar or fruit juice for another liquid) would cause the delicate balance of the recipe to become unbalanced. Of course, some homemakers delight in experimenting with recipes; therefore, these homemakers should continue to do so, while the young and inexperienced homemakers should continue to follow recipes until they have a full understanding of ingredients and how they react to each other.

NUTS

Whole, halved, quartered, slivered, shredded, chopped, or grated—nuts add flavor and more flavor to any cookie recipe. Almost every nut known today will add flavor to one or another of the hundreds of delicious cookie recipes. Among the nuts used most frequently are almonds, brazil nuts, cashews, peanuts, pecans, and walnuts. Through research, two leading food trade magazines have found that walnuts and pecans are favored by today's consumer for recipes requiring nuts. Walnuts were preferred by 65 per cent of the consumers, while pecans were preferred by 18 per cent.

These nuts can be purchased shelled or unshelled in most grocery markets. When buying unshelled nuts, homemakers should select those stamped with a packer's brand. Today, most nuts can be purchased shelled and in cellophane bags or cans. No matter which kind is bought, they should be stored in an air-tight container in the refrigerator until used. And the nuts should not be chopped until time to use.

Most nuts are easy to shell—the shell just needs to be cracked and the kernels removed. If pecans are difficult to crack, they should be covered with boiling water and let stand until cool. After cooling, they should be crushed from one end to the other. To shell brazil nuts, a little salt water should be poured into a saucepan; the nuts should be placed into the pan and simmered about three minutes before the water is drained off the nuts. The nuts should be allowed to cool before the shells are removed.

BLANCHED NUTS

When a recipe requires blanched nuts, the nuts should be dropped into boiling water for one minute—after the nuts have been removed from their shells. After one minute, the nuts should be removed and chilled in cold water. Then they need to be popped from their skins and dried on a towel.

Since nuts are easier to slice or shred when they are warm, they should be placed in an oven 400°F. a few minutes before they are to be sliced or shredded. If a nut grinder (never a meat grinder!) is not available, nuts should be ground by being placed between the folds of a clean towel and a rolling pin pushed back and forth across the covered nuts several times.

If nuts happen to become stale, they can be freshened by being heated in the oven for a few minutes. Stale (not rancid) nuts should be scattered about a baking sheet; placed in an oven 400°F. for a few minutes. They should be watched carefully to prevent scorching. When heated, the nuts should be removed from oven, cooled, and used immediately.

The natural goodness of nuts do more than merely add flavor and variety to cookies. Nuts are rich in food value. They provide essential vitamins and minerals and are a high energy food. For example, one pound of walnut kernels can provide almost one day's dietary requirements; yet walnuts, as a fuel food, are not extremely high in calories.

MEASURING NUTS

Nuts should be measured in one of the standard measuring cups that has the one-cup measuring line below the top of the cup. And, like all ingredients, nuts should be measured accurately. Too many nuts can ruin a cookie recipe just as easily as too much shortening or flour.

EXTRACTS

Extracts, like spices and herbs, must be used in small quantities because they are so concentrated in flavor. Vanilla, a fruit, or a nut extract is a necessary ingredient for most cookie recipes. Vanilla, orange, lemon, banana, walnut, and almond extracts are by far the most popular extracts.

Extreme care should be taken in the measurement of extracts. Since these are so strong in flavor, they should be measured accurately in one of the standard measuring spoons—not a teaspoon or soup spoon that belongs at the dining table. While measuring extracts, the measuring spoon should not be held over the batter. Instead, they should be measured while holding the spoon over an empty measuring cup.

In the long run it is more economical to purchase the better flavoring extracts, because less of the extract is required to obtain the desired flavor. Besides, more of the true flavor will be retained after baking if the better extracts are used. The better extracts have been processed in oil, while the cheaper ones have been processed in alcohol. The oil extracts require only two or three drops as compared to a teaspoon of the alcoholic extracts.

Extracts should be stored in the bottles in which they are purchased. These should be kept tightly sealed and stored in a dark place in the kitchen cabinets. When left open, the extracts will evaporate.

There is little or no food value in the various extracts. The main purpose for using these in cookie recipes is to make the cookies a little tastier—nothing more and nothing less.

CONDIMENTS

Condiments do not add flavor; instead, they enhance the flavor of other ingredients. Only one of the condiments is of any value to cookie recipes, and that is salt.

A very small quantity of salt is often used in cookie recipes, and extreme care should be taken to measure salt accurately. To do this, the measuring spoon should be dipped down into the salt container; after being filled and lifted out of the container, the salt should be leveled by gently raking a knife over the top of the spoon. Salt should be added to the dry ingredients (flour, etc.) and sifted before being added to cookie batters.

CHOCOLATE

Chocolate, like vanilla, has become one of the most valuable of all flavors. And, like vanilla, in reality it belongs to the world of spices and herbs because chocolate is made from ground-roasted cacao beans, which grow on the cacao tree that is native to warm regions such as Mexico.

Chocolate is extremely valuable to many cookie recipes, because to some it is the key flavor. For example, imagine brownies without chocolate. At this point, it is necessary to discuss chocolate and cocoa. These are two entirely different products, and they should never be used as a substitute for one another—unless it is absolutely necessary. In that case, allow three level tablespoons of cocoa for each square of chocolate. And, when substituting cocoa for chocolate, one tablespoon of shortening must be added for three table-spoons of cocoa used. This should be done for cake recipes as well as for cookie recipes. The additional shortening has to be used because chocolate contains more natural cocoa butter than cocoa—this is the reason it makes a richer, more flavorful batch of cookies than cocoa.

Since there are various kinds of chocolate products (unsweetened chocolate, semi-sweet chocolate, German's sweet chocolate, etc.) available at the grocers, the kind of chocolate designated in a recipe should be used.

Chocolate should be stored in a fairly cool place, around 75°F.; a temperature over 90°F. will cause the chocolate to lose some of its natural flavor. Also, excessive temperatures will cause chocolate to become crumbly and the paper it is wrapped into to become oily; thus, this is an indication that some of the cocoa butter has been lost and the chocolate is deteriorating. If chocolate becomes gray during storage, none of the flavor has been damaged; therefore, this chocolate should be kept and used.

MELTING CHOCOLATE

Four methods can be used to melt chocolate. The one used should depend upon the homemaker and the equipment in her kitchen. Chocolate can be melted: (1) over hot water; (2) over very low heat; (3) in the oven; (4) in liquid mixtures.

To melt it over hot water, the chocolate should be placed into a small bowl and the bowl should be set over hot water. The chocolate squares do not need to be cut into small pieces, because they will melt rapidly without it. And there is no need for the water under the bowl to be boiling—just hot. A bowl that fits directly over the top of the double boiler or tea kettle is ideal for melting chocolate. After the chocolate has been melted, it should be poured directly into the batter (unless the recipe directs otherwise). A rubber scraper is perfect for getting every bit of chocolate from the bowl and into the batter.

Chocolate can be melted by placing the squares into a small saucepan and placing the pan directly over a low heat. When this method is used, the chocolate must be stirred constantly to prevent scorching. Chocolate scorches very easily because it contains fat and starch, but little water. When the heat is too high and hot, it will cause the chocolate to lose its aroma and to develop a burned taste.

The third method of melting chocolate is to place the wrapped pieces of chocolate onto a piece of foil or a pie pan and slip it into the oven while the oven is preheating, or even while it is cooling. A careful check should be kept while chocolate is melting in the oven to prevent it from scorching.

In a few recipes, the chocolate can be combined with the liquids and melted by slowly heating the liquids in a saucepan over a low heat. As the liquid mixture gradually heats, it should be stirred constantly. After the chocolate has melted, it should be blended thoroughly with the other liquids by being beaten with a rotary egg beater.

The food value of chocolate is extremely high; therefore, it is a perfect ingredient for that batch of cookies to feed the children and dad after school and work. Chocolate contains fats, carbohydrates, proteins, minerals, and sometimes it has additional vitamins.

PART II

cookie skills

7. baking

The proper baking process is as important to a successful batch of cookies as the ingredients used in the recipe.

The oven, of course, plays the biggest role in baking. Each cookie recipe in this book designates the exact temperature the oven should be for the best baking results. All cookies, with the exception of chocolate cookies, should be baked in an oven that has been preheated between 375° and 425°F.; the cookies should bake at this range of temperature from 5 to 15 minutes, depending upon the particular recipe. Chocolate cookies normally should be baked at least 25°F. lower than the average cookies.

One of the first steps toward becoming a successful cookie baker is for the homemaker to know the oven in her kitchen. Is the heat uneven in certain areas inside the oven? If so, the sheet of cookies must be turned when they are half baked.

PREPARING THE OVEN

When cookie dough has been prepared and placed on the baking sheet, it is ready for the oven. But is the oven ready for the cookies? Has the oven been preheated to the required temperature? Has one of the oven racks been placed slightly above the middle of the oven? If not, the oven rack should be moved, because this allows the heat to circulate freely around the baking sheet of cookies.

For the best results, only one sheet of cookies should be baked at a time; that is, unless the oven being used is one of the large 23-inch kind, then two 14-inch baking sheets can be placed side by side (not touching!). The baking sheet should always be smaller than the oven in order that the heat can circulate more freely. At least one trial cookie should be baked to determine how much room each cookie will require for spreading. Then, each cookie placed on the sheet for baking should be approximately the same size in circumference and depth.

Using the proper pans is as important to a successful batch of cookies as the correct baking temperature. Flat baking sheets of shiny aluminum, tin, stainless steel, or even glass, that have no (or very small) sides, are best for cookie baking. According to one manufacturer of stoves, aluminum baking sheets are best for baking cookies, because "aluminum is a very efficient material for transferring heat to the food, giving even browning results." Dark pans tend to absorb heat and will cause cookies to burn on the bottom. In an emergency, regular cake or bread pans can be turned upside down and be used to bake cookies.

VARY TEMPERATURE

When a glass baking dish is used, the temperature of the oven should be lowered about 25°F. Also, enamel or dark pans require a lower baking temperature than the one desig-nated in the recipe. If pans are dark or, for that matter, if the homemaker wants to save work, the baking sheets can be lined with a piece of clean, shiny, aluminum foil. Also, commercial liners are now on the market.

Just as cookies must be baked in pans without sides, because the sides will shield the cookies from the heat and prevent them from browning, bar-type cookies must be baked in pans with sides. It is of utmost importance that bars be baked in the exact pan designated in the recipe. Other-wise, when baked in a pan too small, the dough will not bake all the way through; and when baked in a pan too large, the dough will spread thin and have a tendency to burn. So the correct size pan for bar cookies is a *must*.

GREASED VS. UNGREASED SHEET

Whether the baking sheet should be greased or not should depend entirely upon the particular recipe being used; how-ever, when the recipe does require the baking sheet to be greased, it should be greased very lightly. If a pan is greased too heavily, cookies will tend to spread more than they should during the baking process, and they, also, will burn more easily on the bottom.

Greased or ungreased cookie sheets may be used for each batch of cookies without being washed. The baking sheets should be scraped clean, wiped with a paper towel, and allowed to cool before placing the next batch of cookies on them. Unbaked cookies will absorb hot grease and then have a greasy taste after being baked. So this should be prevented by giving the baking sheet time to be thoroughly cooled before placing the next batch of cookies on it.

As for the effect of altitude on cookies being baked, there is very little. The temperature of the oven need not be changed for the higher altitudes. Instead, the cookies should be baked a few minutes longer. Care should be taken to not overcook the cookies. Drop and bar cookies are done when they will spring back after being touched lightly with a finger and when they are lightly browned. Other kinds of cookies are done when they are delicately and evenly browned.

BAKED COOKIES

When the cookies are done, they should be removed at once (unless the recipe states otherwise) from the baking sheet with a spatula or pancake turner and placed on a wire rack to cool. The cookies should be left on the wire rack until they are cooled completely, at which time they should be stored in the appropriate cookie jar. Hot cookies should never be placed on top of each other.

In the event that cookies cool before being removed from the baking sheet, the pan should be returned to the oven until slightly reheated. Then the cookies should be transferred immediately to the cooling rack. To cool cookies containing a large quantity of shortening, a paper towel should be placed on the cooling rack before the cookies are placed on it.

8. equipment

Correct equipment is the key to a professional job, regardless of the particular task—sewing, gardening, or baking cookies.

In the case of cookie baking, the correct equipment is a must for lovely, delicious cookies. Probably the most essential piece of equipment for cookie baking is a stove with a dependable oven.

Other equipment that is essential to successful cookie baking includes:

Mixing bowls—a nest of mixing bowls that contains at least three different sizes. One of the sets now on the market has handles molded in such a manner that they also can be used as pouring spouts. These bowls are ideal for mixing cookies, especially the bar-type.

Measuring cups—one standard one-cup size cup with the measuring line below rim of cup; one standard two-cup size cup with measuring line below rim of cup; one standard one-cup size cup with measuring line at rim of cup; and one set of measuring cups ($\frac{1}{8}$, $\frac{1}{4}$, $\frac{1}{2}$, and 1 cup). Also, a large measuring cup that will hold more than one cup is handy, but not essential.

Measuring spoons—one set of standard measuring spoons that are attached by a ring and will measure from $\frac{1}{4}$ teaspoon to 1 tablespoon.

Flour sifter—a four-cup sifter is best.

Mixing spoons—one or two large wooden spoons with long handles, one or two large metal mixing spoons, and several teaspoons and tablespoons.

Spatula—at least one broad spatula or a pancake turner.

Scraper—at least one rubber or plastic scraper.

Forks—several forks of various sizes.

Racks—two square cake racks for cooling cookies, or else a couple of round cake racks.

Miscellaneous—knives, sieve, egg beater, bowls, saucepans, can opener, double-boiler, towels, pot holders, and many other items.

To begin with, a homemaker who is especially interested in baking cookies frequently should purchase several shiny, aluminum baking sheets that are 12 x 15 x $\frac{1}{4}$-inch in size. Besides these, she should purchase two small rectangular cookie sheets without sides, two rectangular bread pans for baking bars, and two square bread pans with sides for baking brownies and other bars.

These baking pans can be made from one of many materials: aluminum, stainless steel, tin, cast iron, glass, or even enamel. Most home economists prefer aluminum pans due to the ability of this material to conduct heat; however, all the other materials are fine for baking cookies. Wise homemakers will keep their pans shiny and bright by covering the pans with a piece of aluminum foil before placing the cookie dough on them to be baked. This saves lots of work and keeps the pans shiny and clean.

COOKIE CUTTERS

Cookie cutters of various sizes and shapes are an absolute must for the homemaker with several small children or grandchildren. Cutters improve the appearance of almost any cookie dough. For plain round cookies, the open end of a tin can will serve very well. For the unusual shapes, a pattern can be drawn on a piece of heavy cardboard. After the pattern is cut out, it should be placed on the rolled cookie dough and cut around with the point of a sharp knife or a pastry wheel.

There is a limitless supply of items on the market today that will help the homemaker prepare cookies better and more easily than ever before. Among these extras that are becoming more essential each day are: a pastry cloth and rolling-pin, electric mixer, electric timer, cookie press, pastry bag and tubes, refrigerator cookie molds, nut mill, nutcracker, graters, wooden chopping bowl, and chopper. The list is endless; nevertheless, the items listed here, and those not listed, should be purchased only as a homemaker becomes aware of a need for them and can afford them.

PAPER EQUIPMENT

Waxed paper, aluminum foil, saran wrap, paper towels, and paper napkins will save a homemaker much work and time. These items always should be on hand. For example, waxed paper can be used in sifting and measuring the dry ingredients. Aluminum foil can be used to line pans, cool cookies, or to wrap and store or mail cookies. And saran wrap can be used to cover a bowl or any container holding the freshly baked cookies or to wrap cookies for the lunch or gift box. There is no end to the countless ways that paper towels and napkins can be used.

Cookie jars, like cookie cutters, are not an absolute necessity; nevertheless, these add joy to cookie baking and eating. Besides, the children always know where to look for those freshly baked cookies. It is best to have several of various sizes and materials (pottery, glass, metal).

Regardless of how little or how much equipment a homemaker has, she should use it. Because only through using it can she provide her family and friends with fresh, tasty, home-baked cookies.

9. cooling and storing

Properly cooling and storing a batch of cookies is the key to lovely and delectable cookies.

When a baking sheet of freshly baked cookies is removed from the oven, the homemaker immediately should remove the hot cookies from the baking sheet by gently lifting each delicately browned cookie with a broad spatula or a pancake turner and placing it on a rack to cool. The cookies should never touch each other while they are warm.

COOLING RACKS

In case a square cake rack, or even a round one, is not available, there are several items that can serve as a cooling rack. For example, the oven should never be filled while baking cookies; therefore, before preheating the oven, one of the oven racks could be removed and used later as a cooling rack.

A large strip of aluminum foil can be spread on top of the

75

cabinet or work table and serve as a cooling place. Using foil is not ideal, because the cookies do not have air constantly circulating underneath them; therefore, it takes longer to cool on foil than on a wire rack. The main advantage of using foil for cooling is that, when cooled, the cookies can be wrapped in the same foil and be stored; thereby, handling is held at a minimum and the cookies retain their oven-freshness and crispness.

Paper products, china, and other glassware can serve as a make-shift cooling rack; however, none of these are too good for this purpose. In the case of paper, sometimes the cookies will stick. And, in the case of china and glassware, cookies have a tendency to sweat and become soft.

Regardless what type of rack or makeshift rack is used, cookies absolutely must be cooled before storage. To lay one hot cookie on top of another is like pouring fresh cement on top of a form containing more fresh cement. It is usually impossible to tell (when cookies are stored without cooling) where the bottom of one cookie ends and the top of another begins. So, cookies *must be cooled* before storing.

Cookies should be left in the open on the cooling rack for just a few minutes before they are cooled and ready for storage in the cookie jar. Selecting the proper cookie jar for a batch of cookies is as important as selecting the correct female to wear a size nine dress. Cookies and the right cookie jar just naturally go together the same as the right female and the right dress.

COOKIE JARS

There are two major types of cookie jars—earthenware and glass. But there are several items in the average kitchen that can serve, and well, as cookie jars. For example, a big glass jar that has a tight fitting lid; a deep casserole with a tight fitting top, a canister with a snug fitting lid, coffee or shortening cans that have tight fitting lids. Or, for that matter, any large container (bowl, pan, jar) can serve the purpose if aluminum foil or saran wrap is used as a cover. The main thing is that cookie containers be covered tightly.

One very important thing should be remembered in connection with the storage of cookies—only one flavor in each cookie jar. For example, it is unwise to store mince meat and oatmeal cookies in the same container, even though they are considered the same basic type of cookies. And it is just as unwise to store a crisp sugar cookie with a moist oatmeal drop cookie; the sugar cookie would become limp and soggy.

Although only cookies of one flavor are stored in a cookie jar, sometimes they will eventually become too dry or too soft. Moist cookies, such as mince meat and oatmeal cookies, have a tendency to become dry and hard; therefore, moist cookies should be stored in an earthenware jar or a tightly covered casserole, and to this should be added a slice of apple, orange, lemon, or even a piece of fresh bread. The slice of fruit or bread keeps the moist cookies soft and mellow plus adding a delicate flavor to the cookies. Crisp cookies, such as rolled or refrigerator cookies, should be stored in a glass jar or canister with a loose fitting lid.

FRESHEN COOKIES

If cookies happen to lose their freshness, they can be freshened. The oven should be preheated to 300°F. Into this oven the cookies should be placed for a matter of minutes. To freshen moist cookies, they should be placed into a large casserole, covered with a lid, and placed in the oven for about 10 minutes. To freshen rolled, refrigerator, and other crisp cookies, they should be placed on an ungreased baking sheet and placed in the oven for about 5 minutes.

Cookie jars can do a much better job of protecting and keeping cookies fresh tasting if they are stored in a cool, dark place. A lower shelf of the cabinet is usually a fairly good place for storing cookie jars. A pantry shelf is also ideal for the cookie jars.

Bar cookies can be stored in the very pan in which they are baked. The pan should be covered tightly with aluminum foil, saran wrap, waxed paper, or even a towel. Of course, bars can be stored in a tightly covered container, such as an earthenware cookie jar.

Freshly baked and cooled cookies can be stored by being wrapped in heavy aluminum foil or freezer paper and being stored in the freezer for six to eight months. When time to serve frozen cookies, they should be removed from the freezer and allowed to thaw (still wrapped) at room temperature for about 15 minutes. However, if the homemaker desires, the cookies can be thawed in the oven. To do this, the cookies should be unwrapped and placed on an ungreased baking sheet and be put into an oven 350°F. for several minutes. When thawed, the cookies should be removed from the oven and placed on a rack to cool before being served or stored.

FREEZING COOKIE DOUGH

Any type of cookie dough can be frozen and stored in the freezer from three to six months. Unbaked drop cookies can be stored in the freezer by first being dropped about $\frac{1}{4}$ inch apart on a baking sheet. The baking sheet should be set into the freezer until the cookie dough has frozen; then, the sheet of dough should be removed and packaged into a carton. If desired, several baking sheets of dough can be stored together by merely placing parchment or freezer paper between the layers before packaging. When it is time to bake the frozen drop cookies, the baking sheets should be removed and placed directly into an oven of the temperature designated in the recipe.

To store unbaked rolled or pressed cookies in the freezer, the dough should be prepared and cut out or pressed as desired. Two pieces of parchment or freezer paper should be placed between each cookie and stacked to the desired height. This prevents the cookies from sticking together. When it is time to bake these cookies, they should be removed from the freezer and placed on a baking sheet. They should be baked at the temperature directed in the recipe. These cookies should not require thawing before being baked.

To store unbaked refrigerator cookies, the dough should be formed into rolls, wrapped in freezer paper, and stored in the freezer. To use this dough, it should be removed from the freezer, unwrapped, and sliced while frozen. The slices should be placed on a baking sheet and baked at the temperature designated in the recipe.

FREEZING BARS

Bars can be frozen before or after baking. The pan containing the bars (uncut) should be wrapped in freezer paper and placed in the freezer. When needed, the pan should be removed from the freezer and thawed at room temperature; or it can be thawed by being placed in a moderate oven for a few moments. Of course, the unbaked dough can be removed from the freezer, unwrapped, and placed directly into the oven and be baked as the recipe directed.

If desired, bars can be cut after they are baked, removed from the pan, and wrapped in waxed paper or be arranged on a cardboard. Either way, the bars should be placed into a freezer bag, sealed, and stored in the freezer. When needed, these bars should be removed from the freezer and be left standing at room temperature for 15 minutes or until thawed.

It doesn't matter too much how a cookie is stored—just so long as it is fresh when served.

10. decorating

The decorations on a cookie can do more than just add glamor to it. They also add flavor and "yumminess." But, just as accessories to a costume must be selected with care and thought, so must decorations for a cookie (a batch of cookies, that is).

Merely preparing a batch of frosting is only the beginning and only one of many ways to add beauty and flavor to cookies. There are a number of colorful decorations that may be applied to cookies before or after baking.

Before baking, cookies can be glazed by brushing each cookie with milk or with an egg white or egg yolk that has been beaten and thinned with one tablespoon of water. This will provide the cookies with a shiny appearance. More color and flavor can be added to the cookies by sprinkling the glaze with tinted granulated sugar, cinnamon and sugar, confectioner's sugar, brown sugar, chopped nuts, grated lemon or orange rind, plain or colored coconut, and many other decorations.

Baked cookies can be decorated by brushing corn syrup over the tops and then sprinkling, or arranging in a particular design, colored sugar, cinnamon or other candies, chocolate shots, or candied fruit on top of the syrup. The cookies should be placed on a rack until the corn syrup has dried; then they can be stored safely. The corn syrup not only makes the cookies shiny, but it also helps keep the decorations securely in place.

AVAILABLE DECORATIONS

Numerous food items are available at the average grocery store that will add glamor to cookies—in a hurry, and either before or after baking. A wise homemaker will tarry at this counter in her favorite grocery store every so often just to see what is new in cookie and baking decorations. Among the items now available (many of these also can be prepared at home) are:

Angelique
Brown sugar
Candied cherries
Candied citron
Candied pineapple
Caraway seeds
Chocolate shots or bits
Cinnamon candies
Cinnamon sugar
Colored decorates
Colored granulated sugar
Confectioner's sugar
Food coloring
Fondant mints

Gum drops
Jam
Jelly
Jelly beans
Maraschino cherries
Marshmallows
Poppy seeds
Shaved chocolate
Shredded coconut
Silver candy beads
Tinted coconut
Whole or chopped nuts

Each homemaker should decorate cookies to suit her family, just as she decorates the home to suit their personalities. Through the decorations she has a chance to become truly creative and use her imagination. There is no limit to the things that can be done in decorating cookies.

METHODS FOR FROSTING

As for frosting cookies, almost any icing recipe can be used to an advantage on cookies. Cookies should be cooled slightly before the icing is applied. It then can be applied with a cake decorator, a paper pastry tube, pastry bag with different shaped tips, or the icing can be poured over the cookies. Also, cooled cookies can be iced with hot liquid icing by dipping the cookies directly into the icing.

Frostings also can be used merely for decorations on a cookie. For example, names can be written in icing across the face of the cookies, or numbers can be drawn. Also, frostings can be used to make flowers, leaves, faces, fancy borders, or other decorations on the cookies. Homemakers should attempt to make the decorations have a theme relating to something connected with the particular season.

And Christmas is not the only time to bake and decorate cookies! Any season is cookie time. The shortening and other ingredients in cookies provide food energy; thus, cookies are wonderful to serve to children and adults the year round.

11. serving

The true pleasure should come when a homemaker can serve with pride the cookies that she has prepared so carefully.

Cookies are perfect for serving:
1. At morning coffee sessions
2. At teas
3. At parties
4. At showers
5. In lunchboxes
6. After school
7. Between meals
8. For bedtime snacks
9. As a dessert
10. As part of dessert

One key to making people get the greatest amount of eating enjoyment from a batch of cookies is to serve the proper kind of cookie with the right drink or dessert. For instance, a plain cookie can be served with almost any type of cold or hot drink, from milk to hot lemonade, whereas a rich cookie cannot be served with extremely rich or sweet drinks, such as a cola drink. A wise homemaker will create a balance in the food value and eating pleasure if she will serve cookies with only those drinks that complement the flavor and texture of the cookies. Among the drinks that are delicious with a large variety of cookies are milk, coffee, tea, chocolate drinks, fruit juices, punches, ades, ice cream sodas, cola drinks, and carbonated drinks.

SERVING WITH FRUIT

Fresh fruit is an excellent complement for almost any type of cookie. According to an outstanding home economist, the juicier fruits, such as oranges, peaches, and plums, are the best fresh fruits to serve with cookies. This home economist suggests that tangerines and oranges be packed along with cookies in lunch boxes, especially during the winter months.

Canned fruits, such as crushed pineapple or berries, frozen fruits, or freshly cooked fruits, are perfectly scrumptious to serve with cookies. This is especially true following a light meal. Even greater food value can be provided to such a dessert by the addition of a few pieces of fresh fruits. As far as that goes, several fresh fruits (grapefruit sections, diced apple, and sliced banana) can be served with cookies following a dinner; this is especially tasty on hot summer nights. Ambrosia dishes are wonderful complements for macaroons.

SERVING WITH FROZEN DESSERTS

Ice cream and sherberts cannot, and must not, be overlooked when planning a dessert to go along with a batch of freshly baked cookies. Moist cookies and bars that have lots of fruit and nuts in them are extremely delicious with ice cream; the crisper, richer types of cookies go well with the fruit-flavored sherberts.

Various types of ice cream and sherbert dishes, such as ice cream sodas, sundaes, and banana splits, are also nice to serve with almost any type of cookie (and anytime)—so long as the cookies are oven fresh.

Gelatinous desserts are also wonderful for serving with a fresh batch of cookies. Since most of the gelatinous desserts are so colorful, one of the plainer types of cookies, such as sugar cookies, or even one of the moist cookies, like oatmeal cookies, are better. If a plain gelatinous dessert is for dessert, then chocolate, nutty, or fruit cookies are best. However, when fruits, nuts, or other ingredients have been added to the gelatinous desserts, a very plain cookie is best.

SERVING WITH PUDDINGS

Puddings—cold or hot—can make cookies extra-yummy. Almost any cookie is a complement to puddings and almost any pudding is a complement to cookies. Many people seem to prefer one of the richer, more moist cookies, such as fruit or spice drop cookies, with puddings (especially hot puddings). Iced cookies go very well with plain puddings.

Cookies are just plain good and a complement to almost any dessert from plain fruit to parfait or mousse. And, of course, cookies can be served alone anytime for dessert.

12. mailing

Fresh, home-baked cookies make a wonderful gift to send to some member of the family who is away at school, in service, or living in another area. Also, cookies are perfect gifts to send to relatives, friends, children's and nursing homes, schools, hospitals, or anyone.

There is a large variety of sturdy cookies that can be shipped by mail without damage. The moist drop cookies and rich bars travel best. The proper method of packaging and mailing helps insure a safe journey for cookies, whether the journey is across town or across the nation.

THE CONTAINER

When mailing cookies, the first step is to select a sturdy, air-tight container. Gift-cookies are usually even more delightful to the receiver if the cookies have been packed in some kind of re-usable container, such as a plastic box, a decorative metal can, or a lovely decorative canister. Any kind of coffee, shortening, or other tin can that has a tight fitting lid can be used successfully for mailing cookies. Heavy cardboard boxes can be used, too.

Once the container has been selected, the next step is to clean and dry it thoroughly. In the case of a heavy box, it should be wiped with a damp cloth and let stand momentarily in the open. The containers should be lined with aluminum foil, saran wrap, or waxed paper. A cushion should be made of shredded waxed paper, crumpled paper, or popped popcorn (unbuttered and unsalted) in the bottom of the container.

Cookies should be separated into pairs and a layer of waxed paper placed between each pair before wrapping in aluminum foil, saran wrap, waxed paper, or something similar. Next, the cookies should be packed snugly and systematically into the container. More shredded or crumpled paper, or plain popped popcorn, should be used to fill all crevices. The package of wrapped cookies should be covered with a layer of aluminum foil or paper; and on top of this another layer of shredded or crumpled paper or plain popped popcorn should be placed.

When the container (metal box, plastic box, metal can, or such) has been packed, the lid should be put into place. The container then should be set down inside a heavy cardboard box that is just a little larger. Shredded or crumpled paper, or popped popcorn, should be distributed all around and over the contents. The box should be wrapped with heavy paper, tied securely, and addressed. The package should be marked on both sides with the words PERISHABLE and HANDLE WITH CARE.

In the case of packaging bars, it is best to select a container first. Then, bake the batter so that it will fit snuggly into the bottom of the container (preferably, a heavy carboard box) that has been lined with aluminum foil, saran wrap, or waxed paper. The big bar should be covered with a layer of foil or paper. If several bars are to be mailed, each should be separated by a layer of foil or paper and then the last one covered with foil or paper. Then, the box is ready to have the lid placed on top. The box should be wrapped with a heavy paper and tied securely. After properly addressing the box, PERISHABLE and HANDLE WITH CARE should be marked on both sides of the box.

If the season happens to be a rainy or damp one, the mailing address should be protected by covering the address (after the ink has dried!) with scotch tape or clear nail polish.

THE GIFT PACKAGE

There is no end to the pleasure that can be given and received through sending or taking gifts of cookies to relatives, friends, and others. The gift-cookies are of even greater value and delight if some type of gift (usually an inexpensive one) goes along as the container. For example, a batch of cookies can be placed on a big lid. No homemaker ever seems to have enough lids for the kitchen pans. The cookie-covered lid can be wrapped with saran wrap and then tied with a big bow. A few flowers, fresh or plastic ones, can be added to the bow for extra beauty.

Limitless are the little extra gifts that can be sent to homemakers along with the gift-cookies. For example, the little extra gift could be: a casserole, bowl, cup, saucer, freezer dish, deep-fryer basket, angel-food pan, loaf pan, pie pan, baking sheet, metal tray, basket, candy dish, colander, cornucopia basket, muffin pan, ring mold, glass or set of glasses, watering can, copper jug, hanging basket, flower pot, fish bowl, cooky jar, flour canister, tea pot, mixing bowl, or a set of bowls.

Any of the items mentioned can be used by cleaning and lining them with aluminum foil, saran wrap, or waxed paper. The cookies can be wrapped individually or as a batch and placed inside the gift-container. Then, if desired, the container can be wrapped and decorated in keeping with the season or occasion.

EXTRA GIFTS

The men? Oh, there are numerous extra gifts that can carry gift-cookies to men. For instance, a metal box that can be used for storing an assortment of nails and screws or for holding fish hooks, a lunch box, a paper paint pail, a straw hat, brandy snifter, drinking glass, extra large coffee cup, small metal file box, pencil box, cigarette dish, large ash tray, or something for the patio chef to use.

The children? Toys that can be purchased and filled with cookies are as numerous as the kitchen items that can be used as extra gifts for women. Among the more appropriate toys are: sand bucket, dump truck, wheelbarrow, toy cart, toy bird cage, spring drum, tambourine, cowboy or cowgirl hat, boy or girl scout neckerchief, or even a lunch box. These can be lined with foil or paper and can be filled with individually wrapped cookies.

There are many items that can be found around the average home that can be covered, decorated, and made into lovely cookie containers. Among these are: paper bags, milk cartons, cans of all kinds and sizes, wide-mouthed jars, oatmeal and other boxes. With a little imagination, a pair of scissors, glue, scotch tape, paper, ribbon, and odds and ends of trimming—there is no limit to what a homemaker can do to change these plain containers into something of value and beauty, not to mention the fun.

But, the important thing is to prepare a delectable batch of cookies!

PART III

cookie recipes

13. drop cookies

LITTLE TWINKS

2 cups enriched flour, sifted
½ teaspoon salt
⅔ cup butter or margarine
1 cup confectioners' sugar
2 eggs, separated
1 teaspoon vanilla
½ cup flaked coconut
⅓ cup red raspberry preserves
   dash of salt
½ cup confectioners' sugar

Sift together sifted flour and salt. Cream together butter or margarine and 1 cup confectioners' sugar until light and fluffy. Add egg yolks and vanilla to creamed mixture; beat well. Gradually blend the sifted dry ingredients into

95

creamed mixture; stir until batter is smooth. Add coconut to batter; mix thoroughly.

Drop dough by tablespoonfuls onto ungreased baking sheet. Make a depression in the center of each cookie and fill with preserves.

Beat egg whites with $\frac{1}{8}$ teaspoon salt until frothy. Gradually add $\frac{1}{2}$ cup confectioners' sugar and continue beating to form stiff peaks. Top each cookie with a teaspoonful of meringue to cover preserves. Bake in oven 300°F. about 30 minutes.

Makes about 2 dozen cookies.

FRUIT DROPS

        1 cup shortening
        2 cups brown sugar
        2 eggs, well-beaten
     3$\frac{1}{2}$ cups all-purpose flour, sifted
        1 teaspoon salt
        1 teaspoon baking soda
        1 teaspoon nutmeg
        1 teaspoon cinnamon
     $\frac{1}{2}$ cup instant coffee, cold
     $\frac{3}{4}$ cup seeded raisins
     $\frac{3}{4}$ cup dates, chopped
        1 cup nuts, coarsely chopped

Thoroughly cream shortening; add brown sugar and cream well. Add eggs to creamed mixture; beat thoroughly. Sift together sifted flour, salt, soda, nutmeg, and cinnamon. Stir sifted dry ingredients into creamed mixture alternately with coffee. Blend fruits and nuts into batter.

Drop by teaspoonfuls onto greased baking sheet. Bake in oven 400°F. 15 minutes.

Makes about 8 dozen cookies.

APPLE DROP COOKIES

$\frac{1}{2}$ cup shortening
1 cup brown sugar
2 eggs, well-beaten
$\frac{1}{2}$ teaspoon vanilla
$\frac{1}{2}$ cup walnuts
$\frac{1}{2}$ cup dates
1 small apple
1$\frac{3}{4}$ cups flour, sifted
$\frac{1}{2}$ teaspoon baking soda
$\frac{1}{2}$ teaspoon baking powder
$\frac{1}{2}$ teaspoon cinnamon
$\frac{1}{2}$ cup rolled oats, uncooked

Cream shortening; add brown sugar. Beat eggs and vanilla into creamed mixture. Grind nuts, dates, and apple through a food chopper; mix into creamed mixture. Sift together sifted flour, soda, baking powder, and cinnamon; stir into creamed mixture along with rolled oats. Mix well.

Drop by teaspoonfuls onto greased baking sheet. Bake in preheated oven 425°F. 10 to 12 minutes.

Makes about 4 dozen cookies.

APPLESAUCE NUT COOKIES

$\frac{1}{2}$ cup shortening
$\frac{1}{2}$ cup brown sugar, packed

$\frac{1}{2}$ cup granulated sugar
1 large egg
2 cups flour, sifted
$\frac{1}{4}$ teaspoon cinnamon
$\frac{1}{4}$ teaspoon salt
$\frac{1}{4}$ teaspoon baking soda
1 teaspoon baking powder
$\frac{1}{2}$ cup applesauce
$\frac{1}{4}$ cup raisins
$\frac{1}{2}$ cup nuts, chopped
1 teaspoon vanilla

Cream together shortening and sugars. Add egg to creamed mixture; mix thoroughly. Sift together sifted flour, cinnamon, salt, soda, and baking powder; add to creamed mixture and blend well. Add applesauce, raisins, nuts, and vanilla to batter; mix well.

Drop by teaspoonfuls, about $1\frac{1}{2}$ inches apart, onto baking sheet. Bake in oven 400°F. about 10 minutes or until brown.

Makes about $2\frac{1}{2}$ dozen cookies.

BANANA OATMEAL COOKIES

$1\frac{1}{2}$ cups all-purpose flour, sifted
1 cup granulated sugar
$\frac{1}{2}$ teaspoon baking soda
1 teaspoon salt
$\frac{1}{4}$ teaspoon nutmeg
$\frac{3}{4}$ teaspoon cinnamon
$\frac{3}{4}$ cup shortening

1 egg, well-beaten
1 cup ripe bananas, mashed
1¾ cups rolled oats, uncooked
½ cup nuts, chopped

Sift together into mixing bowl: sifted flour, sugar, soda, salt, nutmeg, and cinnamon. Cut shortening into sifted ingredients. Add egg, bananas, rolled oats, and nuts to shortening mixture; beat until thoroughly blended.

Drop by teaspoonfuls, about 1½ inches apart, onto ungreased baking sheet. Bake in preheated oven 400°F. 15 minutes, or until edges are browned. Remove from pan immediately and cool on rack.

Makes about 3½ dozen cookies.

COCONUT CRISP COOKIES

½ cup butter
½ cup granulated sugar
½ cup brown sugar, packed
1 egg
1 teaspoon vanilla
1 cup flour, sifted
1 teaspoon double-acting baking powder
1 teaspoon baking soda
½ teaspoon salt
¼ teaspoon nutmeg
1 cup rolled oats, uncooked
1 cup coconut

Cream butter. Gradually add sugars to creamed butter;

mix well after each addition. Add egg and vanilla to creamed mixture; beat until light and fluffy. Sift together sifted flour, baking powder, soda, salt, and nutmeg; blend into creamed mixture. Stir rolled oats and coconut into batter.

Drop by teaspoonfuls onto baking sheet. Bake in oven 350°F. 12 to 15 minutes.

Makes about 3 dozen cookies.

COCONUT CRUNCHIES

$\frac{1}{2}$ cup margarine
$\frac{1}{2}$ cup granulated sugar
$\frac{1}{2}$ cup brown sugar, packed
$\frac{1}{2}$ teaspoon vanilla
1 egg
1 cup flour, sifted
$\frac{1}{4}$ teaspoon baking soda
$\frac{1}{2}$ teaspoon double-acting baking powder
$\frac{1}{8}$ teaspoon salt
1 cup rolled oats, uncooked
1 cup cornflakes
$\frac{1}{2}$ cup coconut

Cream together margarine, sugars, and vanilla. Add egg; mix until smooth. Sift together sifted flour, soda, baking powder, and salt; stir into creamed mixture. Blend rolled oats, cornflakes, and coconut into batter.

Drop by teaspoonfuls onto baking sheet. Bake in oven 325°F. 15 to 20 minutes.

Makes about 4 dozen cookies.

Tropical Oatmeal Nuggets *(Dole Pineapple Co.)*

Coconut-filled Honeys *(American Honey Institute)*

COFFEE COCONUT MERINGUES

2 egg whites
$\frac{1}{4}$ teaspoon salt
1 tablespoon instant coffee
$\frac{1}{2}$ cup granulated sugar
1 cup flaked coconut
$\frac{1}{4}$ teaspoon vanilla

Beat egg whites and salt until foamy throughout. Mix instant coffee and sugar together; add, 2 tablespoons at a time, to the beaten egg whites, beating after each addition until sugar mixture is well blended. Continue beating until mixture stands in peaks. Fold coconut and vanilla into the mixture.

Drop by teaspoonfuls onto well-greased baking sheet. Bake in oven 250°F. 30 minutes, or until done.

Makes $2\frac{1}{2}$ dozen meringues.

PENOCHE COCONUTS

1 cup shortening
2 cups brown sugar, packed
1 teaspoon vanilla
2 eggs
2 cups flour, sifted
$\frac{1}{2}$ teaspoon salt
1 teaspoon baking soda
2 cups coconut

Cream together shortening and brown sugar until

thoroughly blended. Mix in vanilla. Add eggs, 1 at a time, beating well after each addition. Sift together sifted flour, salt, and soda. Add sifted dry ingredients to shortening mixture; blend thoroughly. Stir in coconut.

Drop by teaspoonfuls onto baking sheet. Bake in oven 375°F. 8 to 10 minutes.

Makes about 8 dozen cookies.

CARAMEL–CHOCOLATE–COCONUT CHEWS

$\frac{1}{4}$ cup chocolate chips
$\frac{1}{2}$ cup caramel chips
$2\frac{1}{4}$ cups cornflakes, well-packed but not crushed
$\frac{1}{2}$ cup flaked coconut
$\frac{3}{4}$ cup granulated sugar
2 eggs, well-beaten
1 teaspoon vanilla

Combine chocolate chips, caramel chips, cornflakes, coconut, and sugar; mix well. Add well-beaten eggs and vanilla to chocolate chip mixture; mix well. Let batter set in the mixing bowl 5 minutes.

Drop by teaspoonfuls onto greased and floured baking sheet. Bake in oven 350°F. 10 to 12 minutes. After baking, immediately remove cookies from baking sheet. If cookies begin to stick, hold baking sheet over direct heat for several seconds.

Makes about 3 dozen cookies.

CHOCOLATE COCONUT CRISPIES

2½ cups enriched flour, sifted
½ teaspoon baking soda
½ teaspoon salt
2 one-ounce squares unsweetened chocolate
1 cup shortening
2½ cups brown sugar
2 eggs
½ cup nuts, chopped
½ cup flaked coconut

Sift together sifted flour, soda, and salt. Melt chocolate in top of double boiler over hot water. Cream together shortening and brown sugar until light and fluffy. Add eggs to creamed mixture; beat well. Stir melted chocolate into creamed mixture. Beat well. Add sifted dry ingredients to creamed mixture; mix well. Stir nuts and coconut into batter.

Drop by teaspoonfuls onto greased baking sheet. Bake in oven 350°F. 12 to 15 minutes.

Makes about 5 dozen cookies.

DATE DROPS

½ cup shortening
¾ cup brown sugar, packed
2 eggs
¼ cup milk
1½ cups flour, sifted
1 teaspoon baking powder

1 cup quick-cooking rolled oats, uncooked
1 cup nuts, chopped
1 cup dates, pitted and chopped

Cream together shortening and brown sugar. Add eggs and milk to creamed mixture; combine well. Sift together sifted flour and baking powder; add gradually to shortening mixture. Blend rolled oats, nuts, and dates into batter.

Drop by teaspoonfuls onto baking sheet. Bake in oven 350°F. 15 to 20 minutes.

Makes about 3 dozen cookies.

DATE–NUT DROP COOKIES

1 package yellow cake mix
$\frac{1}{4}$ cup water
2 eggs, unbeaten
$\frac{1}{4}$ cup butter or shortening, soft
1 cup dates, chopped
$\frac{1}{2}$ cup almonds, blanched and shredded

Place half of cake mix into large mixing bowl. Add water, eggs, and butter to the cake mix; blend well. Blend other half of cake mix into the batter; beat smooth. Stir chopped dates and almonds into the batter.

Drop dough by teaspoonfuls onto a greased baking sheet. Bake in oven 375°F. 12 to 14 minutes. These cookies should be stored in a tightly covered container.

Makes about 4 dozen cookies.

SPICY DATE COOKIES

$\frac{1}{2}$ cup shortening
$\frac{3}{4}$ cup brown sugar
1 egg, well-beaten
$1\frac{1}{2}$ cups all-purpose flour, sifted
$\frac{1}{2}$ teaspoon cinnamon
1 teaspoon cloves
$\frac{1}{4}$ teaspoon baking soda
1 teaspoon baking powder
1 tablespoon milk
$\frac{3}{4}$ cup dates, finely chopped
$\frac{1}{4}$ cup walnuts, coarsely chopped

Cream shortening. Add brown sugar to shortening; cream until light and fluffy. Add egg to shortening mixture; beat well. Sift together sifted flour, cinnamon, cloves, soda, and baking powder. Mix sifted dry ingredients and milk into shortening mixture. Stir dates and nuts into batter.

Drop by teaspoonfuls onto greased baking sheet. Bake in oven 375°F. 8 to 10 minutes.

Makes about 3 dozen cookies.

LEMON CREAM COOKIES

1 cup shortening, soft
2 cups granulated sugar or corn syrup
4 cups flour, sifted
$\frac{1}{4}$ teaspoon baking soda
$\frac{1}{4}$ teaspoon baking powder
1 teaspoon salt
1 teaspoon nutmeg

2 eggs, beaten
$\frac{1}{4}$ cup cream or evaporated milk
$\frac{3}{4}$ cup bottled lemon juice

Cream together shortening and sugar. Sift together sifted flour, soda, baking powder, salt, and nutmeg; blend into creamed mixture. Combine beaten eggs, cream, and bottled lemon juice; add to the creamed mixture. Mix well.

Drop dough by teaspoonfuls onto well-greased baking sheet. Allow room for dough to spread during baking process. Bake in oven 375°F. 10 minutes.

Makes 4 dozen cookies.

LEMON DROP COOKIES

1 cup shortening
2 cups granulated sugar
2 eggs
1 tablespoon lemon rind, grated
3 cups flour, sifted
1 teaspoon baking soda
2 teaspoons salt
3 teaspoons baking powder
$\frac{1}{2}$ cup lemon juice
$\frac{1}{2}$ cup cold water

Cream together shortening and sugar. Add eggs and lemon rind to creamed mixture; beat well. Sift together sifted flour, soda, salt, and baking powder. Add sifted dry ingredients, lemon juice, and water. Mix until blended.

Drop by teaspoonfuls onto baking sheet. Bake in oven 400°F. 10 minutes.

Makes about $5\frac{1}{2}$ dozen cookies.

LEMON SPICE COOKIES

2 eggs, beaten
$\frac{1}{4}$ cup cream
$\frac{3}{4}$ cup bottled lemon juice
4 cups flour, sifted
$\frac{1}{4}$ teaspoon baking soda
$\frac{1}{4}$ teaspoon baking powder
1 teaspoon salt
1 teaspoon nutmeg
1 cup shortening, soft
2 cups granulated sugar
1 cup nuts, chopped

Combine beaten eggs, cream, and bottled lemon juice in small bowl. Sift together sifted flour, soda, baking powder, salt, and nutmeg. Cream shortening and sugar in large mixing bowl; add egg mixture alternately with sifted dry ingredients. Mix well. Stir chopped nuts into dough. Raisins or diced candied fruits can be used in place of chopped nuts.

Drop by teaspoonfuls onto well greased baking sheet, allowing room for dough to spread during baking process. Bake in oven 375°F. for 10 minutes.

Makes approximately 6 dozen cookies.

MINCE MEAT PRIZE COOKIES

$3\frac{1}{4}$ cups flour, sifted
$\frac{1}{2}$ teaspoon salt
1 teaspoon baking soda

1 cup shortening
1½ cups granulated sugar
3 eggs, well-beaten
1 nine-ounce package of mince meat

Sift together sifted flour, salt, and soda. Cream shortening; gradually add sugar and cream until fluffy. Add eggs to creamed mixture; beat until smooth. Break mince meat into small pieces; stir into creamed mixture. Add sifted dry ingredients; mix well.

Drop by teaspoonfuls, 2 inches apart, onto greased baking sheet. Bake in oven 400°F. about 12 minutes.

Makes about 4 dozen cookies.

MINCE MEAT JUMBLES

2 cups flour, sifted
2 teaspoons baking soda
½ cup shortening
½ teaspoon salt
1 cup granulated sugar
3 eggs
2 cups semi-sweet chocolate morsels
1 nine-ounce package condensed mince meat, finely crumbled

Sift together sifted flour and soda; set aside. Combine shortening and salt; beat until light. Gradually beat sugar into shortening mixture; add eggs, 1 at a time, and beat until light. Stir sifted dry ingredients, morsels, and mince meat into shortening mixture.

Drop dough by tablespoonfuls onto greased baking sheet. Bake in oven 375°F. 10 minutes. When done, remove from oven and immediately lift jumbles from baking sheet; place on wire racks to cool.

Makes about 4 dozen jumbles.

MINCE MEAT OATMEAL COOKIES

$1\frac{1}{4}$ cups flour, sifted
1 teaspoon instant coffee
$\frac{3}{4}$ teaspoon baking soda
$\frac{1}{2}$ teaspoon salt
$\frac{1}{2}$ cup shortening
1 cup brown sugar, firmly packed
1 egg, slightly beaten
$1\frac{1}{3}$ cups mince meat
$1\frac{1}{2}$ cups rolled oats, uncooked

Sift together sifted flour, instant coffee, soda, and salt. Cream shortening. Gradually add brown sugar to creamed shortening; beat until fluffy. Add egg to creamed mixture; beat thoroughly. Stir mince meat into creamed mixture. Add sifted dry ingredients in 3 parts; blend well after each addition. Mix rolled oats into batter.

Drop by teaspoonfuls, 2 inches apart, onto greased baking sheet. Flatten cookies slightly. Bake in oven 350°F. about 15 minutes or until lightly browned.

Makes about 4 dozen cookies.

FLORIDA ORANGE COOKIES

$\frac{2}{3}$ cup shortening
1 cup granulated sugar
2 eggs
1 tablespoon orange rind, grated
$2\frac{1}{2}$ cups cake flour, sifted
$\frac{1}{2}$ teaspoon salt
$\frac{1}{2}$ teaspoon baking soda
$\frac{1}{2}$ cup orange juice
$\frac{1}{2}$ cup nuts, chopped

Cream together shortening, sugar, eggs, and orange rind. Sift together sifted flour, salt, and soda. Blend sifted dry ingredients, alternately with orange juice, into creamed mixture. Stir nuts into batter.

Drop by level tablespoonfuls onto baking sheet. Bake in oven 400°F. 10 minutes.

Makes about 6 dozen cookies.

ORANGE HONEY COOKIES

$\frac{1}{2}$ cup shortening
$\frac{1}{2}$ cup granulated sugar
1 egg
1 teaspoon orange rind, grated
$\frac{1}{2}$ cup honey
3 cups all-purpose flour, sifted
3 teaspoons baking powder
$\frac{1}{2}$ teaspoon salt
$\frac{1}{2}$ cup orange juice
$\frac{1}{4}$ cup fresh nuts, chopped

$\frac{1}{4}$ cup raisins
4 dozen orange sections*

Cream together shortening and sugar until light and fluffy.
Add egg and grated orange rind; beat thoroughly. Blend
honey into creamed mixture. Sift together sifted flour,
baking powder, and salt; add to creamed mixture alternately
with orange juice. Stir nuts and raisins into the batter.

Drop by teaspoonfuls onto greased baking sheet. Press an
orange section into each unbaked cookie. Bake in oven
375°F. about 15 minutes.

* Approximately 4 oranges.

Makes about 4 dozen cookies.

PINEAPPLE DROP COOKIES

1 cup light brown sugar
$\frac{1}{2}$ cup shortening (part butter)
1 egg, unbeaten
1 teaspoon vanilla
$\frac{3}{4}$ cup crushed pineapple
2 cups flour, sifted
1 teaspoon baking powder
$\frac{1}{2}$ teaspoon baking soda
$\frac{1}{2}$ teaspoon salt
$\frac{3}{4}$ cup walnuts, chopped
$\frac{1}{2}$ cup raisins

Put brown sugar, shortening, egg, and vanilla into a
mixing bowl; mix until well blended. Spoon pineapple (with
as little syrup as possible) into a measuring cup; measure
accurately and blend into sugar mixture. Sift together sifted

flour, baking powder, soda, and salt; stir into sugar mixture. Mix walnuts and raisins into the batter.

Drop by heaping teaspoonfuls onto ungreased baking sheet. Bake in preheated oven 375°F. about 12 minutes or until lightly browned.

Makes 3 dozen cookies.

PRUNE–APRICOT MORSELS

$\frac{1}{2}$ cup butter, soft
6 tablespoons granulated sugar
6 tablespoons brown sugar
1 egg
$\frac{1}{2}$ teaspoon vanilla
$\frac{1}{4}$ teaspoon water
1 cup and 2 tablespoons all-purpose flour, sifted
$\frac{1}{2}$ teaspoon baking soda
$\frac{1}{2}$ teaspoon salt
$\frac{1}{2}$ cup dried prunes, pitted and coarsely chopped
$\frac{1}{2}$ cup dried apricots, coarsely chopped
1 cup semi-sweet chocolate morsels

Cream together butter and sugars; add egg and mix well. Blend vanilla and water into creamed mixture. Sift together sifted flour, soda, and salt; blend into creamed mixture. Add prunes, apricots, and chocolate morsels to batter; mix thoroughly.

Drop by half teaspoonfuls onto ungreased baking sheet. Bake in oven 375°F. 10 to 12 minutes. Cool on wire rack.

Makes about 4 dozen morsels.

RAISIN BUTTER COOKIES

$\frac{3}{4}$ cup golden seedless raisins
$\frac{3}{4}$ cup butter or margarine
$\frac{1}{2}$ cup granulated sugar
1 egg yolk
2 cups all-purpose flour, sifted
$\frac{1}{2}$ teaspoon salt
1 teaspoon vanilla
2 drops almond extract
$\frac{1}{4}$ cup candied cherries, chopped

Rinse and drain raisins. Cream together butter and sugar. Add egg yolk to creamed mixture; beat well. Sift together sifted flour and salt; blend into creamed mixture. Stir vanilla, almond extract, raisins, and cherries into batter.

Drop by teaspoonfuls onto greased baking sheet. Bake in oven 400°F. 8 to 10 minutes. Cool on baking pan. Remove carefully with spatula.

Makes about $3\frac{1}{2}$ dozen cookies.

RAISIN ROUGHS

1 cup shortening
$\frac{1}{2}$ cup peanut butter
2 cups granulated sugar
3 eggs
1 cup all-purpose flour, sifted
$\frac{3}{4}$ teaspoon salt
$\frac{3}{4}$ teaspoon baking soda
$1\frac{1}{2}$ teaspoons cinnamon

$\frac{1}{4}$ cup milk
$1\frac{1}{2}$ teaspoons vanilla
$3\frac{1}{2}$ cups rolled oats, uncooked
2 cups seedless raisins

Cream together shortening, peanut butter, and sugar. Add eggs, 1 at a time, beating well after each addition. Sift together sifted flour, salt, soda, and cinnamon; blend into creamed mixture. Add milk and vanilla. Stir in rolled oats and raisins.

Drop by heaping teaspoonfuls onto greased baking sheet. Bake in oven 385°F. about 15 minutes. Remove to wire rack to cool.

Makes about 5 dozen cookies.

RAISIN MOLASSES COOKIES

1 cup seedless raisins
$\frac{1}{2}$ cup shortening
$\frac{1}{4}$ cup granulated sugar
1 egg
$\frac{3}{4}$ cup molasses
2 cups all-purpose flour, sifted
1 teaspoon ginger
1 teaspoon cinnamon
$1\frac{1}{2}$ teaspoons baking powder
$\frac{1}{2}$ teaspoon salt
$\frac{1}{4}$ teaspoon baking soda

Rinse and drain raisins. Cream shortening and sugar. Add egg to creamed mixture; beat well. Blend molasses into creamed mixture. Sift together sifted flour, ginger, cinnamon, baking powder, salt, and soda. Blend sifted dry ingredients into creamed mixture. Stir raisins into batter.

Drop by teaspoonfuls onto greased baking sheet. Bake in oven 350°F. 15 to 18 minutes. Remove to wire rack to cool.

Makes about 3 dozen cookies.

CHOCOLATE RAISIN DROPS

$\frac{1}{2}$ cup shortening
$\frac{1}{2}$ cup brown sugar, packed
$\frac{1}{4}$ cup granulated sugar
1 egg
$\frac{1}{2}$ teaspoon vanilla
1 cup and 2 tablespoons flour, sifted
$\frac{1}{2}$ teaspoon salt
$\frac{1}{2}$ teaspoon baking powder
$\frac{3}{4}$ cup chocolate-covered raisins
$\frac{1}{4}$ cup nuts, chopped

Cream together shortening and sugars. Add egg and vanilla to creamed mixture; beat thoroughly. Sift together sifted flour, salt, and soda; blend sifted dry ingredients into creamed mixture. Stir chocolate-covered raisins and chopped nuts into batter.

Drop dough by teaspoonfuls onto greased baking sheet. Bake in oven 375°F. 12 minutes or until lightly browned. When done, remove from baking sheet to a rack and cool before storing.

Makes about 4 dozen cookies.

RAISIN HONEY DROPS

$\frac{1}{2}$ cup shortening
$\frac{1}{2}$ cup margarine
$1\frac{1}{4}$ cups honey
2 eggs, well-beaten
2 one-ounce squares unsweetened chocolate, melted
$1\frac{1}{2}$ cups quick-cooking rolled oats, uncooked
$2\frac{1}{2}$ cups cake flour, sifted
1 teaspoon baking powder
$\frac{1}{4}$ teaspoon baking soda
1 teaspoon salt
1 teaspoon cinnamon
$1\frac{1}{2}$ cups golden seedless raisins
$\frac{1}{2}$ cup nuts, chopped

Blend together shortening, margarine, and honey. Blend well-beaten eggs into shortening mixture. Stir melted chocolate and rolled oats into shortening mixture. Sift together sifted flour, baking powder, soda, salt, and cinnamon; mix into shortening mixture. Blend raisins and nuts into the batter.

Drop by teaspoonfuls, about $1\frac{1}{2}$ inches apart, onto greased baking sheet. Bake in oven 325°F. 20 minutes. When done, remove from pan and place on wire racks to cool.

Makes 6 dozen cookies.

SPICY RAISIN COOKIES

1 cup water
2 cups raisins

1 cup shortening
2 cups granulated sugar
3 eggs
1 teaspoon vanilla
4 cups flour, sifted
1 teaspoon baking powder
1 teaspoon baking soda
1 teaspoon salt
$\frac{1}{4}$ teaspoon allspice
$1\frac{1}{2}$ teaspoons cinnamon
$\frac{1}{4}$ teaspoon nutmeg

Boil the water and raisins in a saucepan over medium heat for 5 minutes; set aside to cool. Thoroughly cream together shortening and sugar. Add eggs to creamed mixture; beat well. Add vanilla to the cooled raisin mixture. Sift together sifted flour, baking powder, soda, salt, allspice, cinnamon, and nutmeg; blend, alternately with raisin mixture, into creamed mixture.

Drop by teaspoonfuls onto greased baking sheet. Bake in oven 350°F. 12 to 15 minutes.

Makes 4 dozen cookies.

CHOCOLATE DROP COOKIES

$1\frac{1}{2}$ cups flour, sifted
$1\frac{1}{2}$ teaspoons baking powder
$\frac{1}{2}$ teaspoon salt
3 one-ounce squares unsweetened chocolate
4 tablespoons butter or shortening
1 cup granulated sugar

1 egg, unbeaten
$\frac{3}{4}$ cup milk
$\frac{1}{2}$ teaspoon vanilla

Sift flour once and measure; add baking powder and salt, and sift together 3 times. Melt chocolate and butter in top of double boiler over hot water; cool to lukewarm. Add sugar to chocolate mixture; mix well. Add egg to chocolate mixture; beat thoroughly. Blend sifted dry ingredients, alternately with milk, into chocolate mixture; add vanilla.

Drop dough by teaspoonfuls onto an ungreased baking sheet. Bake in oven 375°F. 9 minutes, or until done. When done, remove from the oven and cool slightly before transferring from pan to a rack. Ice, if desired, with Chocolate Frosting or Java Cocoa Icing.

Makes 3 dozen cookies.

FROSTED CHOCOLATE DROP COOKIES

$\frac{1}{2}$ cup shortening, soft
1 cup light brown sugar
1 egg, unbeaten
$\frac{1}{2}$ cup milk
2 one-ounce squares chocolate, melted
$1\frac{3}{4}$ cups all-purpose flour, sifted
$\frac{1}{4}$ teaspoon baking soda
1 teaspoon baking powder
$\frac{1}{2}$ teaspoon salt
$\frac{1}{2}$ cup walnuts, chopped
Chocolate Frosting

Cream together shortening and brown sugar. Add egg, milk, and melted chocolate to creamed mixture; mix well. Sift together sifted flour, soda, baking powder, and salt; blend into creamed mixture. Add nuts to batter; blend well.

Drop by teaspoonfuls onto greased baking sheet. Bake in preheated oven 375° to 400°F. 12 to 15 minutes. Immediately after removing from oven, place a small amount of Chocolate Frosting on each cookie. The heat will cause the frosting to spread and form a glaze.

Makes 4 dozen cookies.

CHOCOLATE MUNCHERS

1 cup semi-sweet chocolate morsels
8 marshmallows
1 tablespoon water
$\frac{3}{4}$ cup all-purpose flour, sifted
$\frac{1}{2}$ cup granulated sugar
$\frac{3}{4}$ teaspoon salt
$\frac{1}{2}$ teaspoon baking soda
$\frac{1}{2}$ cup shortening, soft
$\frac{1}{3}$ cup brown sugar, firmly packed
1 egg
2 teaspoons almond extract
$\frac{1}{2}$ teaspoon vanilla
$1\frac{1}{4}$ cups quick-cooking rolled oats, uncooked
1 cup pecans, chopped

Melt morsels in top of double boiler over hot (not boiling) water. Add marshmallows and water to melted morsels; stir until melted, then set aside. Sift together sifted flour, sugar, salt, and soda. Slowly blend shortening, brown sugar, egg, almond extract, and vanilla into sifted dry ingredients. Mix well. Stir rolled oats, chopped pecans, and melted morsels mixture into the batter; blend thoroughly.

Drop dough by teaspoonfuls onto well-greased baking sheet. Bake in oven 350°F. 12 to 15 minutes. When done, immediately remove cookies from the baking sheet.

Makes about 4 dozen cookies.

DOUBLE CHOCOLATE HE-MAN COOKIES

$\frac{1}{2}$ cup margarine
$2\frac{1}{2}$ one-ounce squares unsweetened chocolate
1 cup granulated sugar
1 teaspoon vanilla
2 eggs
2 cups flour, sifted
1 teaspoon baking powder
$\frac{1}{2}$ teaspoon baking soda
$\frac{1}{2}$ cup sour cream or buttermilk
He-Man Frosting

Slowly melt together margarine and chocolate in a large saucepan over low heat. Remove the saucepan from heat; add sugar, vanilla, and eggs and beat well. Sift together sifted flour, baking powder, and soda. Stir the sifted dry ingredients, alternately with the sour cream, into the chocolate mixture in the saucepan. Thoroughly beat the mixture.

Drop the dough by teaspoonfuls, about 2 inches apart, onto a greased baking sheet. Bake in oven 350°F. about 15 minutes. Cool and ice the cookies with He-Man Frosting.

Makes 4 dozen cookies.

CHOCOLATE MERINGUE COOKIES

2 cups confectioners' sugar, sifted
1 tablespoon flour
¼ teaspoon salt
3 egg whites
2 or 3 one-ounce squares unsweetened chocolate, melted and cooled
¾ cup shredded coconut
1 teaspoon vanilla

Sift together confectioners' sugar, flour, and salt. Beat egg whites until stiff. Add sifted dry ingredients, 2 tablespoons at a time, to egg whites; after each addition beat until well blended. Fold chocolate, coconut, and vanilla into batter.

Drop by teaspoonfuls onto lightly greased baking sheet. Bake in oven 375°F. about 10 minutes. For best results, start cookies on lower shelf of oven and move to upper shelf after first 5 minutes of cooking to complete the baking process. When done, immediately remove cookies from baking sheet with a knife or spatula. Cool on racks. Store in an airtight container.

Makes about 2½ dozen cookies.

CHOCOLATE SUGAR DROP COOKIES

½ cup butter or margarine
¼ cup shortening
1 cup granulated sugar
3 one-ounce squares unsweetened chocolate, melted
2 eggs
2 teaspoons vanilla

2½ cups all-purpose flour, sifted
¾ teaspoon baking powder
1 teaspoon salt

Cream together butter, shortening, and sugar until light and fluffy. Add melted chocolate to creamed mixture; mix well. Add eggs, 1 at a time, to creamed mixture and stir thoroughly after each addition. Add vanilla. Sift together sifted flour, baking powder, and salt; slowly add sifted dry ingredients to creamed mixture. Mix thoroughly.

Drop by teaspoonfuls onto ungreased baking sheet. Flatten each cookie with bottom of glass. Bake in oven 400°F. 7 minutes.

Makes about 5 dozen cookies.

CHOCOLATE RAISIN DROP COOKIES

1 package devil's food cake mix
¼ cup water
2 eggs, unbeaten
¼ cup butter or shortening, soft
1 cup raisins
½ cup walnuts, chopped

Place about half the cake mix into mixing bowl; add water, eggs, and butter, and blend well. Add rest of the cake mix; beat until smooth. Stir raisins and nuts into batter.

Drop dough by teaspoonfuls onto a greased baking sheet. Bake in oven 375°F. 12 minutes. These cookies should be stored in tightly covered container.

Makes about 4 dozen cookies.

CHOCOLATE RAISIN CLUSTERS

$1\frac{1}{2}$ cups raisins, light or dark
$\frac{1}{2}$ cup shortening
1 cup brown sugar, packed
1 egg
2 one-ounce squares unsweetened chocolate, melted
$1\frac{1}{4}$ cups all-purpose flour, sifted
$\frac{1}{2}$ teaspoon baking powder
$\frac{1}{2}$ teaspoon salt
$\frac{1}{3}$ cup milk
1 teaspoon vanilla
$\frac{1}{2}$ cup walnuts, chopped

Rinse and drain raisins. Cream together shortening and brown sugar. Add egg to creamed mixture; beat thoroughly. Blend melted chocolate into creamed mixture. Sift together sifted flour, baking powder, and salt; blend, alternately with milk, into creamed mixture. Blend vanilla, raisins, and walnuts into batter.

Drop by teaspoonfuls onto greased baking sheet. Bake in oven 350°F. 15 minutes. Remove to wire rack to cool.

Makes about 4 dozen cookies.

CHOCOLATE PUFFS

2 egg whites, well-beaten
$\frac{1}{2}$ cup granulated sugar
$\frac{1}{4}$ teaspoon salt
1 teaspoon vanilla
1 six-ounce package chocolate pieces, melted

$1\frac{1}{3}$ cups coconut
$\frac{1}{2}$ cup walnuts, chopped

Beat egg whites until stiff. Gradually add sugar to egg whites and continue beating until blended. Stir salt and vanilla into egg white mixture. Fold melted chocolate, coconut, and walnut into egg white mixture.

Drop by teaspoonfuls onto baking sheet. Bake in oven 300°F. 10 to 15 minutes.

Makes 3 dozen cookies.

CHOCOLATE CHIP COOKIES

$\frac{1}{2}$ cup shortening, soft
6 tablespoons granulated sugar
6 tablespoons brown sugar
1 egg, well-beaten
$\frac{1}{2}$ teaspoon vanilla
1 cup and 2 tablespoons all-purpose flour, sifted
$\frac{1}{2}$ teaspoon baking soda
$\frac{1}{2}$ teaspoon salt
$\frac{1}{2}$ cup nuts, chopped
1 cup chocolate pieces

Cream together shortening and sugars. Add egg and vanilla to creamed mixture; blend well. Sift together sifted flour, soda, and salt; blend into creamed mixture. Fold nuts and chocolate pieces into batter.

Drop by teaspoonfuls onto greased baking sheet. Bake in preheated oven 375° to 400°F. 12 to 15 minutes.

Makes 3 dozen cookies.

CHOCOLATE CHIP ORANGE DROPS

1 cup flour, sifted
$\frac{1}{4}$ teaspoon salt
$\frac{1}{2}$ cup butter or shortening
3 ounces cream cheese
1 teaspoon orange rind, grated
$\frac{1}{2}$ cup granulated sugar
1 egg yolk
1 teaspoon vanilla
1 cup semi-sweet chocolate chips

Sift flour once and measure; add salt and sift again. Cream together butter, cream cheese, and orange rind; add sugar, egg yolk, and vanilla, and beat until light. Blend sifted dry ingredients into the batter; add chocolate chips and mix well.

Drop by teaspoonfuls onto lightly greased baking sheet. Flatten each drop with back of a spoon. Bake in oven 350°F. 15 minutes. When done, remove from oven and transfer to rack and cool.

Makes 3 dozen cookies.

CHOCOLATE CHIP OATMEAL COOKIES

$\frac{2}{3}$ cup flour, sifted
$\frac{1}{2}$ teaspoon baking powder
1 cup quick-cooking rolled oats, uncooked
$\frac{3}{4}$ cup butter or shortening
$\frac{1}{2}$ cup granulated sugar
$\frac{1}{4}$ cup brown sugar, firmly packed

1 egg
½ cup salted peanuts, chopped
1 cup semi-sweet chocolate chips

Sift flour once and measure; add baking powder and sift again. Blend rolled oats into sifted dry ingredients. Cream butter in a large mixing bowl until soft; gradually add sugars and cream together until light and fluffy. Stir egg into the creamed mixture. Gradually add sifted dry ingredients into creamed mixture; mix well. Blend peanuts and chocolate chips into the batter; mix well.

Drop by teaspoonfuls onto ungreased baking sheet. Press each cookie flat with a fork. Bake in oven 375°F. 13 or 14 minutes. When baked, remove from oven and allow cookies to stand on baking sheet about ½ minute before removing to a rack to cool.

Makes about 3 dozen cookies.

INSTANT CHIP COOKIES

1 package white cake mix
¼ cup water
2 egg whites, unbeaten
¼ cup butter, soft
1 cup chocolate chips
½ cup walnuts, chopped

Place half of the cake mix into a large mixing bowl; add water, egg whites, and butter. After thoroughly blending mixture, add remaining cake mix and beat smooth with a wooden spoon. Blend chocolate chips and chopped walnuts into dough.

Drop dough by teaspoonfuls onto lightly greased baking sheet. Bake in oven 375°F. 12 minutes.

Makes about 4 dozen cookies.

CHOCO-WALNUT DROPS

1 cup and 2 tablespoons flour, sifted
$\frac{1}{2}$ teaspoon baking soda
$\frac{1}{2}$ teaspoon salt
$\frac{1}{2}$ cup granulated sugar
$\frac{1}{4}$ cup brown sugar, firmly packed
1 egg, unbeaten
1 teaspoon vanilla
$\frac{1}{2}$ cup shortening (part butter)
$\frac{1}{2}$ cup walnuts, chopped
1 cup semi-sweet chocolate pieces

Sift together sifted flour, soda, salt, and granulated sugar into a mixing bowl. Add brown sugar, egg, vanilla, and shortening to the sifted dry ingredients; stir with spoon about 1 minute until well mixed. Fold walnuts and chocolate pieces into the dough.

Drop by small teaspoonfuls, about 2 inches apart, onto an ungreased baking sheet. Bake in preheated oven 375°F. 10 to 12 minutes.

Makes about 4 dozen cookies.

COCOMALT COOKIES

½ cup shortening
¾ cup brown sugar
¾ cup cocomalt
1 egg, well-beaten
½ cup milk
1½ cups flour
¼ teaspoon salt
½ teaspoon baking soda
1 teaspoon baking powder
1 cup nuts, chopped

Cream shortening. Add sugar and cocomalt to creamed shortening; cream until fluffy. Add egg to creamed mixture; beat thoroughly. Sift together flour, salt, soda, and baking powder. Blend sifted dry ingredients, alternately with milk, into creamed mixture; mix well. Fold nuts into dough.

Drop by teaspoonfuls onto greased baking sheet. Bake in oven 375°F. 15 minutes.

Makes 2 dozen cookies.

DEVIL'S FOOD CHIP COOKIES

1 package devil's food cake mix
⅓ cup water
2 eggs, unbeaten
¼ cup butter, soft
1 cup chocolate chips
½ cup walnuts, chopped

Place half of the cake mix into a mixing bowl; add water, eggs, and butter. After thoroughly blending mixture, add remaining cake mix and beat smooth with a wooden spoon. Stir chocolate chips and chopped walnuts into dough.

Drop dough by teaspoonfuls onto lightly greased baking sheet. Bake cookies in oven 375°F. 15 minutes.

Makes about 4 dozen cookies.

CORNFLAKE MORSELS

1 cup and 2 tablespoons flour, sifted
$\frac{1}{2}$ teaspoon baking soda
$\frac{1}{2}$ teaspoon salt
$\frac{1}{2}$ cup butter, soft
6 tablespoons granulated sugar
6 tablespoons brown sugar
1 egg, slightly beaten
$\frac{1}{2}$ teaspoon vanilla
$\frac{1}{4}$ teaspoon water
2 cups cornflakes, uncrushed
1 cup semi-sweet chocolate morsels

Sift together sifted flour, soda, and salt; set aside. Cream together butter and sugars; add slightly beaten egg, vanilla, and water. Mix well. Thoroughly blend cornflakes and chocolate morsels into batter.

Drop by half teaspoonfuls onto an ungreased baking sheet. Bake in oven 375°F. 10 to 12 minutes. Cool on wire racks.

Makes about 4 dozen cookies.

BEST OATMEAL COOKIES

$\frac{2}{3}$ cup shortening
1 cup brown sugar, packed
1 egg, unbeaten
1 cup all-purpose flour, sifted
1 teaspoon salt
1 teaspoon baking powder
1 teaspoon vanilla
2 cups rolled oats, uncooked
1 cup seedless raisins

Melt shortening; add brown sugar and mix well. Add unbeaten egg to shortening mixture; beat until well blended. Sift together sifted flour, salt, and baking powder; stir into shortening mixture. Blend vanilla, rolled oats, and raisins into batter.

Drop by teaspoonfuls onto greased baking sheet. Bake in oven 350°F. 15 to 20 minutes. Remove to wire rack to cool.

Makes about 5 dozen cookies.

JUST-RIGHT OATMEAL COOKIES

$\frac{1}{2}$ cup shortening
1 cup granulated sugar
1 egg, unbeaten
$\frac{1}{3}$ cup buttermilk
1 cup flour, sifted
$\frac{1}{2}$ teaspoon salt
$\frac{1}{2}$ teaspoon baking soda
$\frac{1}{2}$ teaspoon baking powder

$\frac{1}{2}$ teaspoon nutmeg
$\frac{1}{2}$ teaspoon cinnamon
$1\frac{1}{4}$ cups rolled oats, uncooked
$\frac{3}{4}$ cup walnuts, chopped
$\frac{1}{2}$ cup raisins or dates, chopped

Beat together shortening, sugar, and egg until well blended; add buttermilk. Sift together sifted flour, salt, soda, baking powder, nutmeg, and cinnamon; blend into shortening mixture. Mix rolled oats, walnuts, and raisins (or dates) into batter.

Drop dough by teaspoonfuls, 2 inches apart, on an ungreased baking sheet. Bake in preheated oven 400°F. 9 to 12 minutes.

Makes about 3 dozen cookies.

OATMEAL DROP COOKIES

1 cup shortening, soft
1 cup brown sugar
1 cup granulated sugar
1 teaspoon salt
2 eggs
1 teaspoon vanilla
5 tablespoons water
1 cup all-purpose flour, sifted
1 teaspoon baking soda
1 teaspoon baking powder
1 teaspoon ground cinnamon
1 dash nutmeg
$2\frac{1}{2}$ cups rolled oats, uncooked

1 cup raisins or dates, chopped
1 cup shredded coconut
1 cup walnuts, chopped

Cream shortening. Add sugars and salt to creamed shortening; continue creaming until well blended. Beat eggs into creamed mixture; add vanilla and water. Sift together sifted flour, soda, baking powder, cinnamon, and nutmeg; combine with rolled oats and fold into creamed mixture. Fold raisins or dates, coconut, and walnuts into batter.

Drop by teaspoonfuls onto greased baking sheet. Bake in preheated oven 375° to 400°F. 12 to 15 minutes.

Makes 6 dozen cookies.

OATMEAL CRISPIES

1 cup shortening
1 cup brown sugar
1 cup granulated sugar
2 eggs, well-beaten
1½ cups flour, sifted
1 teaspoon salt
1 teaspoon baking soda
1 teaspoon vanilla
3 cups rolled oats, uncooked
½ cup walnuts

Cream shortening until light and fluffy. Stir sugars into creamed shortening; mix well. Add eggs to creamed mixture. Sift together sifted flour, salt, and soda; blend into creamed mixture. Add vanilla to batter. Stir rolled oats, 1 cup at a time, into batter. After last cup of rolled oats has been added, slowly stir dough until well mixed. Blend walnuts into the dough.

Drop by teaspoonfuls onto ungreased baking sheet. Bake in oven 350°F. 10 minutes, or until golden brown.

Makes about 5 dozen cookies.

TROPICAL OATMEAL NUGGETS

$\frac{1}{2}$ cup shortening
$\frac{1}{2}$ cup granulated sugar
$\frac{1}{2}$ cup brown sugar
1 egg
1 cup crushed pineapple
1 cup flour, sifted
$\frac{1}{2}$ teaspoon baking soda
$\frac{1}{2}$ teaspoon salt
$\frac{1}{2}$ teaspoon cinnamon
$\frac{1}{8}$ teaspoon nutmeg
$1\frac{1}{2}$ cups rolled oats, uncooked
$\frac{1}{2}$ cup walnuts, chopped

Cream together shortening and sugars until fluffy. Beat egg and pineapple into creamed mixture. Sift together sifted flour, soda, salt, cinnamon, and nutmeg; mix with rolled oats and blend into shortening mixture. Fold walnuts into batter.

Drop by teaspoonfuls onto ungreased baking sheet. Bake in preheated oven 375°F. 15 minutes.

Makes about 3 dozen cookies.

CHOCOLATE OATMEAL COOKIES

$\frac{1}{2}$ cup butter
1 cup granulated sugar
2 eggs, unbeaten
$\frac{1}{2}$ cup flour, sifted
$1\frac{3}{4}$ cups rolled oats, uncooked
2 one-ounce squares unsweetened chocolate, melted
$\frac{1}{2}$ teaspoon vanilla

Cream butter until soft; gradually add sugar until well blended. Add eggs, 1 at a time; beat after each addition. Sift sifted flour and add to creamed mixture. Stir rolled oats into creamed mixture. Add melted chocolate and vanilla to batter.

Drop by teaspoonfuls, 1 inch apart, onto buttered baking sheet. Bake in oven 350°F. 15 minutes, or until lightly browned. Cool. Store in tightly covered jar.

Makes 3 dozen cookies.

CHOCOLATE OAT DROPS

2 cups flour, sifted
1 teaspoon salt
1 teaspoon baking soda
1 cup shortening, soft
1 cup brown sugar
1 cup granulated sugar
3 eggs, unbeaten
2 teaspoons vanilla
1 teaspoon almond extract

4 one-ounce squares chocolate, melted
1 cup walnuts, chopped
4 cups rolled oats, uncooked

Sift together into a large mixing bowl sifted flour, salt, and soda. Add shortening (soft, but not melted), sugars, eggs, vanilla, almond extract, and melted chocolate to sifted dry ingredients; beat about 2 minutes, or until smooth. Stir walnuts into the batter. Blend rolled oats into the mixture.

Drop dough by heaping teaspoonfuls onto a greased baking sheet. Bake in oven 350°F. 12 minutes. When done, remove to rack; cool before storing.

Makes $7\frac{1}{2}$ dozen cookies.

TOLL OATS COOKIES

$\frac{1}{2}$ cup margarine
$\frac{1}{2}$ cup granulated sugar
$\frac{1}{2}$ cup brown sugar, packed
1 egg
1 tablespoon water
$\frac{1}{2}$ teaspoon vanilla
$\frac{3}{4}$ cup flour, sifted
$\frac{1}{2}$ teaspoon baking soda
$1\frac{1}{2}$ cups rolled oats, uncooked
1 cup semi-sweet chocolate pieces
$\frac{1}{2}$ cup nuts, chopped

Cream margarine. Add sugars, egg, water, and vanilla to creamed margarine; mix well. Sift together sifted flour and soda; add to creamed mixture and blend thoroughly. Add rolled oats, chocolate pieces, and nuts. Mix well.

Drop by teaspoonfuls onto baking sheet. Bake in oven 375°F. about 10 minutes. Do not overbake.

Makes about 3½ dozen cookies.

LACY CORNFLAKE CRISPS

¼ cup butter
¼ cup granulated sugar
⅓ cup light molasses
1 cup semi-sweet chocolate morsels
4 cups cornflakes, uncrushed

Measure butter, sugar, and molasses into a large saucepan; blend and bring to full boil over moderate heat, stirring constantly. Remove the butter mixture from the heat; add chocolate morsels and uncrushed cornflakes, stirring until well mixed.

Drop dough by teaspoonfuls onto ungreased baking sheet. Bake in oven 350°F. 6 to 8 minutes. When baked, remove from oven and let cookies cool 2 or 3 minutes on baking sheet. Transfer slightly cooled cookies with a spatula to a wire rack; cool.

Makes about 6 dozen crisps.

ALMOND TEA COOKIES

½ cup butter, soft
¼ cup brown sugar, firmly packed
¼ teaspoon salt
1 teaspoon vanilla

2 tablespoons water
1 cup flour, sifted
$\frac{1}{2}$ cup almonds, toasted and finely shredded
1 cup semi-sweet chocolate morsels
$\frac{3}{4}$ cup confectioners' sugar, sifted

Blend together butter, brown sugar, salt, vanilla, and water; add sifted flour and almonds. Mix well. Blend chocolate morsels into the batter.

Drop dough by half teaspoonfuls onto an ungreased baking sheet. Bake in oven 350°F. 12 minutes. Remove baked cookies from the oven; while still warm, roll each cookie through sifted confectioners' sugar.

Makes about 4$\frac{1}{2}$ dozen cookies.

ALMOND DIPS

2 cups flour, sifted
2 teaspoons baking powder
$\frac{1}{4}$ teaspoon salt
$\frac{1}{2}$ cup butter or shortening
2 teaspoons vanilla
1 teaspoon almond extract
1 cup brown sugar, firmly packed
2 eggs
1 cup semi-sweet chocolate morsels
$\frac{2}{3}$ cup almonds, unblanched and finely shredded

Sift together sifted flour, baking powder, and salt; set aside. Blend together, in a large mixing bowl, butter, vanilla, and almond extract; gradually beat brown sugar into butter mixture. Beat eggs, 1 at a time, into butter mixture. Slowly blend sifted dry ingredients and morsels into butter mixture.

Drop dough by half teaspoonfuls into a small mixing bowl that contains the finely shredded almonds. Place nut-covered cookies on a greased baking sheet. Bake in oven 325°F. 15 minutes.

Makes about $6\frac{1}{2}$ dozen dips.

FRENCH ALMOND MERINGUES

1 cup semi-sweet chocolate morsels
3 egg whites
$\frac{1}{2}$ teaspoon vanilla
1 cup granulated sugar
$\frac{1}{3}$ cup almonds, blanched and finely shredded

Melt chocolate morsels over hot (not boiling) water; remove from water and cool 5 minutes. Combine egg whites and vanilla in a mixing bowl; beat until stiff, but not dry. Gradually beat sugar into egg white mixture; beat until very stiff. Fold almonds and cooled morsels into egg white mixture.

Drop by teaspoonfuls onto greased baking sheet. Bake in oven 350°F. 10 to 12 minutes.

Makes about 4 dozen meringues.

SWISS ALMOND DROPS

3 eggs
$1\frac{1}{2}$ cups granulated sugar
$\frac{1}{2}$ cup flour, sifted

$\frac{1}{8}$ teaspoon salt
2 cups almonds, toasted and finely shredded
1 cup semi-sweet chocolate morsels, finely chopped
1$\frac{1}{2}$ teaspoons vanilla

In a large mixing bowl, beat eggs until they are thick; gradually beat sugar into eggs and continue beating until mixture is very thick. Add sifted flour, salt, almonds, chopped morsels, and vanilla to egg mixture. Mix well. Chill dough approximately 15 minutes, or until stiff.

Drop chilled dough by half teaspoonfuls onto an ungreased aluminum foil-lined baking sheet. Bake in oven 325°F. 25 minutes.

Makes about 7 dozen drops.

DATE PEANUT BUTTER DROPS

2 cups enriched flour, sifted
2$\frac{1}{2}$ teaspoons baking powder
$\frac{1}{2}$ teaspoon salt
$\frac{1}{2}$ cup shortening
$\frac{3}{4}$ cup peanut butter
1 cup granulated sugar
1 teaspoon vanilla
2 eggs, beaten
1 cup dates, chopped
$\frac{1}{2}$ cup milk

Sift together sifted flour, baking powder, and salt. Cream together shortening, peanut butter, and sugar until light and fluffy. Blend vanilla into creamed mixture; add eggs. Stir dates into creamed mixture. Add sifted ingredients to creamed mixture alternately with milk. Mix well.

Drop by teaspoonfuls onto greased baking sheet. Bake in oven 350°F. 15 to 20 minutes.

Makes about 7 dozen cookies.

PEANUT BUTTER MOUNDS

2 cups granulated sugar
$\frac{1}{3}$ cup cocoa
$\frac{1}{4}$ cup butter
$\frac{1}{2}$ cup milk
3 cups quick-cooking rolled oats, uncooked
$\frac{1}{2}$ cup peanut butter
2 teaspoons vanilla
$\frac{1}{3}$ cup peanuts, chopped

Mix sugar and cocoa in a large saucepan; add butter and milk. Bring the sugar mixture to a rolling boil; stir constantly. Boil just 2 minutes. Remove sugar mixture from heat; add rolled oats, peanut butter, and vanilla. Mix thoroughly. Blend peanuts into mixture.

Drop dough by teaspoonfuls onto waxed paper. Cool completely before storing.

Makes about 4 dozen mounds.

PEANUT POLKA DOTTERS

$1\frac{1}{2}$ cups flour, sifted
1 teaspoon salt

$\frac{1}{2}$ teaspoon baking soda
$\frac{1}{2}$ cup shortening
$\frac{1}{2}$ cup chunk-style peanut butter
$\frac{1}{2}$ teaspoon cinnamon
$\frac{1}{4}$ teaspoon nutmeg
1 cup granulated sugar
2 eggs
$\frac{1}{2}$ cup water
1 cup semi-sweet chocolate morsels
1 cup quick-cooking rolled oats, uncooked

Sift together sifted flour, salt, and soda; set aside. Blend together, in a large mixing bowl, shortening, peanut butter, cinnamon, and nutmeg; gradually beat sugar into the mixture. Beat eggs, 1 at a time, into shortening mixture. Add sifted dry ingredients, alternately with water, to the shortening mixture; stir chocolate morsels and rolled oats into the batter.

Drop dough by heaping teaspoonfuls onto an ungreased baking sheet. Bake in oven 375°F. 12 minutes.

Makes about 5 dozen cookies.

PECAN DELIGHTS

1 cup shortening
2 cups brown sugar, packed
1 teaspoon vanilla
2 eggs
$2\frac{1}{2}$ cups flour, sifted
1 teaspoon salt
2 teaspoons baking powder
1 cup pecans, chopped

Cream together shortening, brown sugar, and vanilla. Add eggs to creamed mixture; beat well. Sift together sifted flour, salt, and baking powder; add to creamed mixture and blend. Add pecans to dough; mix well.

Drop by teaspoonfuls onto baking sheet. Bake in oven 350°F. 10 minutes.

Makes about 7 dozen cookies.

BUTTER PECAN DROP COOKIES

$\frac{1}{2}$ cup butter
$1\frac{1}{2}$ cups brown sugar, packed
1 teaspoon vanilla
1 egg
$1\frac{1}{2}$ cups flour, sifted
1 cup pecans, chopped

Cream butter; add brown sugar and vanilla, and cream until well blended. Add egg to creamed mixture; beat thoroughly. Blend sifted flour, alternately with pecans, into creamed mixture; stir until flour is moistened completely.

Drop by teaspoonfuls onto baking sheet. Bake in oven 375°F. 12 minutes, or until lightly browned around edges.

Makes 4 dozen cookies.

MOCHA PECAN BUTTONS

1 cup semi-sweet chocolate morsels
2 eggs

$\frac{1}{2}$ cup granulated sugar
2 tablespoons flour
$\frac{1}{8}$ teaspoon salt
1 teaspoon baking powder
1 tablespoon instant coffee
    pecan halves

Place chocolate morsels in top of double boiler and melt over hot (not boiling) water; remove from water and let cool approximately 5 minutes. In a large mixing bowl, beat the eggs until thick; gradually beat sugar into eggs until mixture is very thick. Combine flour, salt, baking powder, and instant coffee; blend into egg mixture. Add cooled chocolate morsels to the batter; mix well.

Drop dough by half teaspoonfuls onto greased baking sheet. Gently place 1 pecan half in center of each drop. Bake in oven 375°F. 6 to 8 minutes.

Makes about 6 dozen buttons.

WALNUT CLUSTERS

2 cups walnut halves and large pieces
$\frac{1}{4}$ cup butter or margarine, soft
$\frac{1}{2}$ cup granulated sugar
1 egg, unbeaten
$1\frac{1}{2}$ teaspoons vanilla
$1\frac{1}{2}$ one-ounce squares unsweetened chocolate, melted
$\frac{1}{2}$ cup flour, sifted
$\frac{1}{4}$ teaspoon baking powder
$\frac{1}{2}$ teaspoon salt

Place walnut kernels in a paper or plastic bag and crush slightly with rolling pin or measuring cup to break them coarsely. Stir together butter, sugar, egg, and vanilla; beat with spoon just until smooth. Blend melted chocolate into butter mixture. Sift together sifted flour, baking powder, and salt; blend into butter mixture. Stir broken walnuts into the mixture.

Drop dough by teaspoonfuls onto greased baking sheet. Bake in preheated oven 350°F. 10 minutes (no longer!). Cookies should be soft when done. Cool cookies on a rack before storing.

Makes about 3 dozen cookies.

BLACK WALNUT COOKIES

- 1 package ($\frac{1}{4}$ pound) German's sweet chocolate
- 2 cups flour, sifted
- $\frac{1}{2}$ teaspoon baking soda
- $\frac{1}{2}$ teaspoon salt
- $\frac{3}{4}$ cup butter or shortening
- $\frac{3}{4}$ cup granulated sugar
- 2 eggs, unbeaten
- $\frac{1}{2}$ teaspoon vanilla
- $\frac{1}{2}$ cup black walnuts, chopped

Place chocolate in small bowl and set over hot water until melted; cool. Sift flour once, measure; add soda and salt, and sift again. Cream butter in a large mixing bowl; gradually add sugar and cream together until light and fluffy. Add eggs to creamed mixture and beat well. Slowly blend melted chocolate into creamed mixture; add sifted dry ingredients and mix thoroughly. Stir vanilla and black walnuts into dough.

Drop by teaspoonfuls onto greased baking sheet. Bake in oven 350°F. 10 to 12 minutes.

Makes about 4 dozen cookies.

WALNUT–OATMEAL DROPS

    2 eggs
    ½ cup milk
    1 teaspoon vanilla
    2 tablespoons butter, melted
    1¾ cups biscuit mix
    1 cup rolled oats, quick-cooking or regular, un-
       cooked
    1 cup walnuts, coarsely chopped
    1 cup brown sugar, firmly packed
    1 teaspoon cinnamon
    ½ teaspoon nutmeg
    ¼ teaspoon cloves

In a large mixing bowl place the eggs and beat thoroughly; add milk, vanilla, and melted butter. Blend biscuit mix, rolled oats, walnuts, brown sugar, cinnamon, nutmeg, and cloves into the egg mixture.

When dough is well mixed, drop by teaspoonfuls onto greased baking sheet. Bake in oven 375°F. 12 to 15 minutes. When done, remove immediately to a rack and cool before storing.

Makes 3 dozen drop cookies.

SOFT MOLASSES HERMITS

$1\frac{1}{2}$ cups flour, sifted
$1\frac{1}{2}$ teaspoons baking powder
$\frac{1}{4}$ teaspoon baking soda
$\frac{1}{4}$ teaspoon salt
$\frac{1}{2}$ teaspoon cinnamon
$\frac{1}{4}$ teaspoon cloves
$\frac{1}{4}$ cup shortening
$\frac{1}{4}$ cup granulated sugar
1 egg, well-beaten
$\frac{1}{2}$ cup molasses
$\frac{1}{4}$ cup buttermilk
$\frac{1}{2}$ cup raisins

Sift together sifted flour, baking powder, soda, salt, cinnamon, and cloves. Cream shortening in a large mixing bowl; gradually add sugar and cream together until light and fluffy. Add egg to creamed mixture; beat well. Blend molasses into creamed mixture. Add sifted dry ingredients, alternately with milk, to the creamed mixture; stir only to blend. Fold raisins into dough.

Drop by teaspoonfuls about 2 inches apart onto lightly greased baking sheet. Bake in oven 400°F. 10 minutes, or until done.

Makes about $3\frac{1}{2}$ dozen cookies.

SPICY MOLASSES DROP COOKIES

1 cup shortening
1 cup granulated sugar

1 cup molasses
3 eggs
4 cups flour, sifted
1 teaspoon baking soda
2 teaspoons double-acting baking powder
1 teaspoon cinnamon
$\frac{1}{2}$ teaspoon nutmeg
1 cup sour milk
1 cup raisins

Cream together shortening and sugar until light and fluffy; add molasses. Mix well. Add eggs to creamed mixture, 1 at a time; beat well after each addition. Sift together sifted flour, soda, baking powder, cinnamon, and nutmeg. Add sifted dry ingredients, alternately with sour milk, to creamed mixture. Blend raisins into batter.

Drop by teaspoonfuls onto baking sheet. Bake in oven 400°F. 10 to 12 minutes.

Makes about 8 dozen cookies.

MOLASSES DANDIES

$2\frac{1}{2}$ cups flour, sifted
1 teaspoon baking soda
$\frac{1}{2}$ teaspoon cinnamon
$\frac{1}{4}$ teaspoon salt
$\frac{1}{8}$ teaspoon ginger
$\frac{1}{2}$ cup shortening
$\frac{1}{2}$ cup granulated sugar
1 egg
$\frac{1}{2}$ cup light molasses

$\frac{1}{2}$ cup sour milk
1 cup semi-sweet chocolate morsels

Sift together sifted flour, soda, cinnamon, salt, and ginger; set aside. Blend together, in a large mixing bowl, shortening and sugar; beat egg into mixture. Add sifted dry ingredients, alternately with molasses and sour milk, to shortening mixture; mix well. Stir morsels into the batter.

Drop dough by tablespoonfuls onto greased baking sheet. Bake in oven 350°F. 15 minutes. When done, immediately remove baked cookies from baking sheet and place on wire rack to cool.

Makes about $3\frac{1}{2}$ dozen dandies.

HONEY CHIP COOKIES

$\frac{1}{2}$ cup butter, soft
6 tablespoons brown sugar
6 tablespoons honey
1 egg
$\frac{1}{2}$ teaspoon vanilla
$\frac{1}{4}$ teaspoon water
1 cup and 2 tablespoons all-purpose flour, sifted
$\frac{1}{2}$ teaspoon baking soda
$\frac{1}{2}$ teaspoon salt
$\frac{1}{2}$ cup nuts, chopped
1 cup semi-sweet chocolate morsels

Cream together butter and brown sugar; blend honey, egg, vanilla, and water into creamed butter. Sift together sifted flour, soda, and salt; blend into creamed butter. Add chopped nuts and chocolate morsels to the batter; mix well.

Drop by half teaspoonfuls onto an ungreased baking sheet. Bake in oven 375°F. 10 to 12 minutes. Cool on wire racks.

Makes about 4 dozen cookies.

GINGER DROPS

½ cup shortening
¼ cup brown sugar
1 egg, well-beaten
⅜ cup dark corn syrup
1 cup soya flour, unsifted
½ teaspoon salt
1 teaspoon ginger
¼ teaspoon baking soda
1 teaspoon baking powder
¼ cup milk
½ teaspoon vanilla
1¼ cups rolled oats, uncooked
2¼ teaspoons lemon rind, grated

Cream together shortening and brown sugar. Add egg to creamed mixture; beat well. Add syrup to creamed mixture and beat thoroughly. Sift together unsifted soya flour, salt, ginger, soda, and baking powder. Add sifted dry ingredients, alternately with milk and vanilla, to creamed mixture. Blend rolled oats and lemon rind into batter.

Drop by teaspoonfuls onto greased baking sheet. Bake in oven 400°F. 10 to 12 minutes.

Makes about 3 dozen cookies.

WISCONSIN SOUR CREAM COOKIES

$\frac{1}{2}$ cup shortening
$1\frac{1}{2}$ cups brown sugar
2 eggs
$\frac{1}{2}$ cup sour cream
2 cups flour, sifted
1 teaspoon soda
1 teaspoon vanilla
$\frac{1}{2}$ cup raisins
$\frac{1}{2}$ cup walnuts, chopped

Cream shortening; add brown sugar and cream again. Blend eggs and sour cream into creamed mixture. Sift together sifted flour and soda; blend into creamed mixture. Add vanilla, raisins, and walnuts to batter; mix well.

Drop 1 cookie onto a greased baking sheet. Bake in oven 375°F. 6 to 8 minutes. If cookie spreads too much during baking process, add 1 tablespoon of sifted flour to the cookie batter and mix well.

When test cookie is of desired texture, drop dough by teaspoonfuls onto greased baking sheet. Bake in oven 375°F. 6 to 8 minutes, or until golden brown.

Makes about 6 dozen cookies.

SOFT SOUR CREAM JUMBLES

1 cup granulated sugar
$\frac{1}{2}$ cup butter, soft
1 egg
$\frac{1}{2}$ teaspoon vanilla

Coffee Rum Cookies *(Pan-American Coffee Bureau)*

Flaky Meringue Cookies *(Wheat Flour Institute)*

Bright Lemon Baubles and Christmas Lemon Cookies *(The ReaLemon Co.)*

$\frac{1}{2}$ teaspoon lemon extract
1 cup sour cream
2$\frac{1}{2}$ cups flour, sifted
1 teaspoon baking powder
$\frac{1}{2}$ teaspoon baking soda
$\frac{1}{2}$ teaspoon salt
$\frac{1}{4}$ teaspoon nutmeg
$\frac{1}{2}$ cup raisins, chopped
$\frac{1}{2}$ cup walnuts, chopped
2 tablespoons granulated sugar
$\frac{1}{2}$ teaspoon cinnamon

Gradually add 1 cup sugar to butter; cream thoroughly. Add egg, vanilla, and lemon extract to creamed mixture; beat well. Add sour cream to creamed mixture. Sift together sifted flour, baking powder, soda, salt, and nutmeg; blend into creamed mixture. Stir raisins and walnuts into the soft dough.

Drop by heaping teaspoonfuls onto greased baking sheet. Mix 2 tablespoons sugar with cinnamon; sprinkle tops of cookies with this mixture. Bake in oven 350°F. 15 to 20 minutes. Cool on racks. Double recipe as desired.

Makes about 2 dozen cookies.

SOUR CREAM DROP COOKIES

1 cup brown sugar, firmly packed
$\frac{1}{2}$ cup butter, soft
1 egg
$\frac{1}{2}$ cup sour cream
1 teaspoon vanilla
2 cups flour, sifted

$\frac{1}{2}$ teaspoon nutmeg
$\frac{1}{2}$ teaspoon baking soda
2 teaspoons baking powder
$\frac{1}{2}$ teaspoon salt
1 cup rolled oats, uncooked
1 cup raisins or walnuts, chopped

Add brown sugar to butter; cream until fluffy. Add egg to creamed mixture; beat well. Add sour cream and vanilla to creamed mixture. Sift together sifted flour, nutmeg, soda, baking powder, and salt; blend into creamed mixture. Blend rolled oats into batter. Fold raisins or walnuts into batter.

Drop by teaspoonfuls onto buttered baking sheet. Bake in oven 375°F. 12 to 15 minutes, or until done. Cool on rack.

Makes 4 dozen cookies.

BUTTERMILK DROP COOKIES

2 one-ounce squares unsweetened chocolate
1 cup butter
1 cup granulated sugar
3 eggs, well-beaten
1 teaspoon vanilla
$3\frac{1}{2}$ cups flour, sifted
2 teaspoons baking powder
$\frac{1}{2}$ teaspoon salt
$\frac{1}{2}$ teaspoon baking soda
1 cup buttermilk
Java Cocoa Icing

Melt chocolate in top of double boiler over hot water. Cream butter; gradually add sugar. Add melted chocolate, eggs, and vanilla. Sift together sifted flour, baking powder, salt, and soda; add sifted dry ingredients, alternately with buttermilk, to the creamed mixture.

Drop by teaspoonfuls onto greased baking sheet. Bake in oven 350°F. 12 minutes. A walnut half can be placed on each cookie before baking; or, after baking, cookies can be iced with Java Cocoa Icing.

Makes 5 dozen cookies.

BUTTERSCOTCH DROP COOKIES

$\frac{1}{2}$ cup butter
$1\frac{1}{2}$ cups dark brown sugar, packed
2 eggs
3 cups flour, sifted
$\frac{1}{2}$ cup Pream
$\frac{1}{2}$ teaspoon salt
$\frac{1}{2}$ teaspoon baking powder
1 teaspoon baking soda
$\frac{1}{2}$ cup water
2 tablespoons vinegar
1 teaspoon vanilla
$\frac{3}{4}$ cup nuts, chopped
Confectioners' Sugar Frosting

Cream together butter, brown sugar, and eggs; beat until light and fluffy. Sift together sifted flour, Pream, salt, baking powder, and soda; set aside. Combine water, vinegar, and vanilla. Blend sifted dry ingredients, alternately with vinegar mixture, into creamed mixture; mix thoroughly. Stir nuts into the batter.

Drop dough by teaspoonfuls, about 2 inches apart, on an

ungreased baking sheet. Bake in oven 400°F. 10 to 12 minutes. When done, remove from oven and cool.

If desired, frost cookies, while warm, with Confectioners' Sugar Frosting.

Makes about 5 dozen cookies.

BUTTERSCOTCH DESSERT COOKIES

$\frac{1}{2}$ cup butter
$1\frac{1}{2}$ cups brown sugar, packed
2 eggs
1 teaspoon vanilla
$2\frac{1}{2}$ cups flour, sifted
$\frac{1}{2}$ teaspoon salt
$\frac{1}{2}$ teaspoon double-acting baking powder
1 teaspoon baking soda
1 cup sour cream
$\frac{3}{4}$ cup nuts, chopped
Brown Butter Frosting

Cream together butter and brown sugar. Add eggs and vanilla to creamed mixture; beat until light and fluffy. Sift together sifted flour, salt, baking powder, and soda. Add sifted dry ingredients, alternately with sour cream, to creamed mixture. Mix until all ingredients are combined thoroughly. Stir nuts into batter. Chill.

Drop by tablespoonfuls, about 2 inches apart, onto baking sheet. Flatten slightly with back of spoon. Bake in oven 400°F. 10 to 12 minutes. Cool. Frost with Brown Butter Frosting.

Makes about 3 dozen cookies.

CHERRY BUTTERSCOTCHIES

$\frac{1}{2}$ cup butter
$1\frac{1}{2}$ cups brown sugar, packed
1 teaspoon vanilla
1 egg
$1\frac{1}{2}$ cups flour, sifted
1 cup pecans, chopped
$\frac{1}{2}$ cup candied cherries, chopped

Cream butter. Add brown sugar and vanilla to creamed butter; cream until well blended. Add egg to creamed mixture; beat thoroughly. Blend sifted flour, pecans, and cherries into creamed mixture.

Drop by rounded teaspoonfuls onto a slightly greased baking sheet. Bake in oven 375°F. 12 minutes until browned on edges.

Makes about 4 dozen cookies.

BUTTERSCOTCH PECAN COOKIES

$\frac{1}{2}$ cup butter
$1\frac{1}{2}$ cups brown sugar, packed
1 teaspoon vanilla
1 egg
$1\frac{1}{2}$ cups flour, sifted
1 cup pecans

Cream together butter, brown sugar, and vanilla. Add egg to creamed mixture; blend well. Add sifted flour to creamed mixture; mix until flour is moistened completely. Stir pecans into dough.

Drop by teaspoonfuls onto baking sheet. Bake in oven 375°F. about 12 minutes.

Makes about 4 dozen cookies.

BUTTERSCOTCH CREAM CHEESE DROPS

    1 package butterscotch cake mix
    2 tablespoons water
    1 egg, unbeaten
    2 tablespoons butter, soft
    3 ounces cream cheese
    $\frac{1}{2}$ cup pecans, chopped

Place half of the cake mix into a mixing bowl. Add water, egg, butter, and cream cheese to the cake mix; blend well with a wooden spoon. Add remaining cake mix and beat with spoon until dough is smooth. Stir pecans into the dough.

Drop by teaspoonfuls onto lightly greased baking sheet. Bake in oven 375°F. about 12 minutes.

Makes 4 dozen cookies.

SCOTCH 'N CHIPS COOKIES

    1 package butterscotch cake mix
    2 tablespoons water
    1 egg, unbeaten
    $\frac{1}{4}$ cup butter, soft
    1 cup semi-sweet chocolate chips
    $\frac{1}{2}$ cup walnuts, chopped

Place half of the cake mix into a mixing bowl. Add water,

egg, and butter to cake mix; blend thoroughly. Blend remaining cake mix into the batter; with a wooden spoon, beat batter until smooth. Stir chocolate chips and walnuts into the dough.

Drop dough by teaspoonfuls onto lightly greased baking sheet. Bake in oven 375°F. 12 minutes.

Makes 4 dozen cookies.

ORIGINAL TOLL HOUSE COOKIES

1 cup and 2 tablespoons flour, sifted
$\frac{1}{2}$ teaspoon baking soda
$\frac{1}{2}$ teaspoon salt
$\frac{1}{2}$ cup butter or shortening, soft
6 tablespoons granulated sugar
6 tablespoons brown sugar
$\frac{1}{2}$ teaspoon vanilla
$\frac{1}{4}$ teaspoon water
1 egg
1 cup semi-sweet chocolate morsels
$\frac{1}{2}$ cup nuts, coarsely chopped

Sift together sifted flour, baking soda, and salt; set aside. Blend together, in a large mixing bowl, butter, sugars, vanilla and water; beat egg into this mixture. Add sifted dry ingredients to butter mixture; mix well. Stir chocolate morsels and nuts into the batter.

Drop by half teaspoonfuls onto greased baking sheet. Bake in oven 375°F. 10 to 12 minutes.

To freshen Toll House Cookies, wrap in aluminum foil and place in oven 375°F. 5 minutes.

Makes about 4 dozen cookies.

ICE CREAM WAFERS

$\frac{1}{2}$ cup butter
$\frac{1}{2}$ cup granulated sugar
$\frac{1}{4}$ teaspoon salt
$\frac{1}{2}$ teaspoon flavoring
1 egg
$\frac{3}{4}$ cup flour, sifted

Cream together butter, sugar, salt, and flavoring. Add egg to creamed mixture; beat well. Stir sifted flour into creamed mixture.

Drop by half teaspoonfuls in mounds on lightly buttered baking sheet. Bake in oven 350°F. 12 to 15 minutes, or until browned on edges.

Makes 4 dozen wafers.

SEMI-SWEET KISSES

1 cup semi-sweet chocolate morsels
3 egg whites
$\frac{1}{2}$ teaspoon vanilla
1 cup granulated sugar
$\frac{1}{3}$ cup salted crackers, crumbled

Melt chocolate morsels over hot (not boiling) water; remove from water and cool 5 minutes. Combine egg whites and vanilla; beat until stiff, but not dry. Gradually beat sugar into egg white mixture and continue beating until very stiff. Fold crumbled salted crackers and cooled melted morsels into egg white mixture.

Drop dough by teaspoonfuls onto greased baking sheet.
Bake in oven 350°F. 10 to 12 minutes.

Makes about 4 dozen kisses.

WISCONSIN SUGAR COOKIES

1 cup butter
1 cup confectioners' sugar, firmly packed
2 cups flour, sifted
1 teaspoon cream of tartar
$\frac{1}{2}$ teaspoon baking soda
$\frac{1}{4}$ teaspoon salt
1 teaspoon rum
1 egg, unbeaten
  granulated sugar, colored

Cream together butter and confectioners' sugar. Sift
together sifted flour, cream of tartar, soda, and salt. Blend
sifted dry ingredients and rum into creamed mixture. Add
unbeaten egg; mix well.

Drop by teaspoonfuls onto baking sheet. Press each
cookie with the bottom of a glass that has been dipped in
colored sugar. Bake in oven 375°F. 10 to 12 minutes.

Makes about 3 dozen cookies.

SNACKTIME FAVORITE COOKIES

1 cup butter
1 cup brown sugar
1 cup granulated sugar
2 eggs, beaten

1 teaspoon vanilla
1 cup peanuts, finely chopped
1½ cups wheat flake cereal, crushed
2 cups flour, sifted
1 teaspoon baking powder
1 teaspoon baking soda
¼ teaspoon salt
1¾ cups quick-cooking rolled oats, uncooked

Cream together butter, sugars. Add beaten eggs to creamed mixture; mix well. Blend vanilla into creamed mixture. Chop peanuts fine. Crush wheat cereal. Sift together sifted flour, baking powder, soda, and salt. Blend together sifted ingredients, peanuts, wheat cereal, and rolled oats; add to creamed mixture. Mix well.

Drop by teaspoonfuls onto lightly buttered baking sheet. Bake in oven 350°F. 12 to 15 minutes, or until lightly browned.

Makes 7 dozen cookies.

DESSERT COOKIES

1 cup butter
⅔ cup granulated sugar
2 tablespoons orange rind, grated
1 tablespoon lemon rind, grated
2 eggs, well-beaten
2½ cups flour, sifted
1 teaspoon salt
1 cup shredded coconut

Cream butter; add sugar. Add orange rind, lemon rind,

and eggs to creamed mixture; mix well. Sift together sifted flour and salt. Add half the flour mixture to creamed mixture, then the coconut, and then rest of flour mixture.

Drop by teaspoonfuls onto ungreased baking sheet. Bake in 375°F. oven 10 minutes.

Makes 3 dozen cookies.

FLORENTINES

$\frac{1}{3}$ cup flour, sifted
  dash of salt
$\frac{1}{4}$ teaspoon baking soda
$\frac{1}{4}$ cup butter
$\frac{1}{3}$ cup brown sugar, firmly packed
2 tablespoons light corn syrup
1 egg, well-beaten
$\frac{1}{2}$ teaspoon vanilla
$\frac{1}{2}$ cup flaked coconut
2 squares candy-making chocolate

Sift flour once and measure. Add salt and soda to the sifted flour and sift again. In a large mixing bowl, cream the butter, gradually add brown sugar, creaming until light and fluffy. Add corn syrup and well-beaten egg to the creamed mixture; beat well. Stir sifted dry ingredients, vanilla, and coconut into the batter.

Drop by teaspoonfuls, about 2 inches apart, onto a greased baking sheet. Spread dough into thin rounds. Bake in oven 350°F. about 10 minutes. When done, remove at once from baking sheet. Cool.

While cookies are cooling, heat chocolate in top of double boiler over hot water until partly melted. Remove the pan of partly melted chocolate from hot water and stir rapidly until the chocolate is melted entirely. Dribble the melted chocolate in lacy patterns over the cooled cookies. Let the chocolate-coated cookies stand several hours, or until chocolate is firm.

Makes 4 dozen cookies.

CRUNCHY LUNCHBOX DROPS

$\frac{1}{2}$ cup shortening
$1\frac{1}{3}$ cups brown sugar, firmly packed
1 egg, unbeaten
$\frac{1}{2}$ teaspoon vanilla
$1\frac{1}{4}$ cups flour, sifted
$\frac{1}{4}$ teaspoon salt
$\frac{1}{4}$ teaspoon baking soda
$\frac{1}{2}$ cup walnuts, chopped

With spoon stir together shortening, brown sugar, egg, and vanilla until thoroughly blended. Sift together sifted flour, salt, and soda; blend into shortening mixture. Fold walnuts into mixture.

Drop dough by teaspoonfuls onto ungreased baking sheet. Bake in preheated oven 350°F. about 12 minutes. When done, immediately remove cookies from baking sheet and place on a rack to cool. Cookies will be soft when baked, but will wrinkle slightly while cooling. When cool, wrap cookies in pairs, flat sides together, with foil, saran wrap, or waxed paper. Store in a safe place and pack into lunchbox as needed.

Makes about 4 dozen cookies.

HEIRLOOM COOKIES

2 packages ($\frac{1}{2}$ pound) German's sweet chocolate
$\frac{3}{4}$ cup flour, sifted
$\frac{1}{2}$ teaspoon baking soda
$\frac{1}{2}$ teaspoon salt
$\frac{1}{2}$ cup nuts, chopped
1 cup rolled oats, uncooked
$\frac{1}{2}$ cup butter or shortening
$\frac{1}{2}$ cup granulated sugar
$\frac{1}{4}$ cup brown sugar, firmly packed
1 egg, unbeaten
$\frac{1}{2}$ teaspoon vanilla

Cut each square of chocolate into several pieces. Sift flour once and measure; add soda and salt, sift again. Blend chocolate, nuts, and rolled oats into sifted dry ingredients.

In a large mixing bowl, cream butter; gradually add sugars, and cream together until light and fluffy. Add egg and vanilla to creamed mixture; mix thoroughly. Slowly blend flour mixture into creamed mixture; mix well.

Drop dough by teaspoonfuls, about 2 inches apart, onto ungreased baking sheet. Bake in oven 375°F. about 12 minutes.

Makes about 3 dozen cookies.

POTATO CHIPPERS

$1\frac{1}{3}$ cups sweetened condensed milk
$\frac{1}{2}$ cup peanut butter
2 cups shredded coconut
1 cup potato chips, coarsely broken

Mix condensed milk and peanut butter in a large mixing bowl; add coconut and potato chips. Mix thoroughly.

Drop by teaspoonfuls onto a well-greased baking sheet. Bake in oven 375°F. 15 minutes. Cool on racks and store.

Makes about 4 dozen chippers.

WHEAT COOKIES

$\frac{2}{3}$ cup sweetened condensed milk
$\frac{1}{4}$ cup powdered milk
$\frac{1}{4}$ cup wheat germ
$\frac{1}{2}$ teaspoon salt
2 teaspoons vanilla
$1\frac{1}{2}$ cups shredded coconut

Blend together condensed and powdered milk. Add wheat germ, salt, and vanilla to milk mixture; blend thoroughly. Add coconut; mix well.

Drop by teaspoonfuls onto ungreased baking sheet. Bake in oven 325°F. 15 minutes. Remove from baking sheet while hot.

Makes about 3 dozen cookies.

FIESTA COOKIES

8 one-ounce squares semi-sweet chocolate
2 eggs, well-beaten
1 cup granulated sugar
1 teaspoon vanilla
$\frac{1}{2}$ cup butter or margarine, melted

1½ cups all-purpose flour, sifted
½ teaspoon salt
½ teaspoon baking powder
1 cup seedless raisins

Cut chocolate into small cubes; or use packaged chocolate bits. Beat eggs well. Stir sugar and vanilla into beaten eggs. Let butter cool slightly and stir into egg-sugar mixture. Sift together sifted flour, salt, and baking powder; add to egg mixture. Blend raisins and chocolate into batter.

Drop by teaspoonfuls onto greased baking sheet. Bake in oven 350°F. 15 to 18 minutes. Remove to wire rack to cool.

Makes about 4 dozen cookies.

LACY ENGLISH JUMBOS

1 cup semi-sweet chocolate morsels
¾ cup shortening
¾ cup granulated sugar
⅛ teaspoon salt
¼ teaspoon ginger
½ cup light corn syrup
1½ cups flour, sifted

Combine chocolate morsels, shortening, sugar, salt, and ginger; melt over hot (not boiling) water. Remove melted ingredients from water. Stir corn syrup and sifted flour into the melted ingredients.

Drop dough by teaspoonfuls, 3 inches apart, on a well-greased baking sheet. Bake in oven 350°F. 10 minutes. When done, remove from oven and cool approximately 1 minute.

Roll each cookie at once (top side out) over handle of wooden spoon, or use fingers, to form cones. Seal edges by pressing together. If cookies stick, return to oven for a minute. Then proceed as directed.

Makes about 5 dozen cookies.

CRINKLY PUFFS

2 cups semi-sweet chocolate morsels
$\frac{1}{2}$ cup shortening
$\frac{1}{2}$ teaspoon salt
3 eggs, well-beaten
$\frac{3}{4}$ cup granulated sugar
1 cup quick-cooking rolled oats, uncooked
1 teaspoon vanilla

Melt chocolate morsels in top of double boiler over hot (not boiling) water; remove from water. Cream together shortening and salt; add well-beaten eggs and beat until thick. Gradually beat sugar into creamed mixture; beat until very thick. Add rolled oats, vanilla, and melted morsels to creamed mixture; blend thoroughly.

Drop dough by teaspoonfuls onto greased baking sheet. Bake in oven 375°F. 6 to 8 minutes.

Note: This recipe does not require leavening.

Makes about 7 dozen puffs.

14. rolled cookies

LEMON-OAT COOKIES

4 cups flour, sifted
$\frac{1}{4}$ teaspoon baking soda
$\frac{1}{4}$ teaspoon baking powder
1 teaspoon salt
1 teaspoon nutmeg
1 cup shortening, soft
2 cups granulated sugar or corn syrup
2 eggs, well-beaten
$\frac{1}{4}$ cup cream or evaporated milk
$\frac{3}{4}$ cup bottled lemon juice
$\frac{1}{2}$ cup rolled oats, uncooked

Sift together sifted flour, soda, baking powder, salt, and nutmeg. Cream together shortening and sugar in a large mixing bowl. Blend sifted dry ingredients into creamed mixture. Combine eggs, cream, and bottled lemon juice. Add egg mixture, alternately with rolled oats, to creamed mixture. Mix well.

Chill dough. When chilled thoroughly, roll to $\frac{1}{4}$-inch thickness. Cut with favorite cookie cutters and bake in oven 375°F. 10 minutes.

Makes about 4 dozen cookies.

LEMON GINGER CUT-OUT COOKIES

1 package white cake mix
1 teaspoon lemon rind, grated
1 tablespoon lemon juice
2 tablespoons butter, soft
2 tablespoons crystallized ginger, finely cut
1 egg, unbeaten
   candied fruit, colored granulated sugar, or nuts

Pour half of cake mix into a large mixing bowl. Measure lemon rind, lemon juice, butter, ginger, and egg into the bowl; blend well. Gradually add rest of cake mix to the batter; blend with hands, until thoroughly mixed.

Roll dough to $\frac{1}{8}$-inch thickness on a well-floured board or pastry cloth. Cut rolled dough with fancy cookie cutters. Place cookies on an ungreased baking sheet; decorate with candied fruit, colored sugars, or nuts. Bake cookies in oven 375°F. 6 to 8 minutes.

Makes about $5\frac{1}{2}$ dozen cookies.

MINCE MEAT COOKIE-TARTS

2 cups flour, sifted
1¼ teaspoons baking powder
¼ teaspoon salt
½ cup shortening
1¼ cups granulated sugar
1 teaspoon vanilla
2 eggs, unbeaten
1⅓ cups mince meat

Sift together sifted flour, baking powder, and salt. Cream shortening until fluffy. Gradually add sugar to creamed shortening. Beat until well blended. Stir vanilla into creamed mixture; add eggs and beat. Add sifted dry ingredients in 2 portions to creamed mixture; beat batter smooth after each addition.

Chill dough about 1 hour in refrigerator. Roll dough, ¼ at a time, on a lightly floured board to ⅛-inch thickness. Cut dough with 2-inch cookie cutter of any desired shape; cut 2 alike for each filled cookie.

Cut center from tops of cookies by using a small ¾-inch round, leaf, star, or heart-shape cutter. If doughnut cutter is available with removable center, cut half the dough as plain rounds and the remaining halves with the hole in the center to be used as tops.

Place the bottoms 2 inches apart on well-greased baking sheet. Place 2 rounded teaspoonfuls of mince meat in center of each cookie; cover with tops and press edges firmly together.

Bake in oven 400°F. about 7 minutes, or until tops are light golden brown and bottoms are golden brown. Cool. Store in tightly covered container.

Makes about 2 dozen cookies.

CHOCOLATE SUGAR COOKIES

$\frac{1}{2}$ cup butter
1 cup granulated sugar
2 one-ounce squares unsweetened chocolate, melted
2 eggs
1 teaspoon vanilla
1 tablespoon milk
$2\frac{1}{4}$ cups all-purpose flour, sifted
1 teaspoon baking powder
$\frac{1}{2}$ teaspoon baking soda
$\frac{1}{2}$ teaspoon salt

Cream butter. Add sugar and melted chocolate to creamed butter; continue creaming until blended. Add eggs, vanilla, and milk to creamed mixture; mix well. Sift together sifted flour, baking powder, soda, and salt; add to creamed mixture and blend thoroughly.

Roll dough; wrap in waxed paper. Store dough in refrigerator until ready to bake as refrigerator cookies. Or, chill dough until firm enough to roll; roll dough and cut with cookie cutter. Place on greased baking sheet. Bake in preheated oven 425°F. 8 to 12 minutes.

Makes 4 dozen cookies.

MOCHA JUMBLES

4 tablespoons butter or margarine
1 cup granulated sugar
1 egg, beaten
2 tablespoons coffee, cold and strong

    2 one-ounce squares unsweetened chocolate,
      melted
 1¾ cups enriched flour, sifted
    2 teaspoons baking powder
    ½ teaspoon cinnamon
      granulated sugar

Cream butter until consistency of mayonnaise. Slowly
add 1 cup sugar to creamed butter, while continuing to
cream. Blend beaten egg and coffee into creamed mixture;
add melted chocolate. Mix thoroughly. Combine sifted flour,
baking powder, and cinnamon; sift into creamed mixture.
Mix well.

Lightly flour dough board. Place dough onto board and
roll to ⅓-inch thickness. Cut rolled dough with doughnut
cutter; sprinkle with sugar. Place cut cookies onto greased
baking sheet; bake in oven 350°F. 10 to 12 minutes.

                        Makes about 2 dozen cookies.

COFFEE RUM COOKIES

    2 cups flour, sifted
    2 tablespoons soluble coffee
    ½ teaspoon baking powder
    ⅛ teaspoon baking soda
    ½ teaspoon salt
    ⅓ cup shortening
    ⅓ cup butter or margarine
    ½ cup brown sugar
    ⅓ cup granulated sugar
    1 egg, well-beaten

1 teaspoon imitation rum extract
½ cup nuts

Combine sifted flour, soluble coffee, baking powder, soda, and salt; sift together and set aside. Cream together shortening and butter in a large mixing bowl; gradually add sugars and continue to cream. After adding the sugars, beat creamed mixture until light. Mix well-beaten egg and rum extract into creamed mixture. Blend sifted dry ingredients into creamed mixture; mix thoroughly.

Wrap dough in waxed paper or aluminum foil; place in refrigerator and chill several hours. Remove chilled dough from refrigerator as needed. Roll only a small amount of the dough at a time. Roll the dough to ⅛-inch thickness on a lightly floured board. Cut with cookie cutter. Decorate with nuts, if desired. Bake on ungreased baking sheet in oven 400°F. 8 to 10 minutes.

Note: Dough can be formed into a roll, wrapped in wax paper or aluminum foil, chilled overnight, then sliced thin and baked as needed.

Makes about 3 dozen cookies.

WALNUT KRISPIES

1 cup butter or margarine
1 cup granulated sugar
2 egg yolks
⅓ cup milk
3½ cups all-purpose flour, sifted
1 teaspoon baking powder
½ teaspoon salt
1 cup walnuts, finely chopped

1 one-ounce square unsweetened chocolate, melted
½ teaspoon vanilla
Walnut Krispies' Decoration

Cream together butter and sugar in a large mixing bowl. Add egg yolks to creamed mixture; beat thoroughly. Blend milk into the mixture. Sift together sifted flour, baking powder, and salt; blend, alternately with walnuts, into the creamed mixture.

Divide dough in half. Blend melted chocolate into one half of the dough; blend vanilla into the other half of the dough. Place the two halves into refrigerator and chill.

When chilled, remove small portions of the dough at a time from the refrigerator and roll to ⅛-inch thickness. Cut rolled dough in fancy shapes with knife or cookie cutters. Decorate with Walnut Krispies Decoration and bake in oven 400°F. 8 to 10 minutes.

Makes about 8 dozen cookies.

ROLLED MOLASSES COOKIES

1 cup shortening, soft
1 cup brown sugar
1 cup molasses or white corn syrup
1 egg, beaten
4 cups all-purpose flour, sifted
1 teaspoon salt
1 teaspoon baking soda
2 teaspoons ground ginger
1 teaspoon ground cinnamon
½ teaspoon ground nutmeg

½ teaspoon ground cloves
1 cup raisins

Cream together shortening and brown sugar. Add molasses and egg to creamed mixture; mix well. Sift together sifted flour, salt, soda, ginger, cinnamon, nutmeg, and cloves. Blend raisins and sifted dry ingredients into creamed mixture; mix well.

Chill dough. Roll dough to ⅛-inch thickness and cut to desired shape. Bake in preheated oven 350° to 375°F. 10 to 15 minutes.

Makes 7 dozen cookies.

CRISP MOLASSES COOKIES

1 cup shortening
1 cup molasses
2 eggs, well-beaten
1 cup granulated sugar
3½ cups flour, sifted
½ teaspoon salt
1 teaspoon baking soda
¼ teaspoon cinnamon
½ teaspoon cloves
¼ teaspoon ginger

Heat shortening and molasses in a saucepan until shortening is melted; stir constantly while heating. Place well-beaten eggs into mixing bowl; slowly pour melted shortening mixture over eggs. Sift together sugar, sifted flour, salt, soda, cinnamon, cloves, and ginger; blend into egg mixture. After mixing well, place the dough into refrigerator; chill thoroughly.

When dough is chilled, remove from refrigerator. Roll dough to $\frac{1}{16}$-inch thickness on floured board or pastry cloth. Cut rolled dough with a 2-inch cookie cutter; place on baking sheet. Bake in oven 350°F. 10 minutes.

Makes 10 dozen cookies.

DESSERT HONEY COOKIES

5 cups all-purpose flour, sifted
1 teaspoon baking soda
1 teaspoon baking powder
1 teaspoon salt
1$\frac{1}{2}$ teaspoons mace
1 cup honey
$\frac{1}{2}$ cup fresh orange juice
1 cup butter
2 teaspoons vanilla
$\frac{1}{2}$ teaspoon orange rind, grated
1 cup granulated sugar
   granulated sugar

Sift together sifted flour, soda, baking powder, salt, and mace; set aside. Combine honey and orange juice; blend well. Cream together butter, vanilla, orange rind, and 1 cup of sugar in a large mixing bowl; cream until smooth and well blended. Blend the sifted dry ingredients, alternately with the honey mixture, into the butter mixture; mix thoroughly after each addition.

Cover the dough; place in refrigerator and chill for 2 hours or longer. When dough is chilled thoroughly, prepare a small amount of the dough at a time. Leave dough not being worked in the refrigerator. Roll dough to $\frac{1}{4}$-inch thickness on a lightly floured board; cut with a 3-inch cookie cutter. Transfer the cut cookies with a wide spatula or pancake turner to a baking sheet. Lightly sprinkle the surface of each cookie with sugar. Bake in oven 350°F. 18 to 20 minutes. When done, remove cookies from oven; immediately transfer cookies from baking sheet to a rack and cool.

Makes about 2 dozen large cookies.

GINGER STARS

2 cups flour, sifted
$\frac{1}{2}$ cup granulated sugar
$\frac{1}{2}$ teaspoon baking soda
1 teaspoon salt
1 teaspoon ginger
$\frac{1}{2}$ teaspoon cinnamon
$\frac{2}{3}$ cup molasses
6 tablespoons shortening
Confectioners' Sugar Frosting

Sift together sifted flour, sugar, soda, salt, ginger, and cinnamon. Heat molasses to boiling; remove from heat. Add shortening to molasses; blend thoroughly. Add sifted dry ingredients to molasses mixture; mix well.

Chill dough until it is easy to handle. Roll chilled dough thin on lightly floured board. Cut into stars. Bake on greased baking sheet in oven 350°F. 8 minutes. Cool.

Frost with Confectioners' Sugar Frosting, which has been tinted with green food coloring and flavored with peppermint.

Makes 2 dozen cookies.

GINGER BUTTER COOKIES

$2\frac{3}{4}$ cups flour, sifted
$\frac{1}{2}$ teaspoon baking soda
1 teaspoon ginger
$\frac{1}{2}$ teaspoon cinnamon
$\frac{1}{2}$ teaspoon salt
$\frac{1}{4}$ teaspoon cloves
$\frac{1}{2}$ cup butter
$\frac{1}{4}$ cup brown sugar, firmly packed
$\frac{3}{4}$ cup dark molasses
1 egg, beaten
1 teaspoon hot water
1 teaspoon vinegar

Sift together sifted flour, soda, ginger, cinnamon, salt, and cloves. Cream together butter and brown sugar. Add molasses to creamed mixture; add egg and beat until smooth. Fold sifted dry ingredients into creamed mixture. Add water and vinegar to dough; blend. Cover dough and chill for at least 2 hours.

Roll dough on lightly floured board to $\frac{1}{4}$-inch thickness and cut with cookie cutters. Place on buttered baking sheet. Bake in preheated oven 350°F. 15 to 20 minutes. Remove from oven. Transfer cookies to cake racks to cool.

Frost or decorate as desired.

Makes 2 dozen small cookies or
1 dozen gingerbread men.

SOUR CREAM COOKIES

2 cups granulated sugar
1 cup lard

1 teaspoon baking soda
1 cup sour cream
2 eggs
1 teaspoon vanilla
$4\frac{1}{2}$ cups all-purpose flour, sifted

Cream together sugar and lard. Add soda to sour cream; blend with creamed mixture. Add eggs and vanilla to sugar mixture. Work sifted flour into mixture until dough becomes stiff enough to roll.

Roll on floured board and cut with cookie cutters. Bake in oven 350°F. 10 minutes, or until lightly browned.

Makes about 7 dozen cookies.

ROLLED SOUR CREAM SUGAR COOKIES

2 cups granulated sugar
$\frac{2}{3}$ cup butter
2 large eggs
1 teaspoon vanilla
1 cup sour cream
5 cups flour, sifted
2 teaspoons baking powder
1 teaspoon baking soda
$1\frac{1}{2}$ teaspoons salt
$\frac{1}{2}$ teaspoon nutmeg
$\frac{1}{4}$ cup granulated sugar

Gradually blend 2 cups of sugar into butter; cream thoroughly. Add eggs to creamed mixture; beat until fluffy. Stir vanilla and sour cream into creamed mixture. Sift together sifted flour, baking powder, soda, salt, and nutmeg.

Blend the sifted dry ingredients into creamed mixture until a smooth, soft dough is formed. Thoroughly chill dough.

Roll chilled dough to $\frac{1}{3}$-inch thickness on floured board; cut with large cookie cutter, biscuit cutter, or a drinking glass. Place cookies on a greased baking sheet; sprinkle with granulated sugar (colored if desired). Bake in oven 375°F. until lightly browned. For crisp cookies, roll the dough very thin before cutting.

Makes 3 dozen cookies.

BUTTER CREAM COOKIES

> 1 cup butter
> 1 cup granulated sugar
> 2 eggs, well-beaten
> $3\frac{1}{2}$ cups flour, sifted
> $\frac{3}{4}$ teaspoon baking soda
> 4 tablespoons sour cream
>   dash of salt
> 1 teaspoon vanilla or almond extract
> $\frac{1}{4}$ cup granulated sugar

Cream butter well. Gradually add 1 cup of sugar to creamed butter; cream well. Add well-beaten eggs to creamed mixture. Dissolve soda in sour cream. Add sifted flour, alternately with sour cream mixture, to creamed mixture. Add salt and vanilla; mix well.

Knead dough and roll thin. Sprinkle with remaining $\frac{1}{4}$ cup sugar. Cut with biscuit cutter and place on lightly buttered baking sheet. Bake in oven 375°F. 10 to 12 minutes.

Makes about 6 dozen cookies.

BUTTER COOKIES

1 cup butter
½ cup granulated sugar
1 egg, well-beaten
3 teaspoons vanilla
3 cups flour, sifted
½ teaspoon baking powder

Cream butter; add sugar and cream again until fluffy. Add beaten egg to creamed mixture, then vanilla. Sift together sifted flour and baking powder; work into creamed mixture. Blend well. Chill dough.

Roll chilled dough very thin. Cut with desired cookie cutter. Bake on lightly buttered baking sheet in oven 425°F. 5 to 7 minutes, or until lightly browned.

Makes about 4 dozen cookies.

BUTTER RINGS

½ cup butter
¼ cup brown sugar, packed
1 egg, separated
1 cup flour, sifted
1 cup nuts, chopped*
  raspberry jam

Cream together butter and brown sugar until light and fluffy. Stir egg yolk into creamed mixture. Blend sifted flour into creamed mixture.

Form dough into small balls. Place 1 ball at a time on a fork; dip into egg white, then into chopped nuts.

Place dipped balls on a baking sheet; press hole in center of each ball. Bake in oven 300°F. 8 minutes. Remove from oven, press center again, and return to oven—bake 10 minutes more. Remove from oven; cool slightly. Remove baked cookies from baking sheet. Fill centers with jam.

* For variation, substitute 1 cup of coconut for chopped nuts.

Makes about 3 dozen cookies.

CRISP SUGAR COOKIES

$\frac{1}{2}$ cup butter
1 cup granulated sugar
2 eggs
1 teaspoon vanilla*
1 tablespoon milk
$2\frac{1}{4}$ cups all-purpose flour, sifted
1 teaspoon baking powder
$\frac{1}{2}$ teaspoon baking soda
$\frac{1}{2}$ teaspoon salt

Cream butter. Add sugar to creamed butter; continue creaming until well blended. Add eggs, vanilla, and milk to creamed mixture; mix well. Sift together sifted flour, baking powder, soda, and salt. Add sifted dry ingredients to creamed mixture; blend thoroughly.

Roll dough and wrap in waxed paper and store in refrigerator until ready to bake as refrigerator cookies; or, chill dough until firm enough to roll, then roll dough and cut with cookie cutter. Place on greased baking sheet. Bake in preheated oven 425°F. 8 to 12 minutes.

If desired, these cookies can be filled with Sugar Cookie Filling.

* In place of 1 teaspoon vanilla, 1 teaspoon nutmeg or ½ teaspoon lemon extract may be added to change flavor of cookie.

Makes 4 dozen cookies.

MARY'S SUGAR COOKIES

  ½ cup shortening
  1 cup granulated sugar
  2 eggs, well-beaten
  1 teaspoon vanilla
  2¾ cups cake flour, sifted
  2 teaspoons baking powder
  ½ teaspoon salt

Cream shortening. Add sugar to creamed shortening; cream again. Add eggs to creamed mixture; beat thoroughly. Stir vanilla into creamed mixture. Sift together sifted flour, baking powder, and salt; blend into creamed mixture. Thoroughly chill dough.

Roll dough to ⅛-inch thickness on lightly floured board. Cut with floured cutter. Bake in preheated oven 400°F. 8 to 12 minutes.

Makes about 3 dozen cookies.

SAND TARTS

  ½ cup butter
  1 egg, well-beaten

1 cup granulated sugar
1¾ cups flour, sifted
2 teaspoons baking powder
½ teaspoon salt
¼ teaspoon nutmeg
¼ cup sweet cream
1 tablespoon cinnamon
2 tablespoons granulated sugar
1 cup nuts, unbroken

Cream butter. Blend well-beaten egg into creamed butter. Sift together sugar, sifted flour, baking powder, salt, and nutmeg. Cut sifted dry ingredients into creamed mixture.

Roll dough thin on a lightly floured board. Cut rolled dough with cookie cutter. Place cookies on a large baking sheet. Brush cookies with sweet cream. Mix together the tablespoon of cinnamon and 2 tablespoons granulated sugar; sprinkle on top of cookies. Place 1 nut in the center of each cookie.

Bake cookies in oven 350°F. until golden brown.

Makes 3 dozen cookies.

SCOTCH SHORTBREAD

2 cups butter
1 cup granulated sugar
5 cups flour, sifted
extra-fine granulated sugar

Cream together butter and sugar, until the mixture has the consistency of whipped butter. Add the sifted flour, 1 cup at a time, to the creamed mixture; mix thoroughly after each addition.

Roll dough to $\frac{1}{2}$-inch thickness on a floured pastry cloth. Cut rolled dough into 1-inch squares; place squares on baking sheet, leaving a little space between the squares. Prick tops of squares with a fork.

Bake in oven 275°F. 45 minutes, or until lightly browned. Do not overbrown. Remove shortbread squares from oven; sprinkle tops of shortbread, while still hot, with extra-fine granulated sugar.

Makes 10$\frac{1}{2}$ dozen squares.

PEEK-A-BOO COOKIES

2$\frac{1}{2}$ cups enriched flour, sifted
1 teaspoon baking soda
1 teaspoon salt
1 cup brown sugar
1 cup shortening, soft
$\frac{1}{2}$ cup water
2$\frac{1}{4}$ cups rolled oats, uncooked
$\frac{1}{4}$ cup confectioners' sugar
$\frac{1}{2}$ cup jelly or jam

Sift together sifted flour, soda, and salt into large mixing bowl. Add brown sugar, shortening, and water to sifted dry ingredients; beat about 2 minutes, or until batter is smooth. Fold rolled oats into batter.

Generously sprinkle a bread board with confectioners' sugar. Place dough on board and roll until very thin. Cut rolled dough with a cookie cutter. In half of the cookies, cut a design.

Place plain cookies on lightly greased baking sheet; top with ½ teaspoon jelly and cover with a designed cookie. Lightly press edges of the plain and designed cookies together. Bake in oven 350°F. 10 to 12 minutes.

Makes about 3½ dozen cookies.

ESKIMO COOKIES

    2 cups flour, sifted
    1 teaspoon double-acting baking powder
    ½ teaspoon salt
    ½ cup butter or shortening
    ⅔ cup granulated sugar
    1 egg, unbeaten
    1 tablespoon milk
    ½ square candy-making chocolate
    1⅓ cups flaked coconut
      Butter Frosting

Sift flour once; measure. Add baking powder and salt to sifted flour; sift again. Cream shortening in large mixing bowl; gradually add sugar and cream together until light and fluffy. Add egg and milk to creamed mixture; beat well. Add sifted dry ingredients, a small amount at a time, to creamed mixture. Be sure to beat batter well after each addition of sifted dry ingredients. Chill overnight, or until firm enough to roll.

Roll chilled dough to ⅛-inch thickness on floured board. Cut dough with floured cookie cutter into gingerbread men shapes or other figures. Bake on ungreased baking sheet in oven 375°F. 10 minutes, or until done. Remove from oven and cool.

While cookie figures are cooling, melt chocolate. Draw a face on each cookie with a toothpick or small paint brush that has been dipped into the melted chocolate. Spread Butter Frosting or Confectioners' Sugar Frosting over the body of the cookie figure and around the edges of the face. Sprinkle coconut over the frosting. The entire cookie can be frosted first, then decorated with melted chocolate and coconut.

Makes about 2 dozen cookies.

TWO-TONE WHIRLIGIGS

1 cup semi-sweet chocolate morsels
$2\frac{1}{2}$ cups flour, sifted
$1\frac{1}{4}$ teaspoons baking powder
$\frac{1}{2}$ teaspoon salt
1 cup butter, soft
1 cup granulated sugar
1 egg
1 tablespoon vanilla
1 cup quick-cooking rolled oats, uncooked

Melt chocolate morsels over hot (not boiling) water; remove from water and set aside. Sift together sifted flour, baking powder, and salt; set aside. Cream together butter, sugar, egg, and vanilla; gradually blend sifted dry ingredients, alternately with rolled oats, into creamed mixture. Remove 1 cup of dough; chill.

To remaining dough, add melted chocolate morsels; chill until firm enough to handle. Roll between 2 sheets of waxed paper to an 18 x 10-inch rectangle; peel off top sheet of waxed paper. Roll reserved cup of chilled dough between 2 sheets of waxed paper to an 18 x 8-inch rectangle; peel off top sheet of waxed paper. Invert the smaller rectangle onto the larger one; peel off all waxed paper. Starting along the 18-inch edge, roll the chilled doughs like a jelly roll. Wrap the roll and chill several hours. Unwrap the chilled roll; cut into $\frac{1}{4}$-inch slices. Place slices, 1 inch apart, on an ungreased baking sheet. Bake in oven 375°F. 8 minutes.

Makes about 6 dozen cookies.

15. pressed and formed cookies

COCONUT POMPONS

1 cup butter
½ cup granulated sugar
2 teaspoons vanilla
2 cups flour, sifted
¼ teaspoon salt
2 cups pecan halves*
1 cup shredded coconut, chopped

Cream together butter, sugar, and vanilla until fluffy. Sift together sifted flour and salt; blend into creamed mixture.

Use spoon to dip dough and shape around a pecan half to form 1-inch balls. Roll each ball in shredded coconut; place

* For variation use whole blanched almonds, dates, or candied cherries for surprise center in Coconut Pompons.

188

on a baking sheet. Bake in oven 325°F. 20 minutes. Remove from oven; cool.

Makes 4 dozen pompons.

ORANGE ALMOND DROPS

1 package yellow cake mix
1 egg, unbeaten
2 tablespoons orange juice
1 teaspoon orange rind, grated
$\frac{1}{4}$ teaspoon almond extract
2 tablespoons butter, soft
$\frac{1}{2}$ cup almonds, shredded

Place half of the cake mix into a large mixing bowl. Add egg, orange juice, orange rind, almond extract, and butter to the cake mix in the bowl. With a wooden spoon thoroughly beat the batter. Blend other half of the cake mix into the mixing bowl. Stir shredded almonds into the dough.

Shape dough, with hands, into small balls about the size of a walnut. Place balls about 3 inches apart on an ungreased baking sheet. Bake in oven 375°F. 12 to 15 minutes. Allow cookies to cool about 1 minute on baking sheet before removing.

Makes about 4 dozen cookies.

FUDGE BALLS

$1\frac{1}{2}$ cups enriched flour, sifted
1 cup granulated sugar

$\frac{1}{2}$ teaspoon salt
$\frac{3}{4}$ cup shortening, soft
2 one-ounce squares chocolate, melted
$\frac{1}{4}$ cup coffee, cold
$1\frac{1}{2}$ cups rolled oats, uncooked
$\frac{1}{2}$ cup nuts, chopped

Sift together sifted flour, sugar, and salt into large mixing bowl. Blend shortening, melted chocolate, and cold coffee into sifted dry ingredients; beat about 2 minutes or until smooth. Fold rolled oats into cookie batter.

Shape dough, with hands, into logs, balls, and cones. Roll the shaped dough in chopped nuts. Place shaped dough on an ungreased baking sheet. Bake in oven 350°F. 10 to 12 minutes.

Makes about 3 dozen cookies.

CHOCOLATE SNOWBALLS

2 cups flour, sifted
$\frac{1}{2}$ teaspoon salt
$\frac{3}{4}$ cup butter
$\frac{1}{2}$ cup granulated sugar
2 teaspoons vanilla
1 egg
1 cup nuts, chopped
1 cup chocolate morsels
confectioners' sugar

Sift together sifted flour and salt; set aside. Blend together butter, sugar, and vanilla; cream thoroughly. Beat egg into creamed mixture; blend sifted dry ingredients, nuts, and morsels into this mixture.

Shape dough into 1-inch balls. Place on an ungreased baking sheet. Bake in oven 350°F. 15 to 20 minutes. When done, remove from oven and cool slightly. Then, roll each ball in confectioners' sugar.

Makes about 6 dozen cookies.

CHOCOLATE CRISS CROSSES

1 cup and 2 tablespoons flour, sifted
$\frac{1}{2}$ teaspoon baking soda
$\frac{1}{2}$ teaspoon salt
$\frac{1}{2}$ cup shortening, soft
6 tablespoons granulated sugar
6 tablespoons brown sugar
1 egg
$\frac{1}{2}$ cup peanut butter
$\frac{1}{2}$ teaspoon vanilla
$\frac{1}{4}$ teaspoon water
1 cup semi-sweet chocolate morsels

Sift together sifted flour, soda, and salt; set aside. Cream together shortening and sugars; set aside. Blend together egg and peanut butter; add vanilla and water. Mix egg mixture into creamed mixture; add sifted dry ingredients and blend thoroughly. Stir semi-sweet chocolate morsels into the batter.

Form into 1-inch balls. Place on an ungreased baking sheet. Press each ball with the back of fork prongs to make criss-cross design. Bake in oven 375°F. 10 to 12 minutes.

Makes about 4 dozen cookies.

COCOA NUT BALLS

1 cup butter
½ cup granulated sugar
2 teaspoons vanilla
2 cups flour, sifted
½ teaspoon salt
¼ cup cocoa
2 cups pecans, finely chopped
¼ cup confectioners' sugar

Cream together butter, sugar, and vanilla until fluffy. Sift together sifted flour, salt, and cocoa; blend thoroughly into creamed mixture. Stir pecans into batter; mix well.

Shape dough into 1-inch balls; place on baking sheet. Bake in oven 325°F. 20 minutes. *Caution:* Do not brown. Remove from oven; cool. Roll cookies in confectioners' sugar.

Makes about 6 dozen cookies.

JEANNETTE'S LACE COOKIES

1 cup butter
1 cup brown sugar
1 cup granulated sugar
2 eggs, well-beaten
1 teaspoon walnut extract
1⅓ cups flour, sifted
2 cups quick-cooking rolled oats, uncooked
1 teaspoon baking powder
¾ cup black walnuts, chopped

Cream together butter and sugars. Stir well-beaten eggs and walnut extract into creamed mixture. Combine flour, rolled oats and baking powder; blend into creamed mixture. Fold walnuts into dough.

Form dough into small balls. Place, 2 inches apart, on baking sheet. Bake in oven 375°F. until edges of cookies begin to brown. Cool before removing from baking sheet.

Makes 4 dozen cookies.

PEANUT OATMEAL DROPS

1 cup shortening
1 cup granulated sugar
1 cup brown sugar, packed
1 teaspoon vanilla
2 eggs
1½ cups flour, sifted
1 teaspoon baking soda
3 cups rolled oats, uncooked
½ pound salted Spanish peanuts

Cream shortening; gradually add sugars. Add vanilla and eggs to creamed mixture; beat well. Sift together sifted flour and soda; blend into creamed mixture. Stir rolled oats and peanuts into batter; blend thoroughly.

With hands, form dough into small balls. Place balls on baking sheet. Bake in oven 425°F. 7 minutes.

Makes about 6 dozen cookies.

SCOTCH-OAT PRIZES

1 cup butterscotch morsels
1 cup flour, sifted
$\frac{1}{2}$ teaspoon baking soda
$\frac{1}{2}$ teaspoon salt
$\frac{3}{4}$ cup granulated sugar
$\frac{1}{2}$ cup shortening
1 egg
1 teaspoon orange rind, grated
1 cup quick-cooking rolled oats, uncooked
1 cup flaked coconut

Melt butterscotch morsels over hot (not boiling) water; remove from water and let cool approximately 10 minutes. Sift together sifted flour, soda, and salt. Combine together sugar, shortening, egg, and orange rind; beat until creamy. To the creamed mixture, add rolled oats, coconut, sifted dry ingredients, and melted butterscotch; blend thoroughly.

Shape dough into 1-inch balls. Place on greased baking sheet. Bake in oven 350°F. approximately 15 minutes.

Makes about 5 dozen cookies.

SWEDISH OATMEAL COOKIES

$\frac{2}{3}$ cup butter
$\frac{1}{2}$ cup granulated sugar
3 cups rolled oats, uncooked
1 egg, beaten
1 teaspoon almond extract

Save 1 tablespoon of butter to grease the baking sheet. With fingers, knead together into a solid mass remaining butter, sugar, and rolled oats; blend thoroughly. Add egg and almond extract to kneaded mixture; mix well. Form dough into tiny balls the size of marbles and place on buttered baking sheet. Mash each cookie with tines of fork. Bake in oven 325°F. 10 to 15 minutes, or until golden brown.

Makes about $2\frac{1}{2}$ dozen cookies.

LAURINE'S FAVORITE COOKIES

$\frac{1}{2}$ cup shortening
$\frac{1}{2}$ cup brown sugar
$\frac{1}{2}$ cup granulated sugar
$\frac{1}{2}$ cup peanut butter
1 egg
$1\frac{1}{4}$ cups flour, sifted
$\frac{1}{4}$ teaspoon salt
$\frac{1}{2}$ teaspoon baking soda

Cream shortening; add sugars and cream thoroughly. Add peanut butter to creamed mixture; cream again. Beat egg into creamed mixture. Sift together sifted flour, salt, and soda; blend into creamed mixture.

Shape dough into tiny balls. Place on ungreased baking sheet and flatten with fork. Bake in oven 350°F. 15 to 20 minutes.

Makes about 3 dozen cookies.

NUT BUTTER BALLS

1 cup butter, soft
½ cup confectioners' sugar
½ teaspoon salt
1 teaspoon almond or vanilla extract
2 cups flour, sifted
1 to 2 cups nuts, chopped or ground*
½ cup confectioners' sugar

Cream together butter and ½ cup confectioners' sugar. Add salt, extract, sifted flour, and nuts to creamed mixture; mix thoroughly. Chill dough until easy to handle.

With fingers, shape chilled dough into 1-inch balls or 1-inch by ½-inch rolls, triangles, or crescents. Place on ungreased baking sheet. Bake in oven 350°F. 15 minutes, or until light brown. While cookies are still warm, roll in the remaining ½ cup confectioners' sugar. These cookies keep well.

* Use walnuts, pecans, almonds, black walnuts, or Brazil nuts.

Makes about 5 dozen cookies.

PEANUT BUTTER COOKIES I

3 cups flour, sifted
2 teaspoons baking powder
¼ teaspoon salt
1 cup butter
1 cup granulated sugar
1 cup brown sugar, firmly packed
2 eggs, well-beaten

1 cup peanut butter
$\frac{1}{2}$ teaspoon vanilla

Sift together sifted flour, baking powder, and salt. Cream together butter and sugars. Add well-beaten eggs to creamed mixture; mix until smooth. Add peanut butter to creamed mixture; stir well. Blend vanilla into creamed mixture. Thoroughly blend sifted dry ingredients into creamed mixture. Dough will be stiff.

Form dough into tiny balls; place on buttered baking sheet. Press each ball with back of fork to make a waffle design. Bake in oven 375°F. 10 to 12 minutes.

Makes about 7 dozen cookies.

PEANUT BUTTER COOKIES II

1 cup shortening, soft
1 cup granulated sugar
1 cup brown sugar
2 eggs, well-beaten
1 cup peanut butter
1 teaspoon vanilla
2 cups all-purpose flour, sifted
1 teaspoon baking soda
$\frac{1}{2}$ teaspoon salt

Cream together shortening and sugars. Blend well-beaten eggs, peanut butter, and vanilla into creamed mixture. Sift together sifted flour, soda, and salt. Add sifted dry ingredients to creamed mixture; blend well.

Shape dough into balls the size of walnuts; place on greased baking sheet. Flatten dough with fork to about

$\frac{1}{4}$-inch thickness. Bake in preheated oven 350°F. 12 to 15 minutes.

Makes 4 dozen cookies.

PEANUT BUTTER CRUNCHIES

$\frac{1}{2}$ cup shortening
$\frac{1}{2}$ cup peanut butter
$\frac{1}{2}$ cup brown sugar, packed
$\frac{1}{2}$ cup granulated sugar
$\frac{1}{2}$ teaspoon vanilla
1 egg
1$\frac{1}{2}$ cups flour, sifted
1 teaspoon baking soda
1 teaspoon salt

Combine shortening and peanut butter; add sugars and vanilla, mixing until fluffy. Add egg to shortening mixture; beat well. Sift together sifted flour, soda, and salt; blend into shortening mixture.

Shape dough into small balls. Place balls, 2 inches apart, on baking sheet. Flatten each ball with tines of fork that have been dipped in granulated sugar. Bake in oven 375°F. 10 minutes.

Makes about 5 dozen cookies.

PECAN BUTTER COOKIES

1 cup butter
$\frac{1}{2}$ cup confectioners' sugar

2 cups flour, sifted
$\frac{1}{2}$ teaspoon salt
$\frac{1}{2}$ cup pecans, finely chopped
1 teaspoon vanilla
$\frac{1}{2}$ cup confectioners' sugar

Cream together butter and $\frac{1}{2}$ cup confectioners' sugar. Sift together sifted flour and salt; add to creamed mixture. Stir pecans and vanilla into batter; mix thoroughly.

Roll dough into small balls; place on buttered baking sheet and flatten each ball with tines of a fork. Bake in oven 350°F. 10 minutes, or until lightly browned. Roll cookies, while still warm, in the remaining $\frac{1}{2}$ cup confectioners' sugar.

Makes about 3 dozen cookies.

WALNUT TEA-TIME DAINTIES

$\frac{1}{2}$ cup butter
1 cup brown sugar, packed
1 egg
3 tablespoons milk
1 teaspoon vanilla
$1\frac{3}{4}$ cups all-purpose flour
$1\frac{1}{2}$ teaspoons baking powder
$\frac{1}{4}$ teaspoon salt
$\frac{3}{4}$ cup California walnuts, finely chopped
$\frac{1}{2}$ cup currants
1 egg white, slightly beaten
$\frac{1}{4}$ cup granulated sugar
3 dozen large California walnut pieces

Cream together butter and brown sugar. Add egg, milk, and vanilla to creamed mixture; beat well. Combine flour, baking powder and salt; blend into creamed mixture. Mix finely chopped walnuts and currants into the batter. Chill.

Shape chilled dough into small balls, 1 to $1\frac{1}{2}$ inches in diameter. Dip each ball into slightly beaten egg white, then into granulated sugar.

Place balls, sugared side up, on an ungreased baking sheet. Top each ball with a large piece of walnut. Bake in oven 400°F. about 12 minutes, or until lightly browned.

Note: These are light brown ball-type cookies with a sugary glaze. They are flavorful and have a slightly crisp texture. These cookies keep well if stored in a tightly covered container.

Makes about 3 dozen dainties.

MOLASSES COOKIES

1 cup shortening
$1\frac{1}{2}$ cups brown sugar
2 eggs
$\frac{1}{3}$ cup molasses
3 cups flour, sifted
$1\frac{1}{2}$ teaspoons baking soda
$\frac{1}{2}$ teaspoon salt
1 teaspoon cinnamon
1 teaspoon ginger
$\frac{1}{2}$ cup granulated sugar

Cream together shortening and brown sugar. Add eggs to creamed mixture; beat thoroughly. Slowly blend molasses

Chocolate Honey Brownies *(American Honey Institute)*

Cobana Bars *(Pan-American Coffee Bureau)*

Sour Cream Chocolate Cookies (*Pan-American Coffee Bureau*)

Donut Spinners (*American Dairy Association*)

into creamed mixture. Sift together sifted flour, soda, salt, cinnamon, and ginger; blend into creamed mixture.

With hands, pinch tiny pieces of dough and roll into balls. Place on greased baking sheet. Flatten each ball with a fork; sprinkle with sugar. Bake in oven 350°F. 10 to 15 minutes.

Makes about 4 dozen cookies.

CONFECTIONERS' SUGAR COOKIES

1 cup butter
1 cup confectioners' sugar, sifted
2 egg yolks
1 teaspoon vanilla
2 cups flour, sifted
$\frac{1}{2}$ teaspoon salt
$\frac{1}{2}$ teaspoon baking soda
$\frac{1}{2}$ teaspoon cream of tartar
$\frac{1}{2}$ cup confectioners' sugar, sifted
    pecan halves or red or green maraschino cherries

Cream together butter and 1 cup confectioners' sugar; add egg yolks and vanilla. Sift together sifted flour, salt, soda, and cream of tartar. Add sifted dry ingredients to creamed mixture; mix well.

Shape dough into balls the size of a nickel. Roll balls in $\frac{1}{2}$ cup confectioners' sugar; place on baking sheet. Place a pecan half on top of each ball; or top each ball with a maraschino cherry. Bake in oven 350°F. 12 minutes.

Makes about 3 dozen cookies.

AGATHA'S BROWN SUGAR COOKIES

$\frac{1}{2}$ cup shortening
$\frac{1}{3}$ cup peanut butter
1 cup brown sugar
2 eggs
1 tablespoon buttermilk
2 cups flour, sifted
1 teaspoon baking soda
1 teaspoon baking powder
1 teaspoon vanilla

Cream together shortening, peanut butter, and brown sugar. Add eggs and buttermilk to creamed mixture; beat thoroughly. Sift together sifted flour, soda, and baking powder; blend into creamed mixture. Stir vanilla into dough.

Form dough into small balls; place on well-greased sheet. With tines of a fork, press each ball flat. Bake in oven 350°F. 12 minutes.

Makes about 3 dozen cookies.

CINNAMON PUFFS

2 cups flour, sifted
1 teaspoon baking powder
1 cup granulated sugar
3 teaspoons cinnamon
$\frac{1}{2}$ cup butter, soft
$\frac{1}{2}$ cup shortening, soft
1 egg, separated
1 teaspoon orange rind, grated
1 cup chocolate morsels

½ cup nuts, chopped
⅔ cup granulated sugar
2 teaspoons cinnamon

Sift together sifted flour, baking powder, 1 cup sugar, and 3 teaspoons cinnamon; set aside. Blend together butter, shortening, egg yolk, and orange rind, mix well. Gradually stir sifted dry ingredients into butter mixture; mix thoroughly. Blend morsels and nuts into the batter.

Beat the egg white slightly. Blend together ⅔ cup sugar and 2 teaspoons cinnamon. Shape the dough into 1-inch balls. Dip each ball in the beaten egg white, then roll through the sugar mixture. Place coated balls on a greased baking sheet. Bake in oven 350°F. 15 to 20 minutes.

Makes about 5 dozen puffs.

CINNAMON OATMEAL COOKIES

½ cup butter or margarine, soft
½ cup granulated sugar
½ cup brown sugar
1 egg
1 teaspoon vanilla
1 cup all-purpose flour, sifted
½ teaspoon baking soda
½ teaspoon salt
2 cups quick-cooking rolled oats, uncooked
1 tablespoon granulated sugar
1 teaspoon cinnamon

Beat together in a large mixing bowl until well-blended butter, sugars, egg, and vanilla. Sift together sifted flour, baking soda, and salt; beat into creamed mixture. Stir rolled oats into the batter.

Flour hands lightly; shape dough into balls about the size of walnuts. Place balls, about 3 inches apart, on an ungreased baking sheet.

Mix together in a small dish 1 tablespoon granulated sugar and cinnamon. Butter the bottom of a drinking glass and dip into the cinnamon-sugar mixture. Press each cookie flat (about ¼-inch thick) with the glass bottom. Dip the glass into the cinnamon-sugar mixture before flattening each cookie.

Bake in preheated oven 375°F. about 12 minutes. Remove cookies from baking sheet while still warm; place on rack to cool. Store in dry, airtight container.

Makes about 3 dozen cookies.

GINGERSNAPS

¾ cup shortening
¾ cup brown sugar, packed
1 egg
¾ cup molasses
3 cups flour, sifted
¼ teaspoon salt
2 teaspoons baking soda
½ teaspoon cloves
1 teaspoon cinnamon
1 teaspoon ginger
¼ cup granulated sugar

Cream together shortening and brown sugar; add egg and molasses. Beat creamed mixture well. Sift together sifted flour, salt, soda, cloves, cinnamon, and ginger; blend into creamed mixture and mix well. Place dough in refrigerator and chill. The dough is soft and must be chilled thoroughly in order to shape.

When dough is chilled, remove it from refrigerator; form into small balls. Roll balls in granulated sugar; place balls, 2 inches apart, on baking sheet. Bake in oven 375°F. 10 minutes.

Makes about 10 dozen small cookies.

FRENCH BUTTER CREAM COOKIES

$\frac{1}{2}$ cup butter
$\frac{1}{2}$ cup shortening
$1\frac{1}{2}$ cups confectioners' sugar, sifted
$\frac{1}{4}$ teaspoon salt
1 teaspoon vanilla
1 egg
2 cups flour, sifted
1 teaspoon baking soda
1 teaspoon cream of tartar

Cream together butter and shortening; gradually add confectioners' sugar and continue creaming. Stir salt, vanilla, and egg into creamed mixture; beat thoroughly. Blend sifted flour, soda, and cream of tartar into creamed mixture; mix well. Place dough in refrigerator and chill at least 10 minutes.

Remove dough from refrigerator and form it into $\frac{1}{2}$-inch balls. Place balls on baking sheet; flatten each ball with tines of a fork. Bake in oven 350°F. 13 minutes. Remove from oven; cool slightly before removing from baking sheet.

Makes about 7 dozen cookies.

SPRITZ

¾ cup butter
½ cup granulated sugar
1 egg yolk
¼ teaspoon salt
1 teaspoon vanilla
2 cups flour, sifted
    colored sugar or decorettes

Cream together butter and sugar; add egg yolk and beat thoroughly. Blend salt, vanilla, and sifted flour into creamed mixture; mix well.

Press dough through pastry tube onto baking sheet. Decorate with colored sugar or decorettes, if desired. Bake in oven 425°F. 12 minutes.

Makes 5 dozen cookies.

SWEDISH SPRITZ

1 cup butter
¾ cup granulated sugar
1 egg
1 teaspoon vanilla
2 cups flour, sifted
½ teaspoon baking powder
¼ teaspoon salt

Cream together butter and sugar. Add egg to creamed mixture; beat until fluffy. Stir vanilla into creamed mixture. Sift together sifted flour, baking powder, and salt; add to creamed mixture. Stir until smooth.

Force dough through cookie press onto ungreased baking sheet; or, form dough into $\frac{3}{4}$-inch balls and flatten on sheet with tines of a fork. Bake in oven 400°F. 5 to 8 minutes.

Makes 4 dozen cookies.

RIBBON TEA CAKES

    1 cup butter
    1 cup granulated sugar
    2 eggs
    3$\frac{1}{2}$ cups flour, sifted
    1 teaspoon cream of tartar
    $\frac{1}{2}$ teaspoon baking soda
    2 teaspoons vanilla

Cream together butter and sugar. Add eggs to creamed mixture; beat well. Sift together sifted flour, cream of tartar, and soda; blend into creamed mixture. Add vanilla to dough; blend well.

Put dough into cookie press; use ribbon tube. Press 3-inch strips onto lightly buttered baking sheet. Bake in oven 400°F. 5 to 8 minutes, or until lightly browned.

Makes 10 dozen cookies.

SANDIES

    $\frac{3}{4}$ cup butter or shortening
    5 tablespoons confectioners' sugar
    1 teaspoon ice water
    2 cups flour, sifted

$\frac{1}{4}$ teaspoon salt
1 teaspoon vanilla
1 cup nuts
$\frac{1}{2}$ cup confectioners' sugar

Cream together butter and 5 tablespoons confectioners' sugar. Blend ice water into creamed mixture. Sift together sifted flour and salt; blend into creamed mixture. Add vanilla and nuts to batter; mix thoroughly.

Shape dough into small rolls; place on ungreased baking sheet. Bake in oven 300°F. 35 minutes. Remove from oven and place on a plate containing $\frac{1}{2}$ cup confectioners' sugar. Roll in confectioners' sugar until each sandie is well-coated.

Makes about 4 dozen sandies.

SNOW DROPS

$2\frac{1}{4}$ cups flour, sifted
$\frac{1}{4}$ teaspoon salt
1 cup butter
$\frac{1}{2}$ cup confectioners' sugar, sifted
1 teaspoon vanilla
$\frac{3}{4}$ cup walnuts, chopped
$\frac{3}{4}$ cup confectioners' sugar

Sift together sifted flour and salt. Cream butter. Add $\frac{1}{2}$ cup sifted confectioners' sugar and vanilla to creamed butter; blend thoroughly. Stir sifted dry ingredients and walnuts into creamed mixture; mix thoroughly. Chill dough.

Form chilled dough into balls 1 inch in diameter. Place balls, 1 inch apart, on unbuttered baking sheet. Bake in oven 400°F. 10 to 12 minutes. While cookies are still warm, roll in remaining ¼ cup confectioners' sugar. Cool. Roll in confectioners' sugar again.

Makes 4 dozen cookies.

BUTTERSCOTCH SNAPS

2 cups flour, sifted
2 teaspoons baking soda
¼ teaspoon salt
1 cup butterscotch morsels
½ cup granulated sugar
⅓ cup shortening
3 tablespoons light corn syrup
1 egg
  granulated sugar

Sift together sifted flour, soda, and salt; set aside. Melt butterscotch morsels over hot (not boiling) water; remove from water. Blend together ½ cup sugar, shortening, and corn syrup; add egg and beat thoroughly. Blend melted morsels into sugar mixture. Slowly blend sifted dry ingredients into the mixture.

Form dough into 1-inch balls; roll in granulated sugar. Place sugar-coated balls on a greased baking sheet. Bake in oven 350°F. 10 minutes.

Makes about 5 dozen cookies.

16. filled cookies

DATE PINWHEELS

1 pound dates
$\frac{1}{2}$ cup water
$\frac{1}{2}$ cup granulated sugar
$\frac{1}{2}$ cup shortening
$\frac{1}{2}$ cup granulated sugar
$\frac{1}{2}$ cup brown sugar, packed
1 egg
$\frac{1}{2}$ teaspoon vanilla
2 cups flour, sifted
$\frac{1}{2}$ teaspoon baking soda
$\frac{1}{2}$ teaspoon salt
1 cup nuts, chopped

Cut pitted dates into small pieces. Combine dates, water, and $\frac{1}{2}$ cup granulated sugar in a saucepan; place over heat and cook, stirring constantly, until mixture thickens. It will take 2 or 3 minutes for the mixture to thicken. Cool.

Cream together shortening, remaining $\frac{1}{2}$ cup granulated sugar, and brown sugar until fluffy. Add egg and vanilla to creamed mixture; beat well. Sift together sifted flour, soda, and salt; blend into creamed mixture.

Divide dough in half. Place both halves of dough into refrigerator; chill thoroughly. When chilled, remove dough from refrigerator; roll on waxed paper or on a pastry cloth into a rectangle about 11 inches long and $\frac{1}{4}$ inch thick.

Stir chopped nuts into cooled date mixture. Spread date mixture over rolled dough; roll dough like a jelly roll. Wrap rolled dough in waxed paper; chill in refrigerator until firm. When firm, remove from refrigerator; cut into $\frac{1}{4}$-inch slices and place on a baking sheet. Bake in oven 400°F. 8 to 10 minutes, or until lightly browned.

Makes about 6 dozen cookies.

COCONUT FILLED HONEYS

2 cups flour, sifted
1 teaspoon double-acting baking powder
$\frac{1}{2}$ teaspoon salt
$\frac{1}{2}$ cup butter or shortening
$\frac{2}{3}$ cup brown sugar, firmly packed*
2 tablespoons light cream
1 egg, unbeaten
1 teaspoon vanilla
Honey Coconut Filling

Sift flour once and measure; add baking powder and salt, and sift again. Cream butter in a large mixing bowl;

gradually add brown sugar and light cream together, blending until light and fluffy. Add egg to creamed mixture; beat thoroughly. Blend vanilla into the creamed mixture. Add sifted dry ingredients, a small amount at a time, to the creamed mixture; mix well after each addition.

Divide dough into 3 parts; chill. When thoroughly chilled, remove from refrigerator and roll each part between waxed paper to about ⅛-inch thickness; return to refrigerator and chill again. When chilled again, remove from refrigerator and cut with floured 2½-inch round cookie cutter.

Place half the circles on an ungreased baking sheet; place 1 heaping teaspoon of Honey Coconut Filling on top of each. From the remaining circles, cut small round openings; place these cut-out circles on top of the circles on the baking sheet in such a way that the filling will stick out through the openings. Press outer edges together with tines of a fork. Bake in oven 375°F. 10 minutes, or until edges are lightly browned.

* ⅔ cup granulated sugar can be used in place of brown sugar.

Makes 2½ dozen cookies.

FRUIT FILLS

1 cup shortening
1 cup brown sugar, packed
1 teaspoon salt
1 teaspoon baking soda
½ cup water
2½ cups flour, sifted

$2\frac{1}{2}$ cups rolled oats, uncooked*
Date Filling**

Mix (by hand) shortening, brown sugar, salt, and soda until well blended. Stir water and sifted flour into the shortening mixture; add rolled oats. Mix only enough to blend. This is a very stiff dough.

Place half of the dough in 5 or 6 places on a baking sheet or 10 x 15 x $\frac{1}{2}$-inch jelly roll pan. Spread dough with spatula until it is evenly distributed and $\frac{1}{2}$ inch from edges of the baking sheet. Dip palm of hand into flour and pat dough smooth.

Spread dough with cooled Date Filling. Drop remaining half of dough by teaspoonfuls over the filling. Spread with a spatula until evenly distributed. Pinch edges of dough together to cover filling. The top crust should look rough.

Bake in oven 350°F. 30 minutes, or until crust is crisp. Remove from oven; cool. Cut into squares or rectangles, as desired. Leave Fruit Fills on the baking sheet; cover lightly with waxed paper and store. These store well.

* Quick-cooking rolled oats make a less crunchy crust than if the regular long-cooking rolled oats are used.

** Any of the following can be used for a filling: Apricot Filling, Prune Filling, Fruit Filling, or Mince Meat Filling.

Makes 4 dozen fills.

PEACH FILLED COOKIES

$\frac{1}{2}$ cup shortening
1 cup granulated sugar
2 eggs, well-beaten

1 teaspoon vanilla
2 cups all-purpose flour, sifted
2½ teaspoons baking powder
1 teaspoon salt
  Peach Filling

Cream shortening; gradually add sugar and cream thoroughly. Add well-beaten eggs and vanilla to creamed mixture; blend well. Sift together sifted flour, baking powder, and salt; blend into creamed mixture. When mixture is well blended, place in refrigerator and chill for easy handling.

After dough is chilled, remove half of it from the refrigerator to a floured board. Work enough flour into the chilled dough to make it easy to roll. Roll the dough thin; cut into desired shapes. Place half of the cut cookie dough, 1 inch apart, on an ungreased baking sheet. Put approximately 1 teaspoon of Peach Filling on top of each unbaked cookie. Cut small circles from remaining cut cookie dough. Place on top of Peach Filling. Press edges together. Bake cookies in oven 400°F. 10 to 12 minutes.

Makes about 3 dozen cookies.

RAISIN FILLED COOKIES

½ cup butter or margarine
1 cup granulated sugar
2 eggs
1 teaspoon vanilla
2¼ cups all-purpose flour, sifted
2 teaspoons baking powder
½ teaspoon salt
  Raisin Filling

Cream together butter and sugar. Add eggs, 1 at a time, to creamed mixture; beat well after each addition. Blend vanilla into creamed mixture. Sift together sifted flour, baking powder, and salt; blend into creamed mixture.

Thoroughly chill dough. Roll half of dough on lightly floured board; cut with $2\frac{1}{2}$-inch cookie cutter. Place a teaspoonful of Raisin Filling on center of each cookie.

Roll remaining dough as before. Cut small hole in center of each round; place over filled rounds and lightly press edges together. Bake in oven 375°F. about 15 minutes or until edges are browned. Remove to wire rack to cool.

Makes about $3\frac{1}{2}$ dozen cookies.

SWEDISH BUTTER COOKIES

1 cup butter
$\frac{1}{2}$ cup granulated sugar
1 egg yolk
1 tablespoon cream
1 teaspoon vanilla
2 cups flour, sifted
$\frac{1}{2}$ teaspoon baking powder
1 egg white, beaten
$\frac{1}{2}$ cup pecans, chopped
$\frac{1}{2}$ cup jelly*

Cream butter; add sugar and cream again. Add egg yolk, cream, and vanilla to creamed mixture; mix thoroughly. Sift together sifted flour and baking powder; blend into creamed mixture.

Form dough into small balls and dip into beaten egg white, then chopped pecans. After placing the balls on an ungreased baking sheet, make a small indentation in center of each ball of dough. Fill the indentations with jelly or with a red or green maraschino cherry half. Bake in oven 350°F. 20 minutes. Handle carefully when removing from baking sheet.

* Or 1 jar red or green maraschino cherries.

Makes about 4 dozen cookies.

FANCY FILLED COOKIES

$\frac{1}{2}$ cup butter
1 cup brown sugar
1 egg
1 teaspoon vanilla
1 cup flour, sifted
$\frac{1}{2}$ teaspoon baking soda
$\frac{1}{8}$ teaspoon salt
1 cup rolled oats, uncooked
1 jar maraschino cherries
1 cup confectioners' sugar, sifted
$\frac{1}{2}$ cup nuts, chopped

Cream together butter and brown sugar. Add egg and vanilla to creamed mixture; blend thoroughly. Sift together sifted flour, soda, and salt; stir into creamed mixture. Blend rolled oats into creamed mixture. Chill dough approximately 15 minutes, or until it is easy to handle.

Roll small amounts of dough around a maraschino cherry. Bake in oven 350°F. 12 to 14 minutes. Remove from oven; roll cookies, while still warm, in confectioners' sugar, then in chopped nuts.

Makes about 3 dozen cookies.

THUMBPRINT COOKIES

½ cup butter
¼ cup brown sugar
1 egg, separated
½ teaspoon vanilla
1 cup flour, sifted
¼ teaspoon salt
¾ cup nuts, finely chopped
candied fruit, jelly, or icing

Mix together butter, brown sugar, egg yolk, and vanilla. Sift together sifted flour and salt; thoroughly blend into butter mixture.

Roll dough into 1-inch balls. Dip balls into slightly beaten egg white; roll in finely chopped nuts. Place balls, about 1 inch apart, on ungreased baking sheet. Bake in oven 375°F. 5 minutes.

After baking 5 minutes, immediately remove from oven. Gently press thumb on top (center) of each cookie; return to oven and bake 8 minutes more. When done, remove from oven; cool. Inside thumbprints, place candied fruit, sparkling jelly, or colored Confectioners' Sugar Frosting.

Makes about 3 dozen cookies.

RICH PREAM WAFERS

6 tablespoons Pream
1 cup butter
6 tablespoons boiling water
2 cups all-purpose flour, sifted

granulated sugar
Wafer Filling

Combine Pream, butter, boiling water, and sifted flour; blend thoroughly. Chill dough at least 1 hour.

Roll chilled dough to $\frac{1}{8}$-inch thickness on a lightly floured dough board; cut into rounds. Lightly sprinkle granulated sugar on the cookie rounds.

Place cookies on an ungreased baking sheet. Prick each cookie in 4 places with tines of a fork. Bake in oven 375°F. about 8 minutes, or until slightly puffy. When done, remove from oven and cool.

To make fancy filled wafers, put Wafer Filling between 2 cooled cookies, sandwich style.

Makes about $2\frac{1}{2}$ dozen filled wafers.

17. refrigerator cookies

SOUR CREAM COCONUT WAFERS

3 cups enriched flour, sifted
½ teaspoon baking powder
½ teaspoon salt
¼ teaspoon baking soda
¾ cup butter or margarine
1 cup brown sugar
2 eggs, beaten
1½ teaspoons vanilla
¼ teaspoon orange extract
⅓ cup sour cream
1 cup flaked coconut

Sift together sifted flour, baking powder, salt, and soda. Cream together butter and brown sugar until light and fluffy. Add eggs, vanilla, and orange extract to creamed mixture;

beat well. Blend half of sifted ingredients into creamed mixture. Add sour cream to batter; mix thoroughly. Blend remaining sifted ingredients into batter; add coconut and mix well.

Shape dough into rolls and wrap in waxed paper. Chill overnight in refrigerator. Slice $\frac{1}{8}$- to $\frac{1}{4}$-inch thickness. Bake on lightly greased baking sheet in oven 400°F. about 10 minutes.

Makes about 8 dozen cookies.

LEMON GINGER REFRIGERATOR COOKIES

    1 package white cake mix
    1 teaspoon lemon rind, grated
    2 tablespoons lemon juice
    2 tablespoons butter, soft
    2 tablespoons crystallized ginger, finely cut
    1 egg, unbeaten

Empty half of cake mix into mixing bowl; add lemon rind, lemon juice, butter, ginger, and egg; and blend well. Gradually add rest of cake mix; blend thoroughly.

Shape dough into 2 long rolls. Place both rolls into the refrigerator and chill until firm enough to slice. When properly chilled, remove the rolls and slice into $\frac{1}{8}$-inch thickness. Place the slices on an ungreased baking sheet; bake in oven 375°F. 8 to 10 minutes.

Makes about 5 dozen cookies.

LEMON REFRIGERATOR COOKIES

1 cup shortening
$\frac{1}{2}$ cup brown sugar, firmly packed
$\frac{1}{2}$ cup granulated sugar
1 egg
$\frac{1}{4}$ cup bottled lemon juice
3 cups all-purpose flour, sifted
$\frac{1}{4}$ teaspoon baking soda
$\frac{1}{2}$ teaspoon salt
$\frac{1}{2}$ cup nuts, chopped

Combine shortening, sugars, egg, and bottled lemon juice in a large mixing bowl; cream thoroughly. Sift together sifted flour, soda, and salt. Blend sifted ingredients into creamed mixture; mix thoroughly. Fold nuts into dough.

Form dough into 2 rolls, 2 inches in diameter; wrap in waxed paper. Place wrapped dough into refrigerator and chill until firm. When chilled, remove from refrigerator and unwrap. Cut the chilled dough into $\frac{1}{4}$-inch slices. Place the slices on a greased baking sheet; bake in oven 375°F. 10 to 12 minutes.

Makes about 5 dozen cookies.

ORANGE SUGAR COOKIES

1 cup butter
$\frac{3}{4}$ cup granulated sugar
2 egg yolks
1 tablespoon frozen orange juice concentrate, thawed and undiluted
$2\frac{1}{2}$ cups all-purpose flour, sifted

222

$\frac{1}{2}$ teaspoon baking powder
1 egg white, well-beaten
Brazil nuts, chopped

Cream butter; gradually add sugar, blending thoroughly after each addition. Add egg yolks and orange concentrate to creamed mixture; beat. Sift together sifted flour and baking powder; blend into creamed mixture and beat until smooth.

Put dough into 3 empty 6-ounce concentrate cans that have both ends removed. Place in refrigerator and chill several hours. Push chilled dough from cans by using a slightly smaller bottle. Slice dough into $\frac{1}{8}$-inch thicknesses; place, about 1 inch apart, on an ungreased baking sheet. Brush each cookie slice with beaten egg white; top with chopped Brazil nuts, or decorate with candied fruits. Bake in oven 350°F. 12 to 15 minutes.

Makes about 5 dozen cookies.

ORANGE GINGER REFRIGERATOR COOKIES

1 cup margarine
1$\frac{1}{2}$ cups granulated sugar
1 egg
2 tablespoons corn syrup
2 teaspoons baking soda
1 tablespoon warm water
3 cups flour, sifted
2 teaspoons cinnamon
2 teaspoons ginger
$\frac{1}{2}$ teaspoon cloves
1 large orange rind, grated

Cream together margarine and sugar; add egg and corn syrup. Dissolve soda in warm water; stir into creamed mixture. Sift together sifted flour, cinnamon, ginger, and cloves; blend with orange peel and mix thoroughly into creamed mixture.

Shape the dough into 2 long rolls, 2 inches in diameter. Wrap each roll in waxed paper; place in refrigerator and chill until firm. When chilled, remove rolls from refrigerator; cut into $\frac{1}{8}$-inch slices. Place on baking sheet; bake in oven 400°F. 8 to 10 minutes.

Makes 8 dozen cookies.

ORANGE PECAN CRISPS

1 cup shortening
$\frac{1}{2}$ cup brown sugar, packed
$\frac{1}{2}$ cup granulated sugar
1 egg, well-beaten
1 tablespoon orange rind, grated
2 tablespoons orange juice
$2\frac{3}{4}$ cups flour, sifted
$\frac{1}{4}$ teaspoon baking soda
$\frac{1}{4}$ teaspoon salt
$\frac{1}{2}$ cup pecans, chopped

Cream together shortening and sugars. Blend well-beaten egg, orange rind, and orange juice into creamed mixture. Sift together sifted flour, soda, and salt; blend with pecans and add to creamed mixture. Mix thoroughly.

Shape dough into 2 long rolls, 2 inches in diameter. Wrap each roll in waxed paper; place in refrigerator and chill until firm. When firm, remove dough from refrigerator; cut rolls into ⅛-inch slices. Place slices on baking sheet; bake in oven 400°F. 7 minutes.

For fancy shapes: Divide dough into 4 or 6 portions. Place each portion between 2 sheets of waxed paper. Roll dough to ⅛-inch thickness. Chill. Cut into various shapes with cookie cutter. Bake in oven 400°F. 7 minutes.

Makes 8 dozen cookies.

CHOCOLATE MARBLE COOKIES

2 cups cake flour, sifted
1 teaspoon baking powder
½ teaspoon salt
½ cup shortening
⅔ cup granulated sugar
1 egg, unbeaten
1 tablespoon milk
1 one-ounce square unsweetened chocolate, melted

Sift together sifted cake flour, baking powder, and salt. In a large mixing bowl, cream shortening; gradually add sugar and cream together until light and fluffy. Add egg and milk to creamed mixture; beat well. Blend sifted dry ingredients, a small amount at a time, into the creamed mixture; mix thoroughly after each addition.

Divide dough into 2 parts; leave 1 part in the large mixing bowl and place the other in a smaller mixing bowl. To 1 part of the dough add the melted chocolate; blend.

Shape chocolate and plain doughs into separate rolls about 1½ inches in diameter. Place the 2 rolls together and twist to give a marbled effect. Wrap the twisted roll in waxed paper; place in refrigerator and chill overnight, or until firm enough to slice.

Cut the chilled roll in $\frac{1}{8}$-inch slices; place the slices on ungreased baking sheet. Bake in oven 375°F. 10 minutes, or until done.

Makes about 5 dozen cookies.

COCO–MINTS

$\frac{3}{4}$ cup butter
1 cup granulated sugar
1 egg
2 cups flour, sifted
1 teaspoon baking powder
$\frac{1}{2}$ teaspoon baking soda
$\frac{1}{2}$ teaspoon salt
$\frac{3}{4}$ cup cocoa
$\frac{1}{4}$ cup milk
$\frac{1}{2}$ teaspoon vanilla
  Mint Filling

Cream butter; add sugar and beat until light and fluffy. Add egg to creamed mixture; beat well. Sift together sifted flour, baking powder, soda, salt, and cocoa; blend alternately with milk and vanilla, into creamed mixture.

Shape dough into long rolls, 1 inch in diameter. Wrap each roll in waxed paper; place in refrigerator and chill. When chilled, remove rolls from refrigerator; cut chilled rolls into $\frac{1}{8}$-inch slices. Place slices on baking sheet; bake in oven 325°F. 10 minutes. When done, take from oven and immediately remove cookies from baking sheet. Cool. Put cookies together, sandwich style, with Mint Filling in between 2 cookies.

Makes about 7 dozen cookies.

ALL-BRAN REFRIGERATOR COOKIES

1 cup shortening
2 cups brown sugar
1 egg, well-beaten
1 cup all-bran
3 cups all-purpose flour, sifted
2 teaspoons baking powder

Cream shortening until light and fluffy. Add brown sugar to creamed shortening; cream again. Add egg to creamed mixture; beat well. Stir all-bran into creamed mixture. Sift together sifted flour and baking powder; blend into creamed mixture.

Shape dough into 2 large oblong rolls. Store in refrigerator. When ready to bake, trim $\frac{3}{8}$-inch slices from the roll. Bake on greased baking sheet in oven 425°F. 8 to 10 minutes.

Makes about 5 dozen cookies.

FILBERT WAFERS

3 cups flour, sifted
3 teaspoons baking powder
$\frac{1}{2}$ teaspoon salt
$\frac{1}{2}$ cup butter

$\frac{1}{2}$ cup shortening
1 teaspoon vanilla
1$\frac{1}{4}$ cups brown sugar, firmly packed
2 eggs
1 cup semi-sweet chocolate morsels, finely chopped
$\frac{1}{2}$ cup filberts, finely chopped

Sift together sifted flour, baking powder, and salt; set aside. Blend together, in a large mixing bowl, butter, shortening, and vanilla. Gradually beat brown sugar into butter mixture; beat eggs, 1 at a time, into the mixture. Add sifted dry ingredients, chocolate morsels, and filberts; mix well.

Shape dough on waxed paper into 2 rolls. Wrap in the waxed paper; chill several hours or overnight. Unwrap chilled rolls; cut into $\frac{1}{8}$-inch slices. Place slices on an ungreased baking sheet. Bake in oven 400°F. 8 to 10 minutes.

Makes about 12 dozen wafers.

WALNUT REFRIGERATOR COOKIES

1 cup shortening
2 cups brown sugar, packed
2 teaspoons vanilla
2 eggs
3$\frac{1}{2}$ cups flour, sifted
1 teaspoon salt
1 teaspoon baking soda
1 cup walnuts, finely chopped

Cream together shortening, brown sugar, and vanilla. Add eggs to creamed mixture; mix well. Sift together sifted flour, salt, and soda; blend into creamed mixture. Stir walnuts into dough; blend thoroughly.

Shape dough into 2 long rolls, 2 inches in diameter. Wrap each roll in waxed paper; place in refrigerator and chill until firm. When chilled, remove rolls from refrigerator; cut chilled rolls into ⅛-inch slices. Place on baking sheet. Bake in oven 375°F. 8 minutes.

Makes 9 dozen small cookies.

WALNUT–ORANGE REFRIGERATOR COOKIES

1 cup butter or margarine
¾ cup granulated sugar
1 egg
4 tablespoons frozen orange juice concentrate, partially thawed
2¾ cups all-purpose flour
1 teaspoon baking powder
¼ teaspoon nutmeg
¼ teaspoon salt
1 cup California walnuts, finely chopped

Cream butter. Beat granulated sugar into creamed butter and continue beating until fluffy. Beat egg into creamed mixture; add partially thawed orange juice concentrate and beat. Combine flour, baking powder, nutmeg, salt, and finely chopped walnuts; blend into orange juice mixture.

Chill dough several hours. Shape chilled dough into rolls; slice thinly. Place thin slices on a lightly greased baking sheet. Bake in oven 350°F. about 10 minutes.

If desired, pack the dough into empty 6-ounce frozen juice cans, cover with foil, and store in the freezer. When ready to bake, remove bottom of can, push dough out, and slice. Bake as directed above.

Note: These cookies have a dominant orange flavor and are near white in color with flecks of brown walnut showing. These tender, rich cookies keep well if stored in a tightly covered container. For variation, $\frac{1}{2}$ cup finely snipped dates can be added along with the walnuts.

Makes about 5 dozen cookies.

MOLASSES REFRIGERATOR COOKIES

1 cup shortening
1 cup molasses
2 eggs, well-beaten
1 cup granulated sugar
3$\frac{1}{2}$ cups flour, sifted
$\frac{1}{2}$ teaspoon salt
1 teaspoon baking soda
$\frac{1}{4}$ teaspoon cinnamon
$\frac{1}{2}$ teaspoon cloves
$\frac{1}{4}$ teaspoon ginger

Heat shortening and molasses in a saucepan until shortening is melted; stir constantly while heating. Measure well-beaten eggs into mixing bowl; slowly pour melted shortening mixture over eggs. Sift together sugar, sifted flour, salt, soda, cinnamon, cloves, and ginger; blend into egg mixture. After blending thoroughly, shape dough into 1 large roll and place in refrigerator to chill.

When dough is chilled, remove and cut into $\frac{1}{8}$-inch slices. Place slices on baking sheet; bake in oven 350°F. 10 minutes.

Makes about 10 dozen cookies.

BUTTERSCOTCH REFRIGERATOR COOKIES

2 cups brown sugar, firmly packed
1 cup butter
2 eggs
4 cups flour, sifted
1 teaspoon baking soda
1 teaspoon cream of tartar
1 cup nuts, chopped
1 teaspoon vanilla

Cream together brown sugar and butter until light and fluffy. Add eggs, 1 at a time, to creamed mixture; beat after each addition. Sift together sifted flour, soda, and cream of tartar; blend into creamed mixture. Stir nuts and vanilla into batter.

Form dough into 2 rolls; wrap in waxed paper or aluminum foil and store in refrigerator overnight. Slice with a very sharp knife into $\frac{1}{8}$-inch slices. Place on lightly buttered baking sheet. Bake in oven 350°F. 10 to 12 minutes. Watch carefully to prevent burning.

Makes about 8 dozen cookies.

BUTTERSCOTCH THINS

1 cup butterscotch morsels
$\frac{1}{2}$ cup butter
$\frac{2}{3}$ cup light brown sugar, packed
1 egg
$1\frac{1}{3}$ cups flour, sifted
$\frac{3}{4}$ teaspoon baking soda

$\frac{1}{3}$ cup nuts, chopped
$\frac{3}{4}$ teaspoon vanilla

Melt together butterscotch morsels and butter over hot (not boiling) water; remove from heat. Beat brown sugar and egg into the melted butterscotch mixture. Sift together sifted flour and soda; stir into butterscotch mixture. Blend nuts and vanilla into the batter. Chill.

Shape chilled dough into a 12-inch roll. Wrap the roll in waxed paper; chill thoroughly. Slice the chilled roll into very thin slices. Place the slices onto an ungreased baking sheet. Bake in oven 375°F. 5 to 6 minutes. When done, remove from oven and cool slightly before placing the cookies on a wire rack.

Makes about 8 dozen cookies.

FAVORITE ICEBOX COOKIES

2 cups flour, sifted
1$\frac{1}{2}$ teaspoons baking powder
$\frac{1}{2}$ teaspoon salt
$\frac{1}{2}$ cup shortening
1 cup granulated sugar
1 egg, unbeaten
1 cup shredded coconut
1 tablespoon milk
1 teaspoon vanilla

Sift together sifted flour, baking powder, and salt. In a large mixing bowl, cream shortening; gradually add sugar and thoroughly cream together. Add egg, coconut, milk, and vanilla to creamed mixture; beat well. Gradually blend sifted dry ingredients into creamed mixture; mix well after each addition.

Divide dough into 2 parts; shape each into roll about $1\frac{1}{2}$ inches in diameter. Wrap each roll in waxed paper; or, pack the dough into waxed butter or cookie cartons. Place dough into refrigerator to chill overnight, or until firm enough to slice.

Cut chilled dough in $\frac{1}{8}$-inch slices; place on ungreased baking sheet. Bake in oven 425°F. 5 minutes, or until done.

Makes about 8 dozen cookies.

PINWHEEL COOKIES

$\frac{1}{2}$ cup butter
1 cup granulated sugar
2 eggs
1 teaspoon vanilla
1 tablespoon milk
$2\frac{1}{4}$ cups all-purpose flour, sifted
1 teaspoon baking powder
$\frac{1}{2}$ teaspoon baking soda
$\frac{1}{2}$ teaspoon salt
1 one-ounce square unsweetened chocolate, melted

Cream butter; add sugar and continue to cream until well blended. Add eggs, vanilla, and milk to creamed mixture; mix well. Sift together sifted flour, baking powder, soda, and salt. Add sifted dry ingredients to creamed mixture; blend thoroughly.

Divide dough into 2 equal parts. Blend melted chocolate into 1 part.

Roll each part of dough to ⅛-inch thick rectangle on separate pieces of floured, waxed paper. Place white dough on top of chocolate dough. Remove waxed paper. Roll 2 pieces of dough together like a jelly roll. Wrap in waxed paper. Chill in refrigerator; slice. Bake as refrigerator cookies in preheated oven 425°F. 8 to 12 minutes.

Makes 4 dozen cookies.

REFRIGERATOR DESSERT COOKIES

1 cup butter
⅔ cup granulated sugar
2 tablespoons orange rind, grated
1 tablespoon lemon rind, grated
2 eggs, well-beaten
3 cups flour, sifted
1 teaspoon salt
1 cup shredded coconut
½ cup nuts, chopped

Cream butter; add sugar and cream again. Add orange rind, lemon rind, and eggs to creamed mixture; mix well. Sift together sifted flour and salt. Add half of sifted dry ingredients to creamed mixture. Fold coconut into batter; add remaining sifted dry ingredients. Blend thoroughly.

Shape dough into long rolls. Roll them in chopped nuts; place in refrigerator until chilled. Slice chilled rolls into thin slices and bake in oven 375°F. 10 minutes.

Makes about 4 dozen cookies.

SWEDISH DELICACIES

1¾ cups flour, sifted
½ teaspoon salt
¾ teaspoon ground ammonium carbonate*
½ cup butter
½ cup shortening
½ teaspoon vanilla
1 cup granulated sugar
½ cup almonds, finely shredded
1 cup semi-sweet chocolate morsels, finely chopped

Sift together sifted flour, salt, and ammonium carbonate; set aside. Blend together, in a large mixing bowl, butter, shortening, and vanilla; gradually beat sugar into this mixture. Add sifted dry ingredients, almonds, and chocolate morsels to butter mixture.

Shape dough on waxed paper into 2 9-inch rolls; wrap and chill several hours or overnight. Unroll chilled rolls and cut into ⅛-inch slices. Place on ungreased baking sheet. Bake in oven 375°F. 8 to 10 minutes.

* Ground ammonium carbonate may be purchased at drug store. Or, baking powder can be substituted.

Makes about 10 dozen cookies.

18. holiday cookies

BRIGHT LEMON BAUBLES

$1\frac{1}{2}$ cups vanilla wafers, crumbled
$1\frac{1}{2}$ cups confectioners' sugar, sifted
2 tablespoons cocoa
$\frac{1}{2}$ cup pecans, finely chopped
2 tablespoons light corn syrup
$\frac{1}{4}$ cup bottled lemon juice
   granulated sugar, tinted

Combine vanilla wafers, confectioners' sugar, cocoa, pecans, corn syrup, and bottled lemon juice; let stand 30 minutes.

Form dough into small balls. Add more corn syrup if the mixture seems dry. Roll the balls in tinted granulated sugar, or confectioners' sugar. Chill.

Makes $2\frac{1}{2}$ dozen baubles.

CHRISTMAS LEMON COOKIES

$\frac{1}{2}$ cup butter
1 cup granulated sugar
1 egg
2$\frac{1}{2}$ cups all-purpose flour, sifted
1 teaspoon baking powder
$\frac{1}{2}$ teaspoon salt
$\frac{1}{4}$ cup bottled lemon juice
Ornamental Icing

Cream together butter and sugar; add egg and beat well. Sift together sifted flour, baking powder, and salt; add to creamed mixture, alternately with bottled lemon juice. Chill dough several hours or overnight.

Roll chilled dough to $\frac{1}{4}$-inch thickness; cut into festive shapes. Place on greased baking sheet. Bake in oven 350°F. 10 minutes. Cool. Decorate as desired with Ornamental Icing.

Makes about 4 dozen cookies.

LEMONY BON BONS

1 cup butter
$\frac{3}{4}$ cup confectioners' sugar, sifted
2 tablespoons bottled lemon juice
1$\frac{1}{2}$ cups all-purpose flour, sifted
$\frac{3}{4}$ cup cornstarch, sifted
pecan halves
Lemon Icing

Cream together butter, sifted confectioners' sugar, and

bottled lemon juice. Add sifted flour and sifted cornstarch to creamed mixture. Chill.

Form chilled dough into 4 dozen small balls. For each cookie, place 3 pecan halves on an ungreased baking sheet; press a ball of dough to $\frac{1}{8}$- or $\frac{1}{4}$-inch thickness over the pecan clusters. Bake in oven 350°F. 12 to 14 minutes. Note: These cookies will not brown. When done, remove from oven and cool. Ice with Lemon Icing.

Makes 4 dozen bon bons.

ORANGE CURAÇAO COOKIES

$\frac{3}{4}$ cup shortening
$\frac{1}{4}$ cup butter
$1\frac{1}{2}$ cups brown sugar
2 eggs, well-beaten
$\frac{1}{2}$ cup Hiram Walker's orange curaçao
1 tablespoon orange rind, grated
$\frac{3}{4}$ cup sour milk
$3\frac{1}{2}$ cups flour (or more), sifted
$\frac{1}{4}$ teaspoon salt
2 teaspoons baking powder
1 teaspoon baking soda

Cream shortening, butter, and brown sugar in a large mixing bowl. Add well-beaten eggs, orange curaçao, orange rind, and sour milk to creamed mixture; mix thoroughly. Sift together sifted flour, salt, baking powder, and soda; blend into creamed mixture.

Drop dough by teaspoonfuls onto greased baking sheet. Bake in oven 350°F. 15 minutes.

Makes 5 dozen cookies.

HOLIDAY FLORIDA ORANGE BARS

½ cup brown sugar
½ cup granulated sugar
1 cup shortening
2 teaspoons vanilla
1 tablespoon orange rind, grated
½ teaspoon salt
1 egg
1 teaspoon cinnamon
1 teaspoon ginger
1½ cups all-purpose flour, sifted
¾ cup rolled oats, uncooked
½ cup orange juice
½ cup nuts, chopped
    Holiday Orange Icing
    candied cherries, red and green

Combine sugars in a mixing bowl. Add shortening, vanilla, orange rind, salt, egg, cinnamon, and ginger, to the sugars; thoroughly beat mixture. Blend sifted flour and rolled oats into the sugar mixture; mix well. Stir orange juice and chopped nuts into the batter.

Turn batter into a greased 13 x 9-inch pan. Bake in oven 350°F. 40 minutes. When done, remove from oven and cool. Frost with Holiday Orange Icing. Cut into bars. Decorate with red and green candied cherries.

Makes about 3 dozen bars.

ORANGE SPRITZ

¾ cup butter
½ cup granulated sugar

1 egg yolk
¼ teaspoon salt
1 teaspoon orange rind, grated
½ teaspoon orange extract
2 cups flour, sifted
  colored sugar or decorettes

Cream together butter and sugar; add egg yolk and beat thoroughly. Blend salt, grated rind, orange extract, and sifted flour into creamed mixture; mix well.

Press dough through pastry tube onto baking sheet. Decorate with colored sugar or decorettes, if desired. Bake in oven 425°F. 12 minutes.

Makes 5 dozen cookies.

PARTY RAISIN COOKIES

6 cups cake flour, sifted
2 teaspoons baking powder
3 teaspoons baking soda
1 tablespoon salt
2 cups shortening
5 cups brown sugar, firmly packed
4 eggs, unbeaten
1 cup milk
6 cups grape-nuts flakes or bran flakes
3 cups raisins, chopped

Sift flour and measure. Add baking powder, soda, and salt to sifted flour; sift again. Cream shortening; gradually add brown sugar and cream together until light and fluffy. Add eggs to creamed mixture; beat well. Blend sifted dry ingredients, alternately with milk, into creamed mixture; mix well after each addition. Stir flakes and raisins into batter.

Drop dough by teaspoonfuls onto greased baking sheet. With a fork slightly flatten each cookie. Bake in oven 375°F. 8 minutes or until done. When done, remove from oven; place on a rack to cool.

Makes about 16 dozen cookies.

HOLIDAY FRUIT BARS

2 cups seedless nectar raisins
2 cups golden seedless raisins
1 cup mixed candied fruit, diced
1 cup walnuts, chopped
1 cup butter or margarine
1½ cups brown sugar, firmly packed
¼ cup light molasses
4 eggs
3 cups flour, sifted
1 teaspoon salt
½ teaspoon baking powder
½ teaspoon baking soda
1 teaspoon cinnamon
½ teaspoon cloves
½ teaspoon allspice
2 teaspoons vanilla
  walnut halves
  red and green candied cherries

Cover raisins with boiling water; let stand 5 minutes. Drain raisins; cool and then chop. Combine chopped raisins with candied fruits and chopped walnuts; set aside. Beat together butter, brown sugar, molasses, and eggs. Sift together sifted flour, salt, baking powder, soda, cinnamon, cloves, and allspice; blend into butter mixture. Add vanilla and raisin mixture to the batter; mix well.

Spread dough in 2 greased 10 x 15 x 1-inch baking pans. Decorate with walnut halves, red and green candied cherries. Bake in oven 350°F. 25 minutes. When done, remove from oven and let cool in pans. Cut into squares.

Makes about 8 dozen bars.

CANDIED FRUIT BARS

$1\frac{1}{4}$ cups enriched flour, sifted
1 teaspoon baking powder
$\frac{1}{2}$ teaspoon salt
$\frac{1}{2}$ cup shortening
$\frac{1}{2}$ cup honey
2 eggs, beaten
$\frac{1}{2}$ cup raisins
$\frac{1}{2}$ cup candied cherries, chopped
$\frac{1}{2}$ cup nuts, chopped
Confectioners' Sugar Frosting

Sift together sifted flour, baking powder, and salt. (If self-rising flour is used, omit baking powder and salt.) Cream together shortening and honey. Add eggs to creamed mixture; mix well. Thoroughly mix sifted dry ingredients into creamed mixture. Stir raisins, candied cherries, and half of the nuts into the batter.

Spread dough in greased pan 7 x 11 inches. Bake in oven 325°F. about 35 minutes. When cool, frost with thin

Confectioners' Sugar Frosting; sprinkle with remaining chopped nuts. Cut into 1 x 3-inch bars.

These bars will keep 1 week.

Makes about 2 dozen bars.

YULE FRUITCAKE COOKIES

4 cups flour, sifted
1 teaspoon baking soda
1 teaspoon salt
1 cup shortening
2 cups brown sugar, packed
2 eggs, well-beaten
$\frac{2}{3}$ cup sour milk or buttermilk
2 cups dates, chopped
1 cup nuts, chopped
1 cup candied cherries, chopped
1 cup candied fruit and peel

Sift together sifted flour, soda, and salt. Cream shortening; add sugar and eggs, beating until light and fluffy. Add the sour milk or buttermilk, alternately with sifted dry ingredients, into the creamed mixture; mix well. Fold dates, nuts, candied cherries, candied fruit and peel into the batter. Chill the dough about 1 hour.

Drop the chilled dough by teaspoonfuls, about 2 inches apart, onto a lightly greased baking sheet. Bake in oven 375°F. 8 to 10 minutes, or until set and lightly brown.

Makes 8 dozen cookies.

WINE DROPS

$\frac{1}{2}$ cup shortening
$1\frac{1}{4}$ cups granulated sugar
2 eggs
$\frac{1}{2}$ cup port wine
$\frac{1}{4}$ teaspoon salt
$2\frac{3}{4}$ cups flour, sifted
$\frac{1}{2}$ teaspoon baking soda
$\frac{1}{2}$ teaspoon baking powder
1 cup raisins
1 cup nuts, chopped

Thoroughly cream shortening and sugar in a large mixing bowl. Add eggs, 1 at a time, to shortening mixture; beat after each addition. Blend wine into batter and beat thoroughly. Sift flour once. Add salt, soda, and baking powder to sifted flour; sift again. Blend sifted ingredients into batter; mix well. Add raisins and nuts; mix well.

Drop dough by teaspoonfuls onto an ungreased baking sheet. Bake in oven 375°F. until lightly browned.

Makes about 4 dozen drops.

CHOCOLATE BON BONS

1 six-ounce package chocolate chips
$\frac{1}{4}$ cup water
1 teaspoon orange extract
1 teaspoon orange rind, grated
$\frac{1}{2}$ cup granulated sugar
$\frac{1}{4}$ cup corn syrup

$2\frac{1}{2}$ cups vanilla wafers, crushed
1 cup nuts, chopped
$\frac{1}{4}$ cup granulated sugar

Melt chocolate chips in top of double boiler over boiling water; add $\frac{1}{4}$ cup water. Add orange extract, orange rind, $\frac{1}{2}$ cup sugar, and corn syrup to melted chocolate chips. Blend crushed wafers and nuts into the chocolate mixture.

Roll into 1-inch balls; turn gently through saucer containing the $\frac{1}{4}$ cup sugar. Place in a covered tin; let stand several days. Place bon bons in paper candy cups; serve or store.

Makes $4\frac{1}{2}$ dozen confection-like cookies.

MILK CHOCOLATE CHIP ORANGE DROPS

2 cups flour, sifted
$1\frac{1}{2}$ cups granulated sugar
1 teaspoon baking powder
$\frac{1}{2}$ teaspoon baking soda
1 teaspoon salt
1 teaspoon cinnamon
$3\frac{1}{2}$ cups rolled oats, uncooked
1 large orange rind, grated
1 six-ounce package milk chocolate chips
$\frac{1}{2}$ cup walnuts, coarsely chopped
2 eggs
4 tablespoons fresh orange juice
4 tablespoons milk
1 cup salad oil

Sift together into a large mixing bowl sifted flour, sugar, baking powder, soda, salt, and cinnamon. Stir rolled oats, orange rind, chocolate chips, and walnuts into sifted ingredients. Make a well in the ingredients in the large mixing bowl; add eggs, fresh orange juice, milk, and salad oil. Mix thoroughly.

Drop dough by teaspoonfuls onto a greased baking sheet. Bake in preheated oven 400°F. 8 to 10 minutes. When done, remove from baking sheet onto racks to cool. Store in tin cans or a cookie jar.

Makes about 8 dozen cookies.

CHOCOLATE ICEBOX PARTY COOKIES

4 cups cake flour, sifted
3½ teaspoons baking powder
1½ teaspoons salt
1 cup butter or shortening, soft
1½ cups granulated sugar
2 eggs, unbeaten
4 one-ounce squares unsweetened chocolate, melted
1 teaspoon vanilla
1½ cups walnuts, chopped*

Sift flour and measure. Add baking powder and salt to sifted flour; sift again. In a large mixing bowl, combine butter, sugar, eggs, melted chocolate, and vanilla; beat with spoon until blended thoroughly. Stir walnuts into butter mixture. Gradually add sifted dry ingredients to the butter mixture; mix well after each addition.

Divide dough into halves; shape into rolls 2 inches in diameter. Wrap both rolls with waxed paper; or, pack dough into cookie molds. Place the rolls or molds into the refrigerator and chill until firm.

After chilling dough until it is firm, remove from refrigerator and let stand at room temperature 30 minutes or until the dough is soft enough to dent when pressed with a finger. Cut dough into $\frac{1}{8}$-inch slices with a sharp knife. Place fairly close on an ungreased baking sheet; bake in oven 350°F. about 10 minutes.

For Cookie Sandwiches, spread Raisin Nut Filling between pairs of cookies that match.

* To make Chocolate Coconut Party Cookies, substitute shredded coconut for nut meats in this recipe.

Makes 12½ dozen cookies or
about 6 dozen cookie sandwiches

FROSTY CHOCOLATE SQUARES

1 cup semi-sweet chocolate morsels
2 cups all-purpose flour, sifted
2½ teaspoons double-acting baking powder
1 teaspoon salt
⅓ cup cream cheese
¼ cup shortening
1 cup granulated sugar
2 eggs
1 teaspoon red food coloring
1 cup milk
1 teaspoon vanilla
1 cup heavy cream, whipped and sweetened
2 teaspoons vegetable shortening
Chocolate Cream Frosting

Melt chocolate morsels in top section of double boiler over hot (not boiling) water; remove from water. Sift together sifted flour, baking powder, and salt; set aside. In a large mixing bowl, blend cream cheese and shortening. Gradually blend sugar into cream cheese mixture; beat eggs, 1 at a time, into the mixture. Measure 2 tablespoons of the melted morsels and save to make a glaze. Stir remaining melted morsels and food coloring into cream cheese mixture. Stir together milk and vanilla; add, alternately with sifted dry ingredients, into cream cheese mixture. Mix well.

Spread dough into a greased and floured 13 x 9 x 2-inch baking pan. Bake in oven 350°F. 35 to 40 minutes. When done, remove from oven; cool in pan and then cut into 24 2-inch squares.

Frost tops and sides of 12 squares with the whipped and sweetened heavy cream. Combine 2 tablespoons of reserved melted morsels and 2 teaspoons vegetable shortening in top of double boiler; place over hot (not boiling) water and blend well. Drizzle this glaze over tops of frosted squares.

Frost tops and sides of remaining 12 squares with Chocolate Cream Frosting.

Makes 2 dozen squares.

COFFEE TOFFEE BARS

$2\frac{1}{4}$ cups all-purpose flour, sifted
$\frac{1}{2}$ teaspoon double-acting baking powder
$\frac{1}{4}$ teaspoon salt
1 cup butter
1 cup brown sugar, firmly packed
$1\frac{1}{2}$ tablespoons instant coffee
1 teaspoon almond extract
1 cup semi-sweet chocolate morsels
$\frac{1}{2}$ cup nuts, chopped

Sift together sifted flour, baking powder, and salt; set aside. Blend together butter, brown sugar, instant coffee, and almond extract; gradually blend sifted dry ingredients into butter mixture. Stir chocolate morsels and chopped nuts into the batter.

Press dough into greased 15 x 10 x 1-inch pan. Bake in oven 350°F. 20 to 25 minutes. When done, remove from oven and, if desired, top with sugar glaze. Cut into bars while warm.

Makes about 3 dozen bars.

CANDIED WALNUT BALLS

1 egg
$\frac{3}{4}$ cup brown sugar, packed
1 tablespoon flour
1 teaspoon butter, soft
$\frac{1}{2}$ teaspoon brandy flavoring
2 cups California walnuts, chopped
1 cup candied peel or cherries, chopped
confectioners' sugar

Beat egg. Add brown sugar, flour, soft butter, and brandy flavoring to well-beaten egg; beat thoroughly. Mix walnuts and candied peel into batter.

Pour batter into a greased 9 x 5-inch baking pan. Bake in oven 300°F. 35 minutes. Cool. Cut in 3 rows lengthwise; cut each row into 8 squares.

Carefully remove each small cookie bar, one at a time; with damp hands roll into small balls. Coat each small ball by rolling it through confectioners' sugar.

If desired, freeze the small cookie balls before coating them. When ready to use, thaw the balls, roll through confectioners' sugar, and serve.

Makes about 2 dozen balls.

SALTED PEANUT PARTY COOKIES

6 cups cake flour, sifted
2 teaspoons baking powder
3 teaspoons baking soda
2 teaspoons salt
2 cups shortening
5 cups brown sugar, firmly packed
4 eggs, unbeaten
1 cup milk
6 cups grape-nuts flakes or raisin bran flakes
3 cups salted peanuts, chopped

Sift flour and measure; add baking powder, soda, and salt and sift again. In a large mixing bowl, cream shortening; gradually add brown sugar and cream together until light and fluffy. Add eggs to creamed mixture; beat thoroughly. Blend sifted dry ingredients, alternately with milk, into creamed mixture; mix well after each addition. Stir flakes and peanuts into batter.

Drop dough by teaspoonfuls onto greased baking sheet. Slightly flatten each cookie with a fork. Bake in oven 375°F. 8 minutes or until done.

Makes about 16 dozen cookies.

BUTTER-NUT SNOWBALLS

1 cup butter
½ cup granulated sugar
2 teaspoons vanilla
2 cups flour, sifted
½ teaspoon salt
2 cups pecans, finely chopped
¼ cup confectioners' sugar

Cream together butter, sugar, and vanilla until fluffy. Sift together sifted flour and salt; thoroughly blend into creamed mixture. Stir pecans into creamed mixture; mix well.

Shape dough into 1-inch balls; place on baking sheet. Bake in oven 325°F. 20 minutes. *Caution :* Do not brown. Remove from oven; cool. Roll cookies in confectioners' sugar.

Makes about 6 dozen cookies.

OLD FASHIONED PEPPERNUTS

1 cup butter
1 cup margarine
3 cups dark brown sugar
4 eggs, well-beaten
4 to 5 cups flour, sifted
1 tablespoon anise seed, ground
½ teaspoon cloves, ground
½ teaspoon nutmeg
1 tablespoon salt
2 teaspoons baking soda
2 tablespoons hot water

Pecan Fingers, Candy Canes and Christmas Wreaths, and Christmas Bon Bon Cookies *(American Dairy Association)*

Peach Filled Cookies *(California Foods Research Institute)*

Prune-Apricot Morsels, Cornflake Morsels, Honey Chip Cookies, and Chocolate Chip Cookies *(The Nestlé Co., Inc.)*

1 pint dark syrup
1 lemon, juice and grated rind
2 cups walnuts, chopped

Cream together butter, margarine, and brown sugar. Add eggs to creamed mixture; beat thoroughly. Sift together sifted flour, anise seed, cloves, nutmeg, and salt; blend into creamed mixture. Dissolve soda in hot water. Add syrup, lemon juice, lemon rind, dissolved soda, and walnuts to batter; mix well. Let dough stand overnight.

Roll dough into small rolls. Slice into small pieces and roll each slice by hand, into round balls. Bake in oven 400°F. 10 minutes.

Makes 10 dozen peppernuts.

SHERRY PECAN BALLS

3 cups vanilla wafers, ground
1 cup pecans, ground
1 cup confectioners' sugar
3 tablespoons light corn syrup
$1\frac{3}{4}$ tablespoons cocoa
$\frac{1}{2}$ cup sherry wine
$\frac{1}{4}$ cup confectioners' sugar, sifted

Grind vanilla wafers and pecans in a food chopper until very fine. If desired, other nuts can be used in place of pecans. Blend ground wafers and nuts with 1 cup confectioners' sugar, syrup, cocoa, and sherry wine; mix thoroughly.

Pinch small amounts of dough and roll into tiny balls about the size of a big cherry. Dust each ball of dough with sifted confectioners' sugar. Or, pinch small amounts of dough and shape into little thin rolls. Dip the ends of each roll into colored icing.

Makes about 3 dozen balls.

PECAN FINGERS

    2½ cups flour, sifted
    1 teaspoon baking powder
    1 cup butter
    1 cup granulated sugar
    2 eggs
    1 egg yolk
    1 tablespoon milk
    ½ cup pecans, finely chopped
    ¼ cup granulated sugar
      Butter Frosting or Chocolate Butter Frosting
      pecan halves

Sift together sifted flour and baking powder; set aside. Cream butter in a large mixing bowl; add sugar and mix well. Add 2 eggs to creamed mixture; beat. Gradually blend sifted dry ingredients into creamed mixture; mix thoroughly. Place dough in refrigerator and chill 3 or 4 hours.

Roll chilled dough on a lightly floured board; cut into 1 x 3-inch rectangles. Place unbaked rectangles on an ungreased baking sheet. Beat together egg yolk and milk; lightly brush unbaked rectangles with this mixture. Combine chopped pecans and granulated sugar; sprinkle over unbaked rectangles.

Bake in oven 350°F. 10 to 12 minutes, or until cookies are browned lightly. When done, remove from oven and transfer to cake racks; cool. Top cooled rectangles with 1 teaspoonful of Butter Frosting that has been tinted with food coloring or with Chocolate Butter Frosting. Place a pecan half on top of each frosted rectangle.

Makes about 8 dozen fingers.

NUREMBERG NUT PUFFS

$\frac{1}{2}$ cup butter, soft
2 tablespoons granulated sugar
1 teaspoon vanilla
1 cup all-purpose flour, sifted
1 cup pecans, finely chopped
1 cup confectioners' sugar, sifted

Cream together butter, granulated sugar, and vanilla. Gradually blend sifted flour into creamed mixture. Stir pecans into the batter.

Butter palms of hands. Roll dough into 36 to 40 little balls about the size of large marbles. Place balls of dough onto an ungreased baking sheet. Bake in preheated oven 325°F. 20 to 25 minutes. When baked, remove from oven and, while still hot, gently roll the nut puffs in sifted confectioners' sugar (in pie plate). Cool puffs on paper towelling; store in airtight container.

Makes about $3\frac{1}{2}$ dozen cookies.

ANISE COOKIES

3 cups flour, sifted
1 teaspoon baking powder

        dash of salt
   1½ cups butter
    1 cup granulated sugar
    2 egg yolks, unbeaten
    1 teaspoon vanilla
    2 teaspoons whole anise seeds
      poppy or sesame seeds

Sift together flour, baking powder, and salt. Cream butter thoroughly. Gradually add sugar to creamed butter; work the mixture well after each addition. Stir unbeaten egg yolks and vanilla into creamed mixture; mix until batter is smooth. Gradually add sifted dry ingredients and anise seeds to creamed mixture; blend thoroughly.

Pull off little pieces of dough and roll into balls the size of dessert cherry. Place 3 little balls together on an ungreased baking sheet. Press poppy or sesame seeds over tops. Cookies will resemble 3-leafed clover.

Bake in oven 425°F. 7 to 8 minutes, or until edges turn golden. Let cookies cool slightly before removing from baking sheet.

Makes 6 dozen cookies.

ANISETTE COOKIES

Dough :
     4 cups flour
     2 teaspoons baking powder
     ¼ cup butter
     ¼ cup shortening
     4 eggs
     1 tablespoon anise seed

    5 tablespoons Hiram Walker's anisette
Syrup :
    1 cup granulated sugar
    ½ cup water
    ½ cup triple sec
      confetti candy

To make the dough, sift together flour and baking powder; cut butter and shortening into sifted ingredients. Add eggs, anise seed, and anisette to the flour mixture; knead. Roll dough with rolling pin to about 1-inch thickness; cut with small biscuit or doughnut cutter. Place on baking sheet. Bake in oven 350°F. 15 minutes.

To make the syrup, while dough is baking, combine sugar and water in a saucepan; place over medium heat and bring ingredients to a boil. When the syrup becomes stringy, add triple sec. After the dough is done, dip each cookie into the syrup and sprinkle tops with confetti candy. Place decorated cookies on a baking sheet and return to the oven just long enough to allow syrup to harden.

Makes about 5 dozen cookies.

PARTY BUTTER COOKIES

    2 cups cake flour, sifted
    ¾ cup butter
    ½ cup granulated sugar
    1 egg yolk, unbeaten
    ½ teaspoon vanilla

Sift flour once and measure. Cream butter in a large mixing bowl; gradually add sugar and cream together until light and fluffy. Add egg yolk to creamed mixture; beat thoroughly. Add sifted flour, a small amount at a time, to creamed mixture; mix thoroughly after each addition. Blend vanilla into mixture.

Divide dough into 2 parts; shape rolls $1\frac{1}{2}$ inches in diameter. Wrap each roll in waxed paper; place in refrigerator and chill overnight, or until firm enough to slice. Cut chilled dough into $\frac{1}{8}$-inch slices.

Dough can be left in the mixing bowl and placed in the refrigerator to chill. When chilled properly, remove dough and press through a cookie press.

Bake cookies on an ungreased baking sheet in oven 400°F. 4 to 5 minutes, or until done. These cookies are delicious when sprinkled with chopped walnuts before baking.

Makes about 6 dozen small butter cookies.

BUTTERSCOTCH SLICES

4 cups cake flour, sifted
$2\frac{1}{2}$ teaspoons baking powder
$\frac{1}{2}$ teaspoon salt
1 cup butter or shortening
$1\frac{1}{2}$ cups brown sugar, firmly packed
2 eggs, unbeaten
1 cup walnuts, finely chopped
$1\frac{1}{2}$ teaspoons vanilla
$1\frac{1}{2}$ teaspoons lemon juice

Sift together sifted flour, baking powder, and salt. Cream butter in large mixing bowl; gradually add brown sugar and cream well. Add eggs, 1 at a time, to creamed mixture; beat thoroughly after each addition. Stir walnuts, vanilla, and lemon juice into batter. Blend sifted dry ingredients into batter; mix thoroughly.

Shape dough into rolls, 2 inches in diameter. Wrap rolls in waxed paper; place in refrigerator and chill overnight, or until firm enough to slice. Cut chilled dough into $\frac{1}{8}$-inch slices. Place sliced dough onto ungreased baking sheet; bake in oven 425°F. 5 to 6 minutes.

Makes 10 dozen slices.

FLAKY MERINGUE COOKIES

1 package yeast, compressed or dry
$\frac{1}{4}$ cup water
3 egg yolks, well-beaten
1 teaspoon vanilla
1 cup dairy sour cream
4 cups enriched flour, sifted
1 teaspoon salt
1 cup shortening*
1 cup confectioners' sugar
  Meringue Filling

Soften yeast in water. If compressed yeast is used, soften yeast in lukewarm water. If dry yeast is used, soften yeast in warm water.

Blend together beaten egg yolks, vanilla, sour cream, and softened yeast. Sift together sifted flour and salt. Cut the sifted dry ingredients into shortening. Combine yeast mixture into shortening mixture; stir with a spoon, then knead with hands until thoroughly blended. Wrap dough in waxed paper; chill in refrigerator approximately 4 hours or overnight.

Remove chilled dough from refrigerator. Divide dough into 3 or 4 parts for easier handling. Roll dough to $\frac{1}{8}$-inch thickness on board or pastry cloth that has been sprinkled with enough confectioners' sugar to prevent sticking. Cut with sharp knife into 3-inch squares. Place about 1 teaspoon of Meringue Filling in the middle of each square. Fold corners to center and pinch together. Place on ungreased baking sheet. Bake in oven 350°F. 20 to 25 minutes, or until lightly browned.

* Use part butter in the shortening.

Makes about 6 dozen cookies.

CHOCOLATE CHIP MERINGUES

2 egg whites
$\frac{1}{8}$ teaspoon salt
$\frac{1}{8}$ teaspoon cream of tartar
1 teaspoon vanilla
$\frac{3}{4}$ cup granulated sugar
1 cup semi-sweet chocolate chips
$\frac{3}{4}$ cup walnuts
  granulated sugar, tinted red and green

Beat egg whites, salt, cream of tartar and vanilla until soft peaks form; gradually add sugar and continue beating until stiff peaks form. Fold chocolate chips and walnuts into batter.

Drop by teaspoonfuls onto a baking sheet that has been

covered with waxed paper and then greased. Bake in oven 300°F. about 25 minutes.

At Christmastime, sprinkle tops of unbaked cookies with red or green granulated sugar to give the meringues a very festive appearance.

Makes about 4 dozen meringues.

CARROT COOKIES

1 cup carrots
$\frac{1}{4}$ teaspoon lemon juice
$\frac{3}{4}$ cup shortening
1 cup granulated sugar
2 eggs, well-beaten
2 cups flour, sifted
1 teaspoon baking powder
$\frac{1}{4}$ teaspoon salt
   Holiday Orange Icing

Cook carrots until tender; mash or cut fine and stir lemon juice into the cooked carrots. In a large mixing bowl, cream shortening; add sugar and cream again. Add well-beaten eggs to creamed mixture; beat thoroughly. Sift together sifted flour, baking powder, and salt; blend into creamed mixture and mix well. Stir prepared carrots into creamed mixture; blend thoroughly.

Drop dough by teaspoonfuls onto ungreased baking sheet. Bake in oven 325°F. until brown. Remove and ice cookies, while still warm, with Holiday Orange Icing.

Makes about $3\frac{1}{2}$ dozen cookies.

FATTIGMAND

3 eggs, well-beaten
3 tablespoons cream
3 tablespoons granulated sugar
$1\frac{1}{2}$ tablespoons butter, melted
1 tablespoon lemon juice
$\frac{1}{2}$ teaspoon cardamon seed, ground
$\frac{1}{4}$ teaspoon salt
$4\frac{1}{2}$ to 5 cups flour, sifted
$\frac{1}{4}$ cup confectioners' sugar, sifted

Mix together eggs, cream, and sugar. Stir melted butter, lemon juice, cardamon seed, salt, and 2 cups of the sifted flour into egg mixture; mix well. Slowly blend more flour into egg mixture to make a stiff dough. Wrap dough in waxed paper; place in refrigerator and chill at least 1 hour.

When chilled, remove $\frac{1}{4}$ of the dough at a time and roll on a lightly floured board or pastry cloth until the dough is paper thin. Cut rolled dough into 2-inch diamonds. Cut a slit in the center of each diamond-shaped cookie; pull 1 corner through the slit.

Fry the cookies in deep fat which has been heated to 350°F. about $\frac{1}{2}$ minute or until delicately browned. Remove from deep fat to a paper towel. Drain and dust with confectioners' sugar before serving.

Makes 10 dozen cookies.

FRAPPE COOKIES

4 cups flour
5 eggs

    6 tablespoons milk
    1 lemon rind, grated
   12 tablespoons granulated sugar
   $\frac{1}{2}$ cup butter
      pinch of salt
      pinch of baking powder
    4 tablespoons triple sec
    2 tablespoons apricot brandy
   $\frac{1}{4}$ cup confectioners' sugar, sifted

Combine all ingredients; knead about 20 minutes. Place small portions of dough onto lightly floured board; roll very thin with rolling pin. Cut rolled dough into strips approximately 1 inch wide and 5 or 6 inches long. Tie each strip of dough into a bow.

Drop each dough bow into hot deep fat; fry until golden brown on both sides. Remove from fat; cool. Sprinkle cooled bows with sifted confectioners' sugar.

Makes about 8 dozen cookies.

SPRINGERLE

    2 eggs
    1 cup granulated sugar
   $\frac{1}{4}$ teaspoon anise extract
   $1\frac{1}{2}$ cups enriched flour, sifted

Beat eggs and sugar in top of double boiler over hot (not boiling) water for 10 minutes. Remove from heat; continue to beat until mixture is cool. Add anise extract. Fold flour into the mixture. The dough should be moderately stiff.

Turn dough onto a generously floured board or pastry

cloth. Sprinkle top of dough generously with flour. Roll dough gently to $\frac{1}{4}$-inch thickness. Gently press design into dough with a springerle rolling pin or board. Gently brush off excess flour with a clean, dry pastry brush.

Cut dough; place on baking sheet that has been greased and floured. Bake in oven 300°F. 10 minutes. Turn off heat and allow cookies to remain in oven 5 minutes longer. Remove to cooling rack.

These cookies will keep up to 4 weeks.

Makes about 5 dozen small cookies.

ITALIAN TORTELETTA

Dough:
> 1 cup granulated sugar
> $\frac{1}{2}$ lemon rind, grated
> $\frac{3}{4}$ cup butter
> 2 egg yolks
> $1\frac{1}{2}$ cups all-purpose flour

Topping:
> 1 egg white
> 1 tablespoon water
> 1 cup almonds, blanched and shredded
> $\frac{1}{2}$ cup granulated sugar
> 1 tablespoon cinnamon
> $\frac{1}{4}$ teaspoon nutmeg
> $\frac{1}{8}$ teaspoon salt

To make the dough, measure sugar into large mixing bowl; grate lemon rind into the sugar and blend. Add butter to sugar mixture; cream. Beat egg yolks, one at a time, into creamed mixture. Gradually blend flour into creamed mixture until a stiff dough is formed. Pinch off a teaspoon of dough at a time. Roll the dough into a ball and flatten slightly.

To make the topping, beat the egg white and water. Brush each flattened ball with the egg white mixture. Blanch and shred the almonds. Mix the ½ cup sugar, cinnamon, nutmeg, and salt; combine with the shredded almonds. Sprinkle the topping over the flattened cakes. Bake in oven 375°F. 15 minutes or until the tortelettas are light brown.

Makes about 3 dozen tortelettas.

SCANDINAVIAN COOKIES

½ cup butter
¼ cup brown sugar
1 egg yolk
1 cup all-purpose flour, sifted
2 egg whites, well-beaten
½ cup nuts, chopped
jelly

Cream butter. Add brown sugar; cream well. Blend egg yolk into creamed mixture; and beat until light and fluffy. Stir sifted flour into creamed mixture.

Roll dough into tiny balls. Dip each ball in beaten egg whites, then roll in nuts. Place on greased baking sheet and make a dent in center of each ball.

Bake in oven 300° to 325°F. 5 minutes. Remove from oven and press dent in center of each ball once more. Replace in oven and continue baking 20 to 30 minutes. When done, remove from oven and cool slightly before filling dented centers with jelly.

Makes about 3 dozen cookies.

LIGHT PFEFFERNUESSE

2¾ cups enriched flour, sifted
½ teaspoon cinnamon
½ teaspoon ground cloves
¼ teaspoon salt
1 cup almonds, blanched and finely chopped
¼ cup candied citron, finely chopped
¼ cup candied orange peel, finely chopped
3 eggs
1½ cups granulated sugar

Sift together sifted flour, cinnamon, ground cloves, and salt. Blend almonds, candied citron, and candied orange peel into sifted dry ingredients; set aside. Beat eggs, in a large mixing bowl, until foamy; gradually add sugar and continue beating until thick and light. Add flour mixture to egg mixture; mix thoroughly. Cover dough; chill several hours or overnight.

Dust hands lightly with flour; form chilled dough into balls using about 2 teaspoons dough for each cookie. Place balls on greased baking sheet. Bake in oven 350°F. about 15 minutes.

Makes about 5½ dozen cookies.

VALENTINE COOKIES

2 cups flour, sifted
3 teaspoons baking powder
½ teaspoon salt
3 cups bran flakes, crushed
¾ cup butter or margarine, soft

1 cup granulated sugar
1½ tablespoons orange rind, grated
½ cup milk
Valentine Decoration

Sift together sifted flour, baking powder, and salt. Crush bran flakes into fine crumbs; blend into sifted ingredients. In a large mixing bowl, cream together butter, sugar, and orange rind. Add the sifted dry ingredients, alternately with milk, to the creamed butter mixture; mix well after each addition. Place dough into refrigerator and let stand until chilled (approximately 15 minutes).

Roll chilled dough very thin on lightly floured dough board. Cut dough with floured cookie cutters. For Valentine Cookies, be sure to use heart-shaped cookie cutters. Place cut cookies on lightly greased baking sheets. Bake in oven 400°F. about 10 minutes.

When done, remove cookies from baking sheet. Outline edges of each cookie with Valentine Decoration.

Makes about 5 dozen cookies.

GOBLIN CRISP COOKIES

2 cups all-purpose flour, sifted
⅓ cup granulated sugar
½ teaspoon salt
½ teaspoon baking soda
½ teaspoon ginger
½ teaspoon cinnamon
⅓ cup shortening
½ cup molasses
2 tablespoons bottled lemon juice

Sift together sifted flour, sugar, salt, soda, ginger, and cinnamon. Cut shortening into sifted dry ingredients with a pastry blender or 2 knives until particles are fine. Combine molasses and lemon juice; add to the flour mixture and blend thoroughly. Chill dough.

Roll chilled dough to $\frac{1}{16}$-inch thickness on lightly floured board. Cut rolled dough into cat, pumpkin, owl, and other appropriate Halloween shapes. Place cut cookies on a greased baking sheet. Bake in oven 400°F. about 8 minutes.

Decorate as desired. Use tiny candies, raisins, licorice strings, and other food items to accent features of Halloween creatures.

Makes about 4 dozen cookies.

HOLIDAY TREATS

$\frac{1}{2}$ cup butter or shortening, soft
6 tablespoons granulated sugar
6 tablespoons brown sugar
1 egg
1 tablespoon orange or lemon rind, grated
$\frac{1}{4}$ teaspoon water
1 cup and 2 tablespoons all-purpose flour, sifted
$\frac{1}{2}$ teaspoon baking soda
$\frac{1}{2}$ teaspoon salt
$\frac{1}{2}$ cup nuts, chopped
4 ounces mixed candied fruit
1 cup semi-sweet chocolate morsels

Cream together butter and sugars. Stir egg into creamed butter; add grated orange or lemon rind and water. Sift together sifted flour, soda, and salt; blend into creamed mixture. Add nuts, candied fruit, and chocolate morsels to the batter; mix well.

Drop by half teaspoonfuls onto an ungreased baking sheet. Bake in oven 375°F. 10 to 12 minutes.

Makes about 4 dozen cookies.

LENNIE'S HOLIDAY COOKIES

1 cup shortening
$1\frac{1}{2}$ cups brown sugar
3 eggs, well-beaten
$3\frac{1}{2}$ cups flour, sifted
1 teaspoon salt
$1\frac{1}{2}$ teaspoons mixed spices
1 teaspoon baking soda
$1\frac{1}{2}$ tablespoons hot water
1 cup nuts, chopped
1 tablespoon candied orange peel
$\frac{1}{2}$ cup currants
$\frac{1}{2}$ cup raisins
$\frac{1}{2}$ cup granulated sugar

Cream shortening. Add brown sugar to creamed shortening; cream thoroughly. Add well-beaten eggs to creamed mixture; beat well. Sift together sifted flour, salt, and mixed spices; stir into creamed mixture. Dissolve soda in hot water; stir into batter. Blend nuts, candied orange peel, currants, and raisins into the batter.

Drop by teaspoonfuls onto greased baking sheet. Sprinkle with granulated sugar. Bake in oven 400°F. 8 to 10 minutes.

Makes about 8 dozen cookies.

HOLIDAY TARTS

1 cup butter, soft
6 tablespoons confectioners' sugar, sifted
2 cups flour, sifted
1 teaspoon cinnamon
1 teaspoon nutmeg
1 teaspoon vanilla
1 cup nuts
$\frac{1}{2}$ cup confectioners' sugar, sifted

Let butter stand at room temperature until soft. Blend together butter and 6 tablespoons confectioners' sugar. Sift together sifted flour, cinnamon, and nutmeg; mix into butter mixture. Add vanilla and nuts to batter; blend thoroughly.

Roll dough into tiny balls, about the size of a nickel. Bake in oven 400°F. 15 minutes, or until light brown. When tiny balls are done, remove from oven; cool. Roll in sifted confectioners' sugar.

Makes about 6 dozen tarts.

HOLIDAY PRESS COOKIES

2 cups cake flour, sifted
$\frac{3}{4}$ cup butter, soft
$\frac{1}{2}$ cup granulated sugar
1 egg yolk, unbeaten
$\frac{1}{2}$ teaspoon vanilla
candied cherries

Measure sifted cake flour and sift. Thoroughly cream butter and sugar. Add egg yolk to creamed mixture; beat well. Add sifted flour, a small amount at a time, to creamed mixture; mix thoroughly after each addition. Blend vanilla into dough.

Chill dough. Press chilled dough through cookie press onto ungreased baking sheet. Decorate cookies with candied cherries, multi-colored sprinkles, silver dragees, or nuts. Bake in oven 400°F. 5 to 8 minutes.

Makes 6 dozen cookies.

CHRISTMAS BON BON COOKIES

1 cup butter
1½ cups confectioners' sugar
1 egg
½ teaspoon vanilla
2¼ cups flour, sifted
½ teaspoon salt
½ teaspoon baking powder
food coloring
almond halves, blanched
candied fruit

Cream butter; add confectioners' sugar and mix well. Add egg and vanilla to creamed mixture; beat. Sift together sifted flour, salt, and baking powder; blend into creamed mixture and mix thoroughly.

Divide the dough into 4 parts. Leave 1 part of the dough white; tint 1 part light pink; tint 1 part light green; and tint 1 part light yellow. Chill the 4 parts of dough several hours.

Form the chilled dough into small balls, using 1 teaspoonful of dough for each ball. Place the unbaked cookie balls on a baking sheet; decorate each ball with an almond half, or pieces of candied fruit. Bake in oven 350°F. 8 to 10 minutes, or until bottom edges of the cookies begin to brown. When done, remove from oven and transfer cookies to wire racks to cool.

Makes about 6 dozen cookies.

CANDY CANES AND CHRISTMAS WREATHS

1¼ cups butter
1 cup confectioners' sugar
1 egg
1 teaspoon vanilla
½ teaspoon almond extract
3½ cups flour, sifted
1 teaspoon salt
red and green food coloring
red and green decorating sugar
1 egg white
cinnamon candies

Cream butter; add confectioners' sugar and blend thoroughly. Blend egg, vanilla, and almond extract into creamed mixture. Sift together sifted flour and salt; add to batter and mix well. Set aside half of dough. Divide other half of dough into 2 parts; tint 1 part light red and the other part light green with food coloring.

For candy canes, roll 1 teaspoonful of untinted dough into approximately 4-inch strips; roll 1 teaspoonful of red-tinted dough into approximately 4-inch strips. Place an untinted strip and a red-tinted strip of dough side by side; twist lightly together. Carefully place the twisted strips onto an ungreased baking sheet; curve top part of each dough strip down to form a handle. Brush the unbaked candy canes with egg white and sprinkle with red decorating sugar. Bake in oven 350°F. 10 to 12 minutes.

For wreaths, roll 1 teaspoonful of untinted dough into approximately 4-inch strips; roll 1 teaspoonful of green-tinted dough into approximately 4-inch strips. Place an untinted strip and a green-tinted strip of dough side by side; twist lightly together. Carefully place twisted strips of dough onto an ungreased baking sheet; form into circles. Brush unbaked wreaths with egg white and sprinkle with green decorating sugar. Garnish with cinnamon candies. Bake in oven 350°F. 10 to 12 minutes.

Makes about 5 dozen cookies.

CHRISTMAS NUT STICKS

2 cups cake flour, sifted
$\frac{3}{4}$ cup butter
$\frac{1}{2}$ cup granulated sugar
1 egg yolk, unbeaten
$\frac{1}{2}$ teaspoon vanilla
1 cup nuts, finely chopped
$\frac{1}{4}$ cup confectioners' sugar

Measure sifted flour. Cream butter in large mixing bowl; gradually add sugar, beat until light and fluffy. Add egg yolk to creamed mixture; beat thoroughly. Blend sifted flour, a small amount at a time, into creamed mixture; beat thoroughly after each addition. Blend vanilla into dough.

Chill dough. Roll chilled dough into sticks, $1\frac{1}{2}$ inches long and $\frac{1}{4}$ inch in diameter. Roll each stick in finely chopped nuts. Bake on an ungreased baking sheet in oven 400°F. 3 to 4 minutes. While hot, sprinkle with confectioners' sugar.

Makes 5 dozen yuletide sticks.

MERRY CHRISTMAS PATTERN COOKIES

        6 cups enriched flour, sifted
    1$\frac{1}{2}$ teaspoons baking powder
        1 teaspoon salt
        1 cup butter or margarine
    1$\frac{1}{2}$ cups granulated sugar
     $\frac{1}{2}$ cup light brown sugar
        2 eggs, beaten
     $\frac{1}{4}$ cup water
        1 tablespoon vanilla
     $\frac{1}{2}$ teaspoon lemon extract
          Decorating Frosting

Sift together sifted flour, baking powder, and salt. (If self-rising flour is used, omit baking powder and salt.) Cream together butter, granulated sugar, and light brown sugar until light and fluffy. Add eggs to creamed mixture; beat well.

Combine water, vanilla, and lemon extract. Add the water-flavoring mixture, alternately with sifted ingredients, to creamed mixture. Mix well. Cover and chill several hours, or overnight.

Remove dough from refrigerator; divide dough into 4 parts. Roll 1 portion at a time, returning remainder of dough to refrigerator. Roll dough to $\frac{1}{2}$-inch thickness on floured board or pastry cloth. Cut with floured cookie cutters, or cut around patterns with sharp knife. Bake on lightly greased baking sheet in oven 375°F. 10 minutes.

When cool, frost and decorate with Decorating Frosting.

Makes about 8 dozen cookies.

GERMAN CHRISTMAS COOKIES

1 cup butter
$\frac{3}{4}$ cup confectioners' sugar
2 cups flour, sifted
dash of salt
1 tablespoon cream
1 tablespoon vanilla
$1\frac{1}{2}$ cups walnuts, ground
$\frac{1}{2}$ cup confectioners' sugar, sifted

Cream butter. Sift together $\frac{3}{4}$ cup confectioners' sugar, sifted flour, and salt. Add $\frac{1}{2}$ of the sifted dry ingredients to the creamed butter; mix thoroughly. Add cream and rest of sifted dry ingredients to the creamed mixture; blend vanilla and walnuts into creamed mixture. Mix and knead approximately 20 minutes.

Roll small amounts of the dough into tiny balls; place on baking sheet. Bake in oven 300°F. about 30 minutes. Remove cookies from oven; dust each cookie, while still hot, with sifted confectioners' sugar. Let cookies cool, then dust each cookie again with sifted confectioners' sugar.

Makes about 6 dozen cookies.

SANTA'S BROWNIES

$\frac{3}{4}$ cup cake flour, sifted
$\frac{1}{2}$ teaspoon baking powder
$\frac{1}{4}$ teaspoon salt
$\frac{1}{3}$ cup butter or shortening
2 or 3 one-ounce squares unsweetened chocolate
2 eggs, well-beaten
1 cup granulated sugar
$\frac{1}{2}$ cup walnuts, chopped
1 teaspoon vanilla
Mocha Filling

Measure sifted flour. Sift together sifted flour, baking powder, and salt. Melt butter and chocolate over hot water. Place well-beaten eggs into large mixing bowl; gradually add sugar, then beat thoroughly. Add shortening mixture to egg mixture; blend. Add sifted dry ingredients to egg mixture; mix well. Stir walnuts and vanilla into batter.

Pour batter into greased 8 x 8 x 2-inch pan. Bake in oven 350°F. 25 minutes for moist chewy brownies, or 30 minutes for cake-like brownies. When brownies are done, remove from oven; cool in pan. Cut cooled brownies into squares. Split each brownie and fill with Mocha Filling.

Makes about 2 dozen brownies.

YULE CRISPIES

$\frac{3}{4}$ cup butter
1 cup granulated sugar
4 egg yolks
1 teaspoon vanilla

1½ cups flour, sifted
2 teaspoons baking powder
½ teaspoon salt
3 teaspoons cinnamon
¾ cups pecans, finely chopped
candied cherries
⅛ cup granulated sugar

Cream butter; add 1 cup sugar and beat until fluffy. Stir egg yolks and vanilla into creamed mixture; beat until creamy. Sift together sifted flour, baking powder, and salt; blend into creamed mixture.

Form dough into 1-inch balls. Combine cinnamon and pecans; roll balls in this mixture. Place balls on baking sheet; flatten with bottom of a tumbler, which has been dipped in remaining sugar. Place a candied cherry in center of each flattened ball. Bake in oven 375°F. 8 to 10 minutes.

Makes 5 dozen cookies.

CHRISTMAS JEWEL DROPS

2¼ cups enriched flour, sifted
½ teaspoon salt
1 cup butter or margarine
½ cup granulated sugar
1 teaspoon vanilla
1 cup gumdrops, finely chopped
1 cup flaked coconut

Sift together sifted flour and salt; set aside. Cream butter, sugar, and vanilla until light and fluffy. Blend the sifted dry ingredients into creamed mixture; add gumdrops and coconut. Mix well.

Drop dough by teaspoonfuls onto greased baking sheet. Bake in oven 325°F. 15 to 20 minutes.

Makes about 5 dozen cookies.

FROSTED CHRISTMAS JEWELS

$1\frac{1}{2}$ cups seeded muscat raisins
$\frac{1}{2}$ cup shortening
$\frac{1}{2}$ cup granulated sugar
1 egg
$\frac{1}{2}$ cup light molasses
$2\frac{1}{2}$ cups flour, sifted
1 teaspoon salt
1 teaspoon ginger
$\frac{1}{2}$ teaspoon nutmeg
$\frac{1}{2}$ teaspoon cinnamon
1 teaspoon baking soda
$\frac{1}{2}$ cup warm water
Creamy Browned Butter Icing

Chop raisins; set aside. Beat together shortening and sugar. Blend egg, molasses, and chopped raisins into shortening mixture. Sift together sifted flour, salt, ginger, nutmeg, and cinnamon. Dissolve soda in warm water. Blend the sifted dry ingredients, alternately with dissolved soda, into the shortening mixture. Mix well.

Drop by teaspoonfuls onto greased baking sheet. Bake in oven 375°F. 8 minutes. When done, remove from baking sheet to wire rack; cool. Lightly frost cooled cookies with Creamy Browned Butter Icing.

Makes $4\frac{1}{2}$ dozen jewels.

19. bar cookies

APPLESAUCE BROWNIES

$\frac{1}{2}$ cup shortening
2 one-ounce squares unsweetened chocolate
2 eggs
1 cup granulated sugar
1 teaspoon vanilla
$\frac{1}{2}$ cup applesauce
1 cup flour, sifted
$\frac{1}{2}$ teaspoon baking powder
$\frac{1}{4}$ teaspoon baking soda
$\frac{1}{4}$ teaspoon salt
$\frac{1}{2}$ cup nuts, chopped

Melt together shortening and chocolate in top of double boiler. Beat eggs until foamy; add sugar and beat well. Blend vanilla, applesauce, and chocolate mixture into egg mixture.

277

Sift together sifted flour, baking powder, soda, and salt; blend into egg mixture. Mix thoroughly.

Pour batter into 9 x 13-inch greased pan. Bake in oven 350°F. 35 to 40 minutes. When done, remove from oven; cool slightly before cutting into squares.

Makes about 4 dozen brownies.

LUSCIOUS APRICOT BARS

$\frac{2}{3}$ cup apricots, cooked and diced
$\frac{1}{2}$ cup butter, soft
$\frac{1}{4}$ cup granulated sugar
1 cup flour, sifted
Apricot-Nut Filling
confectioners' sugar

Rinse dried or fresh apricots. Place the fruit in a medium-size saucepan and cover the fruit with water; boil about 10 minutes. After cooking, drain water off the fruit. Let the apricots stand until cool, then dice.

Cream together butter and sugar; add sifted flour and mix until crumbly. Pack mixture into greased 8 x 8 x 2-inch pan. Bake in oven 350°F. 25 minutes, or until lightly browned.

When done, remove from oven and cool. Fill with Apricot-Nut Filling. Spread with cooled apricots. Return to oven and bake in oven 350°F. another 30 minutes. Remove from oven and cool in pan. After thoroughly cooled, cut into bars and roll in confectioners' sugar.

Makes about 2 dozen bars.

SPICY COCONUT BARS

$\frac{1}{2}$ cup butter or shortening
2 eggs, unbeaten
$\frac{1}{4}$ cup milk
1$\frac{1}{2}$ cups flour, sifted
1$\frac{1}{2}$ teaspoons double-acting baking powder
1 teaspoon ground cinnamon
$\frac{1}{4}$ teaspoon ground cloves
$\frac{1}{4}$ teaspoon allspice
$\frac{1}{4}$ teaspoon ground nutmeg
$\frac{1}{4}$ teaspoon ground ginger
$\frac{1}{4}$ teaspoon salt
1 cup granulated sugar
1 teaspoon vanilla
1$\frac{1}{3}$ cups flaked coconut
    Butter Frosting
    Tinted Coconut

Have butter, eggs, and milk at room temperature.

Sift together sifted flour, baking powder, cinnamon, cloves, allspice, nutmeg, ginger, salt, and sugar into large mixing bowl. Add butter, eggs, 2 tablespoons of the milk, and vanilla to the sifted dry ingredients; blend and beat 2 minutes. Add remaining milk and coconut to the batter; beat $\frac{1}{2}$ minute. (Beat vigorously by hand or at a low speed with electric mixer.) Chill dough 2 hours.

Spread chilled dough in 2 greased 8 x 8 x 2-inch pans. Bake in oven 375°F. 20 to 25 minutes. When done, remove from oven and cool in pan. Spread with Butter Frosting and decorate with Tinted Coconut. Cut into bars. To keep these bars soft, store in a tightly covered container with a slice of fresh bread.

Makes 4 dozen bars.

TOASTED COCONUT BROWNIES

- ⅔ cup flour, sifted
- ½ teaspoon baking powder
- ¼ teaspoon salt
- ⅓ cup butter or shortening
- 2 squares unsweetened chocolate
- 1 cup granulated sugar
- 2 eggs, well-beaten
- ¾ cup coconut, finely chopped
- 1 teaspoon vanilla
- Toasted Coconut Topping

Sift together sifted flour, baking powder, and salt. Melt butter and chocolate in top of double boiler over hot water. In a large mixing bowl, gradually add sugar to the well-beaten eggs; beat thoroughly. Blend chocolate mixture into egg mixture. Add sifted ingredients to chocolate-egg mixture; mix well. Thoroughly blend coconut and vanilla into batter.

Pour batter into 2 greased 8 x 8 x 2-inch pans. Cover batter with Toasted Coconut Topping. Bake in oven 350°F. 25 minutes. Cool in pan; cut into squares or rectangles.

Makes about 2 dozen brownies.

COCONUT PECAN SQUARES

Dough:
- ½ cup butter
- ½ cup dark brown sugar
- 1 cup flour

Filling:
- 2 eggs
- 1 cup light brown sugar

$\frac{1}{2}$ cup shredded coconut
2 tablespoons flour
1 cup pecans, coarsely chopped
1 teaspoon vanilla
   dash of salt
Topping:
   $\frac{1}{4}$ cup confectioners' sugar, sifted

To make dough, cream together butter and dark brown sugar; add flour and mix until mixture is a crumbly mass. Press into a greased 8 x 8 x 2-inch square pan. Evenly spread the crumbs into corners of pan. Bake in oven 350°F. 20 minutes.

To make filling, while the dough is baking, beat eggs until frothy; gradually add light brown sugar and beat until mixture is thick. Toss shredded coconut with flour; blend, alternately with pecans, into the egg mixture. Add vanilla and salt to the egg mixture; mix thoroughly. Spread the filling over the baked crumb mixture. Return to oven 350°F. and bake another 20 minutes until top is well browned.

When baked, remove from oven. Allow to cool completely in pan before sprinkling with sifted confectioners' sugar. Cut into 1-inch squares.

Makes 2 dozen squares.

BANANA FRUIT SQUARES

Crumb Mixture:
   $\frac{1}{2}$ cup butter or margarine
   $\frac{3}{4}$ cup brown sugar
   $1\frac{1}{4}$ cups all-purpose flour, sifted
   1 cup rolled oats, uncooked

Filling:

  1 cup bananas, sliced
  ½ cup prunes, cooked and coarsely chopped
  ½ cup apricots, cooked and coarsely chopped
  ½ cup raisins, plumped
  ½ cup liquid from cooked fruits
  1 teaspoon orange or lemon rind, grated
  1¼ teaspoons cinnamon
  ½ teaspoon nutmeg
  ¼ teaspoon ground cloves
  ¼ teaspoon ground ginger

To make crumb mixture: cream butter; gradually add brown sugar and mix until well blended. Add sifted flour and rolled oats to creamed mixture; blend until mixture has coarse-crumb texture. With back of a spoon, firmly and evenly pack half of the crumb mixture into a greased 9 x 9 x 2-inch square pan.

To make filling: combine sliced bananas, prunes, apricots, raisins, liquid from cooked fruits, grated orange or lemon rind, cinnamon, nutmeg, ground cloves, and ground ginger; spread evenly over the firmly packed crumbs. Cover with the remaining half of the crumb mixture and pack down gently, making sure all of the filling is covered.

Bake in preheated oven 400°F. 30 minutes. Chill thoroughly before cutting into squares and removing from the pan. Store in refrigerator.

Makes about 2 dozen squares.

DATE SQUARES

Filling:

  ¾ pound dates, pitted
  2 tablespoons granulated sugar

1 teaspoon lemon juice

¼ cup water

Dough:

1½ cups all-purpose flour

½ teaspoon soda

¼ teaspoon salt

1½ cups rolled oats, uncooked

1 cup brown sugar

¾ cup butter, soft

To make filling: cut dates into small pieces; add granulated sugar, lemon juice, and water. Cook date mixture about 10 minutes, or until dates are tender and mixture thickens to a jam-like consistency. The date mixture should be cooked in a saucepan over a medium flame.

To make dough: sift together flour, soda, and salt. Add rolled oats and brown sugar to sifted ingredients; blend with the butter as for pie crust.

Press half of the dough into an even layer in bottom and sides of well-buttered 8 x 8-inch pan. Add cooled filling; spread evenly. Press remainder of dough to form cover over filling. Bake in preheated oven 350°F. 30 to 45 minutes.

Makes about 1½ dozen squares.

DATE HONEY CHEWS

Filling:

¼ cup butter or margarine

2 tablespoons honey

1 egg, separated

1 cup confectioners' sugar, sifted
¾ cup dates, chopped

Dough:

1½ cups enriched flour, sifted
1 teaspoon baking powder
½ teaspoon salt
½ cup granulated sugar
½ cup rolled oats, uncooked
½ cup shortening
¼ cup milk
1 teaspoon vanilla

To make filling, cream together butter or margarine and honey until light. Add egg white to creamed mixture; beat until light and fluffy. Gradually add sifted confectioners' sugar to creamed mixture; mix well. Stir dates into creamed mixture.

To make dough, sift together sifted flour, baking powder, salt, and granulated sugar. (If self-rising flour is used instead of enriched flour, omit baking powder and salt.) Add rolled oats to sifted dry ingredients. Cut or rub shortening into sifted dry ingredients, until mixture is crumbly. Beat egg yolk; add milk and vanilla. Blend the egg yolk mixture into sifted dry ingredients; stir until sifted dry ingredients are well moistened.

Spread half of dough into bottom of greased, paper-lined pan 7 x 11 inches. Spread filling over dough; cover with remaining dough. Bake in oven 400°F. about 25 minutes. Cut into bars.

Makes about 2 dozen bars.

DATE NUT BARS

3 eggs, well-beaten
1 cup honey
1 lemon rind, grated
1 cup flour, sifted
$\frac{1}{4}$ teaspoon salt
1 teaspoon double-acting baking powder
1 pound dates, pitted and chopped
1 cup nuts, chopped
$\frac{1}{4}$ cup confectioners' sugar

Combine well-beaten eggs, honey, and grated lemon rind in a large mixing bowl. Sift together sifted flour, salt, and baking powder; blend with dates and nuts into egg mixture.

Pour batter into greased 9 x 13 x 2-inch baking pan. Bake in oven 325°F. 40 to 45 minutes. Remove from oven; cool and sprinkle with confectioners' sugar. Cut into bars.

Makes about 3 dozen bars.

FRUIT NUT BARS

3 eggs
1 six-ounce can frozen orange juice concentrate, thawed and undiluted
1 cup granulated sugar
2 cups graham crackers, crumbled*
1 teaspoon baking powder
$\frac{1}{4}$ teaspoon salt
1 teaspoon vanilla
1 eight-ounce package dates, chopped
1 cup nuts, chopped

Break eggs into a large mixing bowl; beat until light and fluffy. Blend undiluted orange juice concentrate into beaten eggs; beat thoroughly. Blend sugar into egg mixture; add graham cracker crumbs, baking powder, salt, vanilla, chopped dates, and nuts. Mix well.

Pour batter into a greased 9-inch square pan. Bake in oven 350°F. about 50 minutes, or until cake tester comes out clean when inserted into center of baked bars. Remove from oven; cool. Cut into bars.

* About 28 graham crackers.

Makes about 2 dozen bars.

MINCE MEAT SQUARES

2 cups enriched flour, sifted
2 teaspoons baking powder
½ teaspoon salt
¾ cup granulated sugar
½ cup shortening, melted
2 eggs
½ teaspoon orange extract
1 tablespoon orange rind, grated
¾ cup prepared mince meat

Sift together sifted flour, baking powder, and salt. (If self-rising flour is used, omit baking powder and salt.) Add sugar to shortening; mix well. Add eggs to shortening mixture; beat until smooth. Stir orange extract and orange rind into shortening mixture. Gradually add sifted dry ingredients to shortening mixture; stir until well blended.

Place half the dough into a well-greased 9-inch square

pan. Spread mince meat over the dough; cover with remaining dough. Bake in oven 375°F. about 30 minutes. When done, remove from oven and cool. Cut into $1\frac{1}{2}$-inch squares.

Makes about 2 dozen squares.

MINCE MEAT BROWNIES

1 nine-ounce package mince meat
$\frac{1}{4}$ cup water
$\frac{3}{4}$ cup flour, sifted
$\frac{1}{2}$ teaspoon baking powder
$\frac{1}{2}$ teaspoon salt
$\frac{1}{2}$ cup shortening
1 cup granulated sugar
2 eggs
2 one-ounce squares unsweetened chocolate, melted
1 teaspoon vanilla

Break mince meat into small pieces; place in small saucepan. Add water to mince meat; place over medium heat and stir until lumps are thoroughly broken. Bring to a boil; boil briskly for 1 minute. Cool.

Sift together sifted flour, baking powder, and salt. Cream shortening in a large mixing bowl; gradually add sugar and beat until fluffy. Beat eggs, 1 at a time, into creamed mixture; blend well after each addition. Stir melted chocolate and vanilla into creamed mixture. Blend sifted dry ingredients into creamed mixture; mix thoroughly. Blend cooled mince meat into batter.

Pour batter into well-greased 9-inch square pan. Bake in oven 350°F. 35 minutes. When done, remove from oven and cool in pan. When cool, cut into 1 x 3-inch bars.

Makes about 2½ dozen brownies.

ORANGE NUT BARS

1 six-ounce can frozen orange juice concentrate, thawed and undiluted
½ cup rolled oats, uncooked
½ cup mixed candied fruit
½ cup walnuts, chopped
2 cups all-purpose flour, sifted
¼ teaspoon salt
1 teaspoon baking soda
1 teaspoon ginger
1 teaspoon cinnamon
½ cup shortening
½ cup granulated sugar
½ cup unsulphured molasses
1 egg
Orange Icing
candied cherries

Combine undiluted orange juice concentrate, rolled oats, candied fruit, and chopped nuts; set aside. Sift together sifted flour, salt, soda, ginger, and cinnamon; set aside. Cream together shortening and sugar; add unsulphured molasses and egg. Mix well. Gradually blend sifted dry ingredients into the molasses mixture; add fruit mixture and stir until thoroughly blended.

Pour batter into greased 13 x 9-inch baking pan; spread evenly. Bake in oven 325°F. 40 minutes. When done, remove from oven and let stand until cool. Frost with Orange Icing and cut into 3 x 1-inch bars. Decorate with candied cherries.

Makes about 3 dozen bars.

ORANGE DATE SKILLET BARS

½ cup margarine
½ cup granulated sugar
1 teaspoon orange rind, grated
2 tablespoons orange juice
1 cup flour, sifted
½ teaspoon baking soda
1 egg
½ cup nuts, chopped
½ cup dates, chopped
Orange Frosting for Bars

Generously grease the bottom of a 9-inch pan with margarine. Melt ½ cup margarine in a large skillet over low heat; remove skillet from heat. Add sugar, orange rind, and orange juice to the melted margarine; blend thoroughly. Stir sifted flour and soda into margarine mixture; add egg and beat well. Fold nuts and dates into the mixture.

Pour batter into the prepared pan. Bake in oven 350°F. 25 minutes. *Caution:* Do not overbake. When baked, cool in pan and frost with Orange Frosting for Bars. After the frosting has set, cut into bars.

Makes 1½ dozen bars.

CHOCOLATE PINEAPPLE BARS

1 package devil's food cake mix
2 eggs
$\frac{1}{4}$ cup shortening, soft
$\frac{2}{3}$ cup canned crushed pineapple, drained
$\frac{1}{2}$ cup pecans, chopped

Measure half of the cake mix into a large mixing bowl. Add eggs and shortening to cake mix; blend thoroughly. Blend the remaining cake mix and crushed pineapple into the batter; beat until smooth. Stir chopped pecans into the batter.

Pour the batter into a greased 13 x 9 x 2-inch pan. Bake in oven 375°F. about 30 minutes. When done, remove from the oven; cool in pan before cutting into rectangular bars. The bars should be stored in a tightly covered container.

Makes 3 dozen bars.

FUDGY PINEAPPLE BROWNIES

2 one-ounce squares unsweetened chocolate
$\frac{1}{2}$ cup shortening
1 cup granulated sugar
$\frac{1}{2}$ teaspoon vanilla
2 eggs, well-beaten
1 cup flour, sifted
1 teaspoon baking powder
1 teaspoon cinnamon
$\frac{1}{2}$ teaspoon mace

$\frac{1}{2}$ teaspoon salt

$1\frac{1}{2}$ cups pineapple, crushed and drained, or $1\frac{1}{2}$ cups apples, finely grated

$\frac{1}{2}$ cup pecans, coarsely chopped

Melt together chocolate and shortening in top of double boiler. Beat together sugar, vanilla, and eggs; blend into chocolate mixture and beat thoroughly. Sift together sifted flour, baking powder, cinnamon, mace, and salt; add sifted ingredients, alternately with crushed fruit, into chocolate mixture. Add coarsely chopped nuts into batter; blend well.

Pour batter into greased 9 x 9-inch pan. Bake in oven 350°F. 30 to 35 minutes.

Makes about $2\frac{1}{2}$ dozen brownies.

GOLDEN RAISIN SQUARES

1 cup light or dark raisins

$\frac{1}{2}$ cup shortening

1 cup brown sugar, packed

1 teaspoon lemon rind, grated

$\frac{1}{2}$ cup canned cling peaches, crushed

$2\frac{1}{2}$ cups all-purpose flour, sifted

1 teaspoon salt

$\frac{1}{2}$ teaspoon baking soda

1 teaspoon cinnamon

Rinse, drain, and chop raisins. Cream together shortening and brown sugar. Blend lemon rind and crushed peaches into creamed mixture. Sift together sifted flour, salt, soda, and cinnamon; blend into creamed mixture. Stir prepared raisins into creamed mixture. Place dough into refrigerator and chill about 1 hour.

Remove chilled dough from refrigerator; divide into halves. Roll each half of the chilled dough on a large greased baking sheet about 14 x 17-inches, keeping edges as square as possible.

Bake in oven 400°F. 7 minutes. When done, remove from oven. Cut while still hot, with pastry wheel or sharp knife.

Makes about 6 dozen squares.

RAISIN FUDGE SQUARES

$\frac{1}{2}$ cup shortening
2 one-ounce squares unsweetened chocolate
2 eggs
1 cup granulated sugar
1 teaspoon vanilla
$\frac{1}{2}$ cup all-purpose flour, sifted
$\frac{1}{4}$ teaspoon salt
1 cup seedless nectars

Measure shortening and chocolate into top of double boiler; melt over hot water. Cool slightly. Beat eggs; gradually beat sugar into eggs. Blend chocolate mixture and vanilla into egg mixture. Blend sifted flour and salt into egg mixture; mix well. Fold raisins into batter.

Spread dough into greased 8-inch square pan. Bake in oven 350°F. 25 to 30 minutes. Cool in pan. Cut into squares.

Makes about 2 dozen small squares.

CHOCOLATE COCONUT CHEWS

½ cup shortening, soft
6 tablespoons granulated sugar
6 tablespoons brown sugar
1 egg
½ teaspoon vanilla
¼ teaspoon water
1 cup and 2 tablespoons all-purpose flour, sifted
½ teaspoon baking soda
¼ teaspoon salt
½ cup flaked coconut
1 cup semi-sweet chocolate morsels

Cream together shortening and sugars; add egg, vanilla, and water. Mix well. Sift together sifted flour, soda, and salt; blend into creamed mixture. Add coconut and chocolate morsels to batter; blend thoroughly.

Spread batter in a greased 9 x 13-inch pan. Bake in oven 375°F. 10 to 12 minutes. Cool in pan. Cut into squares.

Makes about 3 dozen squares.

CHOCOLATE CHIP COCONUT BARS

⅓ cup shortening
½ cup granulated sugar
½ cup brown sugar, packed
1 egg
2 tablespoons water
1 teaspoon vanilla

1 cup flour, sifted
1¼ teaspoons baking powder
¼ teaspoon salt
½ cup moist coconut
1 six-ounce package semi-sweet chocolate pieces
½ cup nuts, chopped

Cream together shortening and sugars; add egg and mix well. Add water and vanilla to creamed mixture; blend. Sift together sifted flour, baking powder, and salt; blend into creamed mixture. Stir coconut, chocolate pieces, and chopped nuts into batter.

Press dough into a greased 7 x 11-inch or 9-inch square cake pan. Bake in oven 350°F. 30 minutes. Remove from oven; cool. Cut into bars.

Makes about 2½ dozen bars.

CHOCOLATE CHIP SCOTCH BARS

1 cup flour, sifted
½ teaspoon baking powder
⅛ teaspoon baking soda
½ teaspoon salt
½ cup nuts, chopped
⅓ cup butter, melted
1 cup brown sugar, firmly packed
1 egg, slightly beaten
1 teaspoon vanilla
½ cup semi-sweet chocolate chips

Sift flour once and measure; add baking powder, soda, and salt, and sift again. Blend nuts (walnuts, pecans, or peanuts) into sifted dry ingredients. Measure brown sugar into a large mixing bowl; mix melted butter into brown sugar and cool slightly. Add egg and vanilla to brown sugar mixture. Blend sifted dry ingredients, a small amount at a time, into brown sugar mixture; mix well after each addition.

Spread batter into a greased 9 x 9 x 2-inch pan. Sprinkle chocolate chips over top of batter. Bake in oven 350°F. 20 to 25 minutes. Do not overbake. When baked, remove from oven and cool in pan. Cut into $1\frac{1}{2}$ x $2\frac{1}{4}$-inch bars.

Makes 2 dozen bars.

CHOCOLATE YUM YUMS

30 graham crackers
1 can Eagle Brand milk
1 package milk chocolate chips
$\frac{1}{4}$ cup nuts, chopped

Roll graham crackers very fine; place in a mixing bowl. Add milk, chocolate chips, and chopped nuts to graham crackers; mix thoroughly.

Spoon the thick mixture into an 8-inch square pan. Bake in oven 350°F. 20 to 25 minutes. When done, remove from oven; cool in pan 5 minutes before cutting into squares. Remove cut squares from pan while still warm.

Makes about 3 dozen squares.

CHOCOLATE CRISPIES

1 one-ounce square unsweetened chocolate
$\frac{1}{4}$ cup butter or shortening
$\frac{1}{2}$ cup granulated sugar
1 egg, unbeaten
$\frac{1}{4}$ cup flour, sifted
$\frac{1}{8}$ teaspoon salt
$\frac{1}{4}$ teaspoon vanilla
$\frac{1}{4}$ cup nuts, finely chopped

Melt together chocolate and butter in top of double boiler over hot water. Remove chocolate mixture from heat; add sugar, egg, sifted flour, salt, and vanilla. Thoroughly beat the batter.

Spread the batter in a thin layer in 2 greased 8 x 8 x 2-inch pans; sprinkle with nuts. Bake in oven 400°F. 12 to 15 minutes. When done, remove from oven and, while warm, mark in 2-inch squares. Cool; break into squares.

Makes 2 dozen crispies.

CHOCOLATE SQUARES

$1\frac{1}{2}$ cups flour, sifted
$1\frac{1}{2}$ teaspoons baking powder
$\frac{1}{2}$ teaspoon salt
3 one-ounce squares unsweetened chocolate
4 tablespoons butter or shortening
1 cup granulated sugar
1 egg, unbeaten
$\frac{3}{4}$ cup milk
$\frac{1}{2}$ teaspoon vanilla

Sift together 3 times sifted flour, baking powder, and salt. Melt chocolate and butter in top of double boiler over hot water; cool to lukewarm. Add sugar to chocolate mixture; mix well. Add egg to mixture and beat thoroughly. Blend sifted dry ingredients, alternately with milk, into chocolate mixture; stir only to blend. Stir vanilla into batter.

Spread batter in 2 greased 9 x 9 x 2-inch pans. Bake in oven 375°F. 12 minutes, or until done. When done, remove from oven and let cool in pans. When almost cool, cut into squares; remove from pans. Ice, if desired.

Makes about 4 dozen squares.

CHOCOLATE FRUIT SQUARES

$1\frac{1}{2}$ cups flour, sifted
$1\frac{1}{2}$ teaspoons baking powder
$\frac{1}{2}$ teaspoon salt
3 one-ounce squares unsweetened chocolate
4 tablespoons butter or shortening
1 cup granulated sugar
1 egg, unbeaten
$\frac{3}{4}$ cup milk
$\frac{1}{2}$ teaspoon vanilla
$\frac{2}{3}$ cup dates, chopped*
$\frac{2}{3}$ cup nuts, chopped

Sift together sifted flour, baking powder, and salt. Melt chocolate and butter over hot water; cool to lukewarm. Add sugar to chocolate mixture; mix well. Add egg to mixture; beat thoroughly. Blend sifted dry ingredients, alternately with milk, into chocolate mixture; stir only to blend. Stir

vanilla into mixture. Add chopped dates and nuts; mix well.
Pour batter into 2 greased 9 x 9 x 2-inch pans. Bake in
oven 375°F. 12 minutes, or until done. Let cool in pans.
When almost cool, cut into squares and remove from pans.
* $\frac{2}{3}$ cup chopped raisins may be substituted for dates.

Makes about 4 dozen squares.

CHOCOLATE NUT SQUARES

1 cup flour, sifted
1 teaspoon baking powder
$\frac{1}{2}$ teaspoon salt
2 eggs, well-beaten
1 cup granulated sugar
1 teaspoon vanilla
1 tablespoon butter or shortening, melted
1 tablespoon hot water
1 cup nuts, chopped
1 cup semi-sweet chocolate chips

Sift flour once and measure; add baking powder and salt,
and sift again. Beat eggs in a large mixing bowl; gradually
add sugar and beat well. Blend vanilla, butter, and hot water
into the egg mixture; add nuts and chocolate chips.
Gradually blend sifted dry ingredients into the mixture;
mix well.

Turn batter into a well-greased 13 x 9 x 2-inch pan. Bake
in oven 325°F. 30 to 35 minutes. Remove from oven when
done and cool. Cut into 1$\frac{1}{2}$-inch squares. Ice, if desired, with
Quick Chocolate Frosting.

Makes about 3 dozen squares.

CHOCOLATE BROWNIES

$\frac{1}{2}$ cup shortening
1 cup granulated sugar
2 eggs, beaten
2 one-ounce squares unsweetened chocolate, melted
$\frac{3}{4}$ cup cake or pastry flour, sifted
$\frac{1}{4}$ teaspoon baking powder
$\frac{1}{4}$ teaspoon salt
$\frac{3}{4}$ cup walnut kernels, chopped

Cream shortening; add sugar and cream thoroughly. Add beaten eggs and melted chocolate to creamed mixture. Sift together sifted flour, baking powder, and salt; blend, alternately with walnut kernels, into the creamed mixture.

Turn batter into a 9-inch square baking pan. Bake in oven 350°F. 30 minutes. When baked, remove from oven; cut into squares at once with a sharp knife.

Makes 2 dozen brownies.

FUDGY BROWNIES

2 eggs
1 cup granulated sugar
$\frac{1}{2}$ teaspoon salt
1 teaspoon vanilla
$\frac{1}{3}$ cup shortening (part butter), melted
2 one-ounce squares unsweetened chocolate
$\frac{3}{4}$ cup flour, sifted
1 cup walnuts, chopped

Break eggs into a large mixing bowl; beat eggs slightly with spoon. Stir sugar, salt, and vanilla, into the eggs. Blend melted shortening and chocolate into the mixture. Add sifted flour and walnuts to the mixture; blend gently. Do not beat the batter at any time.

Turn batter into a greased 8 x 9 x 2-inch pan. Bake in preheated oven 325°F. 30 to 35 minutes. When done, remove brownies from oven (brownies should still be soft); let cool in pan before cutting into squares.

Makes about 2 dozen squares.

DOUBLE-DECK BROWNIES

Bottom Layer :
  $\frac{1}{2}$ cup flour, sifted
  $\frac{1}{4}$ teaspoon baking soda
  $\frac{1}{4}$ teaspoon salt
  1 cup rolled oats, uncooked
  $\frac{1}{2}$ cup brown sugar, firmly packed
  $\frac{1}{2}$ cup butter or margarine, melted

Sift together sifted flour, baking soda, and salt; combine with rolled oats and brown sugar. Blend oat mixture into melted butter. Pat dough into bottom of 7 x 11-inch pan. Bake in oven 350°F. 10 minutes. When done, remove from oven and cool in pan.

Top Layer :
  1 one-ounce square unsweetened chocolate, melted
  $\frac{1}{4}$ cup butter or margarine, melted
  $\frac{3}{4}$ cup granulated sugar
  1 egg

Sour Cream Coconut Wafers *(Wheat Flour Institute)*

Candied Fruit Bars *(Wheat Flour Institute)*

Springerle *(Wheat Flour Institute)*

$\frac{2}{3}$ cup flour, sifted
$\frac{1}{4}$ teaspoon baking powder
$\frac{1}{4}$ teaspoon salt
$\frac{1}{4}$ cup milk
$\frac{1}{2}$ teaspoon vanilla
$\frac{1}{2}$ cup nuts, chopped

Combine melted chocolate, melted butter, and sugar; add egg and beat well. Sift together sifted flour, baking powder, and salt; add, alternately with milk and vanilla, to chocolate mixture. Fold chopped nuts into batter.

Spread batter over baked bottom layer. Bake in oven 350°F. 25 minutes. Cool baked brownies before frosting with a chocolate icing. Cut into squares.

Makes about 3 dozen squares.

CHOCOLATE HONEY BROWNIES

$\frac{2}{3}$ cup flour, sifted
$\frac{1}{2}$ teaspoon double-acting baking powder
$\frac{1}{4}$ teaspoon salt
$\frac{1}{3}$ cup butter or shortening
2 one-ounce squares unsweetened chocolate
2 eggs, well-beaten
$\frac{1}{2}$ cup granulated sugar
$\frac{1}{2}$ cup honey
$\frac{1}{2}$ cup walnuts, chopped
1 teaspoon vanilla

Measure sifted flour; add baking powder and salt, and sift again. Melt together butter and chocolate in top section of double boiler over hot water. Beat eggs in a large mixing bowl; gradually add sugar and beat thoroughly. Blend honey into egg mixture; add chocolate mixture and blend thoroughly. Add sifted dry ingredients; mix well. Blend walnuts and vanilla into the batter.

Pour batter into greased 8 x 8 x 2-inch pan. Bake in oven 350°F. 30 to 35 minutes. When baked, remove from oven; cool in pan. Cut into squares or rectangles.

Makes about 2 dozen brownies.

PECAN BROWNIES

$\frac{1}{3}$ cup shortening
1 cup granulated sugar
2 eggs
$\frac{1}{2}$ teaspoon vanilla
2 one-ounce squares unsweetened chocolate, melted
$\frac{3}{4}$ cup flour, sifted
$\frac{1}{2}$ teaspoon double-acting baking powder
$\frac{1}{2}$ teaspoon salt
1 cup pecans, chopped

Cream together shortening and sugar. Add eggs, vanilla, and melted chocolate to creamed mixture; blend thoroughly. Sift together sifted flour, baking powder, and salt; blend with pecans and stir into creamed mixture.

Pour batter into greased 7 x 11-inch pan. Bake in oven 350°F. 22 minutes. *Caution:* Do not overbake. Cut into squares before removing from pan. Dip in confectioners' sugar, if desired.

Makes 2 dozen brownies.

SPICY PECAN SQUARES

1 cup butter*
1 cup brown sugar, packed
1 teaspoon vanilla
1 egg, separated
2 cups flour, sifted
½ teaspoon salt
1 teaspoon cinnamon
1 cup pecans, chopped

Cream together butter and brown sugar; add vanilla and egg yolk, beating until light and fluffy. Sift together sifted flour, salt, and cinnamon; blend with half of the pecans and stir into creamed mixture.

Press batter into greased 19 x 15 x ½-inch pan. Brush top of batter with lightly beaten egg white and sprinkle remaining pecans on top. Bake in oven 350°F. 20 to 25 minutes. When done, remove from oven; cut, while still warm, into squares. Remove squares from pan; cool on a rack.

* If margarine is used in this recipe, omit salt.

Makes about 3 dozen squares.

PEANUT BARS

1 cup shortening
½ cup granulated sugar
1½ cups brown sugar
1 teaspoon water
1 teaspoon vanilla
2 egg yolks
2 cups flour, sifted

1 teaspoon baking soda
¼ teaspoon salt
1 cup semi-sweet chocolate chips
2 egg whites
½ cup brown sugar
1 cup Spanish salted peanuts

Cream together shortening, granulated sugar, and 1½ cups brown sugar. Stir water, vanilla, and egg yolks into creamed mixture. Sift together sifted flour, soda, and salt; blend into creamed mixture. The mixture should be dry like pie crust.

Press dough into 12 x 18-inch pan. Sprinkle chocolate chips over the mixture. Beat egg whites; gradually add ½ cup brown sugar, continue beating until stiff. Spread over chocolate chips. Cover the mixture with peanuts.

Bake in oven 350°F. 20 to 30 minutes, or until lightly browned. *Caution:* Do not overbake. Remove from oven when done; cool slightly before cutting into squares.

Makes about 2½ dozen bars.

PEANUT BRITTLE SQUARES

Bottom Layer:
¼ cup shortening
¼ cup butter or margarine
¼ cup granulated sugar
1 cup all-purpose flour, sifted
1 cup peanut brittle, finely crushed
Topping:
½ teaspoon salt
½ teaspoon baking powder
1 egg
1 cup granulated sugar

$\frac{1}{2}$ cup all-purpose flour, sifted
2 tablespoons milk
1 teaspoon vanilla
$\frac{1}{2}$ cup coconut, finely shredded
$\frac{1}{4}$ cup confectioners' sugar

To make bottom layer: blend shortening, butter, sugar, sifted flour, and peanut brittle. Mix the ingredients until a soft dough is formed. Evenly pat the dough into greased 8 x 12 x 2-inch baking pan. Bake in oven 350°F. 10 minutes; remove from oven and cover the bottom layer with the topping.

To make topping: sprinkle salt and baking powder over the egg; beat until foamy. Gradually add granulated sugar to the egg mixture; beat thoroughly. Add sifted flour, milk, vanilla, and shredded coconut; blend well. Spread smoothly over the partially baked bottom layer.

Return bottom layer and topping to oven 350°F. and bake 25 to 30 minutes until lightly browned. When baked, remove from oven and cool partially. Sprinkle partially cooled topping with confectioners' sugar; cut into bars.

Makes $1\frac{1}{4}$ dozen squares.

BROWN SUGAR SQUARES

1 egg
1 cup brown sugar
1 teaspoon vanilla
$\frac{1}{2}$ cup flour, sifted
$\frac{1}{4}$ teaspoon baking soda
$\frac{1}{4}$ teaspoon salt
1 cup walnuts, coarsely chopped

In a large mixing bowl stir together egg, brown sugar, and vanilla. Do not beat. Quickly stir sifted flour, soda, and salt into the egg mixture. Blend walnuts into the batter.

Spread batter in buttered 8-inch square pan. Bake in preheated oven 350°F. 18 to 20 minutes. This batter should still be soft in the center when removed from oven. When done, remove from oven, but leave in pan; cut into squares as needed. Keep pan covered with foil until all the squares have been consumed.

Makes about 1½ dozen squares.

ENGLISH TOFFEE SQUARES

¾ to 1 cup almonds, shelled
1 cup butter or margarine
1 cup brown sugar, firmly packed
1 egg
½ teaspoon vanilla
2 cups flour, sifted
½ teaspoon baking powder
½ teaspoon salt
1 six-ounce package semi-sweet chocolate pieces

Drop shelled almonds into boiling water; let stand about 5 minutes until the skins are loosened. Add cold water to cool the nuts. Push off the skins by pinching nuts between the thumb and finger. Put nuts on paper toweling to drain. While nuts are still moist, chop or shred them with a very sharp knife. Spread in a jelly roll pan or other shallow pan and heat in oven 350°F. until delicately browned. Allow 7 to 10 minutes for toasting. Check every 2 or 3 minutes to prevent scorching.

Cream butter in a large mixing bowl. When butter is soft, add brown sugar; beat until light and fluffy. Beat egg and vanilla into the creamed mixture. Sift together sifted flour, baking powder, and salt; stir into creamed mixture. When all ingredients are well blended, spread the thick batter into a buttered 15½ x 10½ x ½-inch jelly roll pan or a baking sheet with low sides. Bake in oven 350°F. 20 minutes.

While batter is baking, melt chocolate pieces in top of double boiler over boiling water. When done, remove from oven and immediately spread the top with the melted chocolate. Sprinkle the toasted almonds over the warm chocolate. While still warm, cut into squares or bars. Chill or freeze until serving time.

Makes about 6 dozen squares.

BUTTERSCOTCH BROWNIES

1 package butterscotch cake mix
¼ cup water
2 eggs, unbeaten
¼ cup butter or margarine, soft
½ cup walnuts, chopped
1 cup semi-sweet chocolate chips

Measure half of the cake mix into a large mixing bowl; add water, eggs, and butter. With a wooden spoon, thoroughly beat the mixture. Blend remaining cake mix into batter; mix well. Stir walnuts and chocolate chips into batter.

Evenly spread batter into a greased 13 x 9 x 2-inch pan. Bake in oven 375°F. 30 to 35 minutes. When done, remove brownies from oven; cool. Cut into bars.

Makes 3 dozen brownies.

CRUNCHY BUTTERSCOTCH FUDGE BARS

- $\frac{3}{4}$ cup flour, sifted
- $\frac{1}{2}$ teaspoon baking soda
- $\frac{1}{2}$ teaspoon salt
- 1 cup brown sugar, firmly packed
- $\frac{1}{2}$ cup shortening
- 1 egg
- $\frac{1}{2}$ teaspoon vanilla
- 1 cup cornflakes, crushed
- 1 cup quick-cooking rolled oats, uncooked
- $\frac{1}{2}$ cup nuts, chopped
- Butterscotch Filling

Sift together sifted flour, soda, and salt. Cream together brown sugar, shortening, egg, and vanilla; gradually blend sifted dry ingredients into creamed mixture. Stir cornflakes, rolled oats, and chopped nuts into the batter. Remove 1 firmly packed cup of the dough; set aside.

Press remaining dough into a greased 9-inch square pan. Prepare Butterscotch Filling. Evenly spread the prepared filling over the dough in the pan. Crumble and sprinkle reserved cup of dough over top of filling.

Bake in oven 350°F. 25 to 30 minutes. When done, remove from oven and cool. Cut into $1\frac{1}{2}$ x 1-inch bars.

Makes $4\frac{1}{2}$ dozen bars.

CHEWY BUTTERSCOTCH BARS

- $\frac{1}{2}$ cup butter
- $1\frac{1}{2}$ cups brown sugar, packed
- 2 eggs

1 teaspoon vanilla
1½ cups flour, sifted
2 teaspoons double-acting baking powder
1 cup nuts, chopped

Melt butter in a large saucepan; add brown sugar and bring to a boil over low heat, stirring constantly. Cool slightly. Drop eggs, 1 at a time, into the saucepan; mix well. Stir vanilla into the butter mixture. Sift together sifted flour and baking powder; add to butter mixture. Stir nuts into the batter.

Pour batter into greased 9 x 13 x 2-inch pan. Bake in oven 350°F. 30 minutes. Remove pan from oven; cool. Cut into bars.

Makes about 3 dozen bars.

BUTTERSCOTCH CONFECTION

½ cup butter
2 cups flour, sifted
4 eggs
¼ cup flour, sifted
½ teaspoon double-acting baking powder
1 teaspoon salt
2 cups brown sugar, packed
2 teaspoons vanilla
1½ cups shredded coconut
1 cup nuts, chopped

Cream butter until soft and fluffy. Add 2 cups sifted flour

to creamed butter; mix thoroughly. Spread into 9 x 13 x 2-inch pan. Bake in oven 350°F. 15 minutes.

Beat eggs. Sift together $\frac{1}{4}$ cup sifted flour, baking powder, salt, and brown sugar; beat into eggs. Add vanilla, coconut, and nuts to egg mixture; mix thoroughly. Pour mixture over baked crust. Bake mixture in oven 350°F. 30 minutes. Remove from oven and cool thoroughly before cutting into 2-inch squares.

Note: This recipe can be divided in half and baked in 8 x 8 x 2-inch pan.

Makes about 3 dozen squares.

BUTTERSCOTCH MERINGUE BARS

$\frac{1}{3}$ cup shortening
$\frac{1}{2}$ cup brown sugar
$1\frac{1}{2}$ cups flour, sifted
1 teaspoon baking powder
$\frac{1}{2}$ teaspoon salt
2 egg yolks
  Butterscotch Meringue Topping

Cream shortening; add brown sugar and mix thoroughly. Sift together sifted flour, baking powder, and salt; blend into creamed mixture. Add egg yolks to creamed mixture and mix until batter becomes crumbly.

Pack batter into a greased 7 x 11-inch pan. Top with Butterscotch Meringue Topping. Bake in oven 350°F. 20 minutes. Cool. Cut into squares.

Makes about 2 dozen bars.

ALLSPICE BARS

1 tablespoon flour, sifted
$\frac{1}{2}$ cup light brown sugar
$\frac{1}{2}$ cup butter
$\frac{3}{4}$ cup light brown sugar
2 eggs, well-beaten
1 cup flour, sifted
1 teaspoon allspice
$\frac{1}{2}$ teaspoon salt
1 teaspoon baking powder
1 cup shredded coconut
1 cup nuts, chopped

Mix the tablespoon of sifted flour and $\frac{1}{2}$ cup light brown sugar until blended thoroughly. Set aside. Cream together butter and $\frac{3}{4}$ cup light brown sugar. Add well-beaten eggs to creamed mixture; mix well. Sift together 1 cup sifted flour, allspice, salt, and baking powder; blend into creamed mixture. Stir coconut and nuts into batter; blend thoroughly.

Pour dough into greased pan. Top with flour and light brown sugar mixture that was set aside. If desired, sprinkle a few additional nuts over top of dough. Bake in oven 375° to 400°F. about 25 to 30 minutes. Remove from oven and cut while slightly warm.

Makes about 2 dozen bars.

BROWNIES

$\frac{1}{3}$ cup butter
2 one-ounce squares chocolate
1 cup granulated sugar

¼ teaspoon salt
2 eggs, beaten
¾ cup all-purpose flour, sifted
½ teaspoon baking powder
1 teaspoon vanilla
1 cup nuts, chopped

Melt butter and chocolate in a large saucepan over medium flame. Add sugar, salt, and beaten eggs to the melted chocolate mixture; mix well. Sift together sifted flour and baking powder; add to chocolate mixture. Blend vanilla and nuts into batter.

Pour batter into well-greased 8 x 8-inch pan. Bake in preheated oven 350°F. 30 to 35 minutes.

Makes 1½ dozen squares.

BETTER-THAN BROWNIES

2 one-ounce squares unsweetened chocolate
½ cup shortening
1 cup granulated sugar
3 eggs
1 teaspoon vanilla
¾ cup cake flour, sifted
1 teaspoon double-acting baking powder
½ teaspoon salt
1 cup nuts, chopped
　　De Luxe Chocolate Frosting

Melt chocolate and shortening in an ovenproof mixing bowl in the oven. Remove the heated mixture and let bowl cool slightly. Beat sugar into the chocolate mixture. Add the eggs, 1 at a time, to the chocolate mixture; beat well after each addition. Blend vanilla into the mixture. Sift together sifted flour, baking powder, and salt; add to chocolate mixture. Fold chopped nuts into the batter.

Pour into greased two-quart ovenproof utility dish. Bake in oven 325°F. about 30 minutes. When done, remove from oven; cool. When cooled, top with De Luxe Chocolate Frosting.

Makes about 2 dozen brownies.

WISCONSIN BROWNIES

$\frac{1}{2}$ cup butter
1 cup brown sugar
1 egg, well-beaten
$\frac{1}{2}$ cup flour, sifted
1 teaspoon baking powder
$\frac{1}{2}$ teaspoon salt
$\frac{1}{2}$ teaspoon vanilla
$\frac{1}{2}$ cup nuts

Melt butter in saucepan over low heat. Remove saucepan from heat. Stir brown sugar into melted butter; beat well. Add egg to butter mixture; mix thoroughly. Sift together sifted flour, baking powder, and salt; blend into butter mixture. Blend vanilla and nuts into butter mixture.

Spoon batter into greased, floured 8 x 8-inch pan. Bake in oven 350°F. 20 to 25 minutes. Cool slightly; cut into squares.

Makes about 1$\frac{1}{2}$ dozen brownies.

ROCKY ROAD BARS

10 marshmallows
$\frac{1}{2}$ cup walnuts, chopped
2 packages ($\frac{1}{2}$ pound) German's sweet chocolate

Line bottom of 9 x 4-inch loaf pan with waxed paper; let paper extend in 2-inch tabs at each end. Cut marshmallows into quarters and arrange in bottom of the pan. Fill spaces between marshmallow quarters with walnuts.

Heat chocolate in top of double boiler over boiling water until partly melted; remove from boiling water and stir rapidly until chocolate is entirely melted. Pour melted chocolate over carefully arranged marshmallows and walnuts. Use fork to distribute chocolate throughout. Tap pan several times to settle chocolate.

Let mixture stand in cool place to harden. Run a sharp knife around sides of pan and lift the hardened mixture out with the paper tabs. Cut into 1 x 2-inch bars.

Makes $1\frac{1}{2}$ dozen bars.

YUMMY FROSTED BARS

$\frac{1}{4}$ cup shortening
$\frac{1}{2}$ cup granulated sugar
1 egg
$\frac{1}{4}$ cup dark molasses
$\frac{1}{4}$ cup dark corn syrup
2 cups flour, sifted
$\frac{1}{4}$ teaspoon salt
$\frac{1}{4}$ teaspoon baking soda

1½ teaspoons baking powder
½ cup milk
1 teaspoon vanilla
1 cup nuts, chopped
1 cup raisins or dates, chopped
Confectioners' Sugar Frosting

Cream together shortening and sugar; add egg, molasses, and corn syrup blending thoroughly. Sift together sifted flour, salt, soda, and baking powder. Measure milk and vanilla; mix. Blend sifted dry ingredients, alternately with milk and vanilla, into creamed mixture. Stir chopped nuts and raisins into batter.

Pour batter into greased 9 x 13 x 2-inch baking pan. Bake in oven 350°F. 25 minutes. When done, remove from oven; cool. Spread with a thin coating of plain Confectioners' Sugar Frosting. Cut into 2-inch squares.

Makes 2 dozen bars.

HONEY STICKS

1½ cups flour, sifted
1 teaspoon baking powder
½ teaspoon salt
½ cup shortening
1 teaspoon vanilla
¼ cup granulated sugar
1 teaspoon cinnamon
1 egg
¾ cup honey
1 cup semi-sweet chocolate morsels

Sift together sifted flour, baking powder, and salt; set aside. Blend together in a large mixing bowl, shortening, vanilla, sugar, and cinnamon. Beat egg into shortening mixture; add honey, alternately with sifted dry ingredients. Mix well. Blend morsels into the batter.

Spread dough into greased 15 x 10 x 1-inch pan. Bake in oven 400°F. 12 minutes. When done, remove from oven; cool. Cut into 3 x 1-inch sticks.

Makes about 4 dozen sticks.

COBANA BARS

1¾ cups flour, sifted
2 teaspoons baking powder
½ teaspoon salt
2 tablespoons instant coffee
½ cup shortening
1 cup granulated sugar
1 teaspoon lemon extract
3 eggs, well-beaten
1 cup bananas, mashed
½ cup walnuts, chopped
 Confectioners' Sugar Frosting

Combine sifted flour, baking powder, salt, and instant coffee; sift together and set aside. Cream together shortening and sugar in a large mixing bowl. Add lemon extract and well-beaten eggs to creamed mixture; mix well. Add sifted dry ingredients, alternately with mashed bananas, to the creamed mixture. Stir walnuts into the batter.

Pour batter into greased 8 x 12 x 2-inch pan. Bake in

oven 350°F. for 30 minutes. When done, remove from oven; cool in pan. Cut into 4 x 1-inch bars. Frost with plain Confectioners' Sugar Frosting and sprinkle with additional chopped walnuts.

Makes 2 dozen bars.

INDIANS

2/3 cup flour, sifted
1/2 teaspoon baking powder
1/4 teaspoon salt
1/3 cup butter or shortening
2 one-ounce squares unsweetened chocolate
1 cup granulated sugar
3 eggs, well-beaten
1/2 cup walnuts or pecans, chopped
1/2 cup dates, chopped
1 teaspoon vanilla

Sift together sifted flour, baking powder, and salt. Melt butter and chocolate in top of double boiler over hot water. In a large mixing bowl, gradually add sugar to the well-beaten eggs; beat thoroughly. Blend chocolate mixture into egg mixture. Add sifted dry ingredients; mix well. Add walnuts, dates, and vanilla to batter; blend thoroughly.

Pour batter into 2 greased 8 x 8-inch pans. Bake in oven 350°F. 25 minutes. Cool in pan; cut into squares or rectangles. Can be frosted, if desired; or, decorated with whole nuts.

Makes about 2 dozen Indians.

ORIENTAL BRITTLE "COOKIES'

1 cup butter
2 tablespoons instant coffee
1 teaspoon salt
½ teaspoon almond extract
1 teaspoon vanilla
1 cup granulated sugar
2 cups flour, sifted
1 cup semi-sweet chocolate morsels, coarsely
  chopped
½ cup almonds, finely shredded

Blend together, in a large mixing bowl, butter, instant coffee, salt, almond extract, and vanilla; gradually beat sugar into butter mixture. Add sifted flour and morsels to butter mixture. Mix well.

Spread dough in a 15 x 10 x 1-inch ungreased pan. Sprinkle finely chopped almonds over top of dough. Bake in oven 375°F. 25 minutes. When done, remove from oven; cool, then break into irregular pieces.

Number of cookies will vary.

20. gems, macaroons, and miscellaneous cookies

COCONUT KISSES

2 egg whites
dash of salt
$\frac{1}{2}$ to 1 cup granulated sugar*
1$\frac{1}{3}$ cups flaked coconut
$\frac{3}{4}$ teaspoon vanilla

Beat together egg whites and salt until foamy throughout; add sugar, 2 tablespoons at a time, and beat after each addition until sugar is well blended. Continue beating until mixture stands in peaks. Fold coconut and vanilla into mixture.

Drop by teaspoonfuls onto greased baking sheet. Bake in oven 325°F. 20 minutes, or until delicately browned.

319

* For a moist, chewy cookie, use ½ cup sugar. For a moist, but less chewy cookie, increase sugar to ¾ cup. For a crisp cookie, use 1 cup sugar.

Makes 2½ dozen kisses.

COCONUT NUGGETS

  2⅔ cups flaked coconut
  1 cup sweetened condensed milk
  ⅛ teaspoon salt
  2 teaspoons vanilla
  ½ teaspoon almond extract

Combine coconut, milk, salt, vanilla, and almond extract in a mixing bowl; mix thoroughly.

Drop by teaspoonfuls, 1 inch apart, onto greased baking sheet. Bake in oven 350°F. 10 to 12 minutes, or until golden brown. After baking, immediately remove nuggets from baking sheet.

Makes about 3 dozen nuggets.

COCONUT MACAROONS

  1⅓ cups flaked coconut
  ½ cup granulated sugar
  1 egg, well-beaten
  1 teaspoon almond extract

Combine coconut and sugar; mix thoroughly. Blend egg

and almond extract into coconut mixture. Let mixture stand
5 minutes.

Drop by teaspoonfuls onto greased baking sheet. Bake in
oven 350°F. 15 minutes, or until golden brown. When done,
immediately remove macaroons from baking sheet to a
rack for cooling.

Makes about 1 dozen large macaroons.

CHEWY COCONUT MACAROONS

2⅔ cups flaked coconut
⅔ cup sweetened condensed milk
1 teaspoon vanilla

Combine coconut, milk, and vanilla; mix thoroughly.

Drop by teaspoonfuls, 1 inch apart, onto a greased baking
sheet. Bake in oven 350°F. 8 to 10 minutes. When done,
remove immediately from baking sheet.

Makes 2½ dozen macaroons.

COCONUT DATE KISSES

2 egg whites
dash of salt
¾ cup granulated sugar
1⅓ cups flaked coconut
1 cup dates, finely chopped
¾ teaspoon vanilla

Beat egg whites and salt until foamy throughout; add

sugar, 2 tablespoons at a time, and beat after each addition until sugar is blended. Continue beating until mixture stands in peaks. Fold coconut, dates, and vanilla into mixture.

Drop by teaspoonfuls onto greased baking sheet. Bake in oven 325°F. 20 minutes.

Makes 2½ dozen kisses.

DATE STICKS

1¼ cups cake flour, sifted
1¼ teaspoons baking powder
½ teaspoon salt
1 cup granulated sugar
2 eggs, well-beaten
1 tablespoon butter or shortening, melted
1 tablespoon water, hot
2 cups dates, finely chopped
½ cup nuts, chopped

Sift together sifted cake flour, baking powder, and salt. In a large mixing bowl, gradually blend sugar with eggs; beat thoroughly. To the egg mixture add butter and hot water; blend thoroughly. Stir dates and nuts into the egg mixture; beat well. Gradually add sifted dry ingredients into the egg mixture; mix thoroughly.

Turn batter into 2 greased 8 x 8 x 2-inch square pans; spread batter thin. Bake in oven 325°F. 30 to 35 minutes. When done, remove from oven; cool. Cut into ⅔ x 1-inch strips. Remove cut strips from pans.

Makes 4 dozen sticks.

STUFFED DATE BUTTER COOKIES

 1 pound soft dates, pitted
 48 walnut halves
 $\frac{1}{4}$ cup butter
 $\frac{3}{4}$ cup brown sugar, packed
 1 egg
 $\frac{1}{2}$ cup sour cream
 $\frac{1}{2}$ teaspoon vanilla
 $1\frac{1}{4}$ cups flour, sifted
 $\frac{1}{4}$ teaspoon double-acting baking powder
 $\frac{1}{2}$ teaspoon baking soda
 Golden Butter Frosting

Stuff each date with a walnut half; press to hold in shape. Cream together butter and brown sugar. Beat egg, sour cream, and vanilla into creamed mixture. Sift together sifted flour, baking powder, and soda; stir into creamed mixture. Blend dates into the batter.

Use a teaspoon to dip the batter-covered dates, 1 at a time, from the batter. Place the dates on a baking sheet. Bake in oven 400°F. 8 to 10 minutes. Cool.

Frost with Golden Butter Frosting.

Makes about 4 dozen cookies.

ORANGE DATE STICKS

 $1\frac{1}{4}$ cups cake flour, sifted
 $1\frac{1}{4}$ teaspoons baking powder
 $\frac{1}{2}$ teaspoon salt
 1 cup granulated sugar

2 eggs, well-beaten
1 tablespoon butter or shortening, melted
1 tablespoon water, hot
2 cups dates, finely chopped
½ cup nuts, chopped
2 teaspoons orange rind, grated
Lemon Cream Icing

Sift together sifted cake flour, baking powder, and salt. In a large mixing bowl, gradually blend sugar with eggs; beat thoroughly. Blend butter and hot water into the egg mixture; add dates and nuts. Beat thoroughly. Gradually add sifted dry ingredients into the egg mixture; mix well. Blend grated orange rind into the batter.

Pour batter into 2 greased 8 x 8 x 2-inch square pans. Bake in oven 325°F. 30 to 35 minutes. When done, remove from oven; cool. Spread with a thin Lemon Cream Icing. Cut into sticks.

Makes 4 dozen sticks.

ORANGE JUICE GEMS

¼ cup butter or margarine
½ cup granulated sugar
1 egg
1 tablespoon orange rind, grated
½ cup pecans, chopped
1¼ cups cake flour, sifted
¼ teaspoon salt
1 teaspoon baking powder
¼ teaspoon baking soda
½ cup orange juice
Orange Syrup

Cream butter; gradually add sugar and blend thoroughly after each addition. Beat egg into creamed mixture. Stir orange rind and pecans into creamed mixture. Sift together sifted flour, salt, baking powder, and soda. Blend sifted dry ingredients, alternately with orange juice, into creamed mixture; mix well, but quickly.

Fill greased 2-inch muffin pans two-thirds full of the dough. Bake in oven 375°F. 20 to 25 minutes. When done, remove from pan; cool. Insert fork into each gem and dip into Orange Syrup; strike fork against edge of pan to allow excess syrup to drain off. Place iced gems on rack to cool.

Makes about 2 dozen gems.

RAISIN BONANZAS

2 cups all-purpose flour, sifted
1 tablespoon granulated sugar
$3\frac{1}{2}$ teaspoons baking powder
1 teaspoon salt
$\frac{1}{3}$ cup shortening
$\frac{3}{4}$ cup milk
   Raisin Bonanza Filling
   melted butter or margarine
   granulated sugar

Sift together sifted flour, sugar, baking powder, and salt. Cut shortening into sifted dry ingredients until in small pieces; add milk and mix until dough is moderately stiff.

Roll dough on lightly floured board or waxed paper to an oblong shape about 12 x 9 inches. Dough will be about $\frac{1}{4}$-inch thick. Cut rolled dough into 12 squares (about 3 inches each).

Drop teaspoonful of Raisin Bonanza Filling into center of each square.

Bring the 4 corners of each square together and twist lightly at the top. Place each Raisin Bonanza into a greased, medium-sized muffin cup. Brush with melted butter and sprinkle with granulated sugar. Bake in oven 400°F. 15 to 20 minutes.

Makes 1 dozen bonanzas.

CHOCOLATE NUGGETS

$\frac{1}{3}$ cup cocoa
1 cup sweetened condensed milk
2$\frac{2}{3}$ cups flaked coconut
$\frac{1}{8}$ teaspoon salt
2 teaspoons vanilla

Combine cocoa and milk in a large mixing bowl; add coconut, salt, and vanilla. Mix well.

Drop by teaspoonfuls, 1 inch apart, onto greased baking sheet. Bake in oven 350°F. 10 to 12 minutes. When done, remove from oven. Transfer the nuggets from baking sheet to a rack at once; cool.

Makes about 3 dozen nuggets.

CHOCOLATE TEA PUFFS

1 cup flour, sifted
$\frac{1}{2}$ cup shortening
1 cup water, boiling

4 eggs, unbeaten
Cocoa Whipped Cream Filling
Chocolate Glaze

Sift flour once; measure. Place shortening in saucepan; add water and bring to boil. Stir sifted flour into steadily boiling water. Cook and stir constantly until mixture leaves sides of pan in a smooth, compact mass. Remove from heat.

Add eggs, 1 at a time, to the mixture; beat thoroughly after each addition. After all eggs are added, constantly beat the mixture until it appears satiny and breaks off when spoon is raised.

Drop dough by teaspoonfuls onto ungreased baking sheet. Bake in oven 450°F. 15 minutes, then decrease heat to 350°F. and bake 10 minutes longer.

When baked, remove from oven, and, with a sharp knife, slit one side of puffs; fill with Cocoa Whipped Cream Filling, Chocolate Walnut Cream Filling, or a favorite custard filling. Cover tops with Chocolate Glaze.

Makes about $2\frac{1}{2}$ dozen puffs.

CHOCOLATE CHIP MACAROONS

1 cup semi-sweet chocolate chips
2 cups flaked coconut
$\frac{1}{2}$ teaspoon baking powder
$\frac{1}{4}$ teaspoon salt
1 teaspoon vanilla*
$\frac{2}{3}$ cup sweetened condensed milk

Blend chocolate chips, coconut, baking powder, and salt. Add vanilla and condensed milk to the mixture; mix well.

Drop by teaspoonfuls onto lightly greased baking sheet. Bake in oven 325°F. 12 minutes, or until delicately browned.

* One teaspoon grated orange rind may be added with vanilla. Or, ½ teaspoon peppermint extract may be substituted for vanilla.

Makes 2 dozen macaroons.

BEACON HILL COOKIES

1 cup semi-sweet chocolate chips
2 egg whites
  dash of salt
½ cup granulated sugar
½ teaspoon vinegar
½ teaspoon vanilla
1 cup walnuts, chopped

Melt chocolate chips in top of double boiler over hot water. Beat the egg whites and salt until foamy. Gradually beat sugar into egg whites; continue beating until stiff peaks form. Beat vinegar and vanilla into the egg mixture. Fold melted chocolate and ¾ cup of walnuts into the batter.

Drop by teaspoonfuls onto greased baking sheet. Decorate with the remaining ¼ cup of chopped walnuts. Bake in preheated oven 350°F. 10 minutes. When baked, remove immediately from oven. Cool on rack.

Makes 3 dozen cookies.

SOUR CREAM CHOCOLATE COOKIES

$\frac{1}{2}$ cup shortening
1 cup brown sugar, firmly packed
1 egg, beaten
1 cup walnuts, chopped
2 one-ounce squares unsweetened chocolate,
  melted
2 cups cake flour, sifted
$\frac{1}{2}$ teaspoon salt
$\frac{1}{2}$ teaspoon baking soda
2 teaspoons baking powder
$\frac{1}{2}$ teaspoon cinnamon
1 cup dairy sour cream

Cream together shortening and brown sugar; add beaten egg and blend thoroughly. Add walnuts and melted chocolate to creamed mixture. Combine sifted flour, salt, soda, baking powder, and cinnamon; sift and add, alternately with sour cream, to the creamed mixture. Mix well.

Drop by teaspoonfuls onto greased baking sheet. Bake in oven 375°F. about 15 minutes.

Makes about 3 dozen cookies.

CEREAL MACAROONS

$\frac{1}{4}$ cup brown sugar
$\frac{1}{4}$ cup granulated sugar
3 tablespoons shortening, melted
1 egg, well-beaten

¼ cup nuts, chopped
¼ cup shredded coconut
2½ cups cornflakes, crushed

Measure sugars into large mixing bowl; blend. Add melted shortening to mixed sugars; blend thoroughly. Add well-beaten egg to sugar mixture; beat thoroughly. Add nuts, coconut, and cornflakes to sugar mixture; blend well.

Drop by tablespoonfuls onto greased baking sheet. Bake in preheated oven 350°F. 10 minutes.

Makes about 2 dozen cookies.

ALMOND MACAROONS

2⅔ cups flaked coconut
1 cup sweetened condensed milk
⅛ teaspoon salt
2 teaspoons vanilla
1 teaspoon almond extract
2 one-ounce squares unsweetened chocolate, melted
1 cup almonds, shredded

Combine coconut, milk, salt, vanilla, and almond extract in large mixing bowl; mix well. Melt chocolate in top of double boiler over hot water; stir shredded almonds into melted chocolate. Mix melted chocolate and shredded almonds into batter.

Drop by teaspoonfuls, 1 inch apart, onto greased baking sheet. Bake in oven 350°F. 10 to 12 minutes. After baking, immediately remove macaroons from baking sheet.

Makes about 3 dozen macaroons.

ALMOND STICKS

2 cups cake flour, sifted
$\frac{3}{4}$ cup butter
$\frac{1}{2}$ cup granulated sugar
1 egg yolk, unbeaten
$\frac{1}{2}$ teaspoon vanilla
   almonds, blanched and finely shredded
   confectioners' sugar

Sift flour once and measure. Cream butter; gradually add granulated sugar and cream until light and fluffy. Beat egg yolk into creamed mixture. Blend sifted flour, a small amount at a time, into creamed mixture; mix well after each addition of sifted flour. Mix vanilla into dough.

Chill dough several hours or overnight. Pinch off pieces of chilled dough; roll into sticks about $1\frac{1}{2}$ inches long and $\frac{1}{4}$ inch in diameter. Twirl the dough sticks through finely shredded almonds.

Place the prepared sticks on an ungreased baking sheet. Bake in oven 400°F. 3 to 4 minutes. Sprinkle baked sticks with confectioners' sugar.

Makes about 5 dozen sticks.

WALNUT SPICE KISSES

1 egg white
2 dashes salt
$\frac{1}{4}$ cup granulated sugar
1 teaspoon cinnamon
$\frac{1}{8}$ teaspoon nutmeg

$\frac{1}{8}$ teaspoon cloves
1 cup walnuts, finely chopped
walnut halves

Beat egg white and salt until stiff in a large mixing bowl. Blend together sugar, cinnamon, nutmeg, and cloves; gradually beat into egg white mixture. Fold finely chopped walnuts into mixture.

Drop dough by teaspoonfuls onto a well-greased baking sheet. Top each teaspoonful of dough with a walnut half. Bake in oven 250°F. 35 to 40 minutes.

Makes about 2 dozen kisses.

WALNUT SURPRISE COOKIES

1 cup brown sugar
1 egg
1 teaspoon vanilla
$\frac{1}{2}$ cup flour
$\frac{1}{4}$ teaspoon salt
$\frac{1}{4}$ teaspoon baking soda
1 cup walnuts, chopped

Mix together brown sugar, egg, and vanilla. Sift together flour, salt, and soda; blend, alternately with walnuts, into the sugar mixture. Mix thoroughly.

Spread batter in a greased 9-inch square pan. Bake in oven 350°F. 20 minutes. After baked, let stand in pan. Cut into squares while still warm. Ice, if desired.

Makes about 2$\frac{1}{2}$ dozen cookies.

TOFFEE BUTTER COOKIES

1 cup butter
1 cup brown sugar
1 egg
1 teaspoon vanilla
2 cups flour, sifted
8 plain milk chocolate bars*
$\frac{1}{4}$ cup nuts, chopped

Cream together butter and brown sugar; beat well. Add egg to creamed mixture; beat until light, then add vanilla. Add sifted flour to creamed mixture; blend thoroughly.

Spread batter in 11 x 17-inch jelly roll pan. Bake in oven 350°F. 15 to 20 minutes. Remove from oven when done and immediately place chocolate bars on top; spread and sprinkle with chopped nuts (pecans, English walnuts, or cashews).

* The small 5-cent size.

Makes about 7 dozen cookies.

LADYFINGER BUTTER TORTE

$\frac{1}{2}$ cup butter
$1\frac{1}{2}$ cups confectioners' sugar, sifted
1 egg
2 teaspoons lemon rind, grated
2 tablespoons lemon juice
21 ladyfingers, split lengthwise
$\frac{1}{4}$ cup almonds, blanched and shredded
2 tablespoons butter, melted

Cream $\frac{1}{2}$ cup butter; add sifted confectioners' sugar and cream well. Add egg, lemon rind, and lemon juice to creamed mixture; blend thoroughly.

Place a layer of split ladyfingers over the bottom of an 8-inch square pan. Spread $\frac{1}{3}$ of batter over layer of ladyfingers. Alternate layers, making 3 layers of ladyfingers and 3 of batter. Top with shredded almonds, which have been browned in 2 tablespoons melted butter.

Let chill several hours in refrigerator. Serve squares topped with whipped cream, if desired.

Makes about 1 dozen tortes.

PEPPERMINT NUGGETS

$2\frac{2}{3}$ cups flaked coconut
1 cup sweetened condensed milk
$\frac{1}{8}$ teaspoon salt
2 teaspoons vanilla
$\frac{1}{2}$ teaspoon almond extract
$\frac{2}{3}$ cup hard peppermint candy, crushed

Combine coconut, milk, salt, vanilla, almond extract, and peppermint candy. Mix well.

Drop dough by teaspoonfuls, 1 inch apart, onto greased baking sheet. Bake in oven 350°F. 10 to 12 minutes. When done, remove immediately from baking sheet.

Makes about 3 dozen nuggets.

ICE CREAM GRADUATION DESSERT

        1 quart vanilla ice cream
        2⅔ cups flaked coconut
        12 chocolate-coated graham crackers
           maraschino cherries
           chocolate chips
           jam

   Scoop ice cream into balls and place in a "ruff" of flaked coconut on a serving plate (a square one is especially pretty). Press a chocolate-coated graham cracker on top of each ball for "mortarboards." Cut a slice of maraschino cherry and place on one side of the scoop of ice cream to make a mouth. Use chocolate chips for eyes. In the center of each "mortarboard," place a bit of jam; fasten a short tassel of ribbon. Serve at once.

Makes 12 servings.

COOKIE LOLLIPOPS

        ½ cup butter or shortening, soft
        6 tablespoons granulated sugar
        6 tablespoons brown sugar
        1 egg
        ½ teaspoon vanilla
        1½ teaspoons water
        ¾ cup all-purpose flour, sifted
        ½ teaspoon baking soda
        ½ teaspoon salt

1 cup rolled oats, uncooked
½ cup seedless raisins
1 cup semi-sweet chocolate morsels
1½ dozen 5-inch wooden spoons
    food coloring

Cream together butter and sugars. Stir egg into creamed mixture; blend vanilla and water into egg mixture. Sift together sifted flour, soda, and salt; add rolled oats and blend thoroughly. Add flour mixture to creamed mixture; mix well. Blend raisins and semi-sweet chocolate morsels into the batter.

Color handles of 5-inch wooden spoons by dipping them into water which has been tinted with red, yellow, green, or blue food coloring. Place spoons, 4 inches apart, on a greased baking sheet.

Drop dough by tablespoonfuls onto bowls of wooden spoons. Bake in oven 375°F. approximately 12 minutes. When done, remove from oven. Using a wide spatula, transfer each lollipop while still warm from the baking sheet to a wire rack. Cool before serving.

Makes 1½ dozen lollipops.

DELECTABITES

½ cup butter
2 tablespoons granulated sugar
1 teaspoon vanilla
1 cup flour, sifted
1 cup walnuts, finely chopped

confectioners' sugar

Mix together butter, sugar, and vanilla. Gradually stir sifted flour and walnuts into butter mixture. Chill dough. When chilled, shape into marble-size balls and place on an ungreased baking sheet.

Bake in oven 350°F. 15 to 17 minutes. Do not brown. Gently roll the baked balls, while hot, in confectioners' sugar. Cool; gently roll the delectabites in confectioners' sugar again.

Makes about 4 dozen delectabites.

DONUT SPINNERS

4 donuts
$\frac{1}{4}$ cup butter, softened
2 tablespoons brown sugar
2 tablespoons walnuts, chopped
$\frac{3}{4}$ teaspoon maple extract

Slice donuts (makes 8 donut rings). Blend together butter, brown sugar, walnuts, and maple extract; spread on cut surface of the donuts. Place under broiler 1 or 2 minutes until bubbly and browned.

Pecan Variation: Add 2 tablespoons chopped pecans and 1 teaspoon cinnamon to butter and brown sugar.

Coconut Variation: Add 1 tablespoon tender, flaked coconut, and 1 teaspoon nutmeg to butter and brown sugar.

Makes 8 spinners.

MACAROON WAFERS

$\frac{1}{4}$ cup butter or shortening
$\frac{1}{2}$ cup brown sugar, firmly packed
$\frac{1}{2}$ cup granulated sugar
1 egg, well-beaten
$\frac{1}{2}$ cup walnuts, finely chopped
3 cups grape-nuts flakes
1 cup flaked coconut

Cream butter in a large mixing bowl. Gradually add sugars to creamed butter; continue to cream until light and fluffy. Add egg to creamed mixture; beat well. Blend walnuts, flakes, and coconut into mixture; stir until thoroughly mixed.

Drop by teaspoonfuls onto greased baking sheet. Bake in oven 350°F. 10 minutes, or until golden brown. When done, remove from oven and allow cookies to cool slightly while still on baking sheet. Place baking sheet over low heat and remove cookies with spatula.

Makes about $5\frac{1}{2}$ dozen cookies.

TUNISIAN GAZELLE HORNS

Flaky Pastry: (Make this first).
2 cups flour, sifted
1 teaspoon salt
$\frac{2}{3}$ cup butter
5 to 6 tablespoons cold water

Prepare the filling before rolling pastry $\frac{1}{8}$-inch thick and cutting diagonally in strips 2 inches wide. Be sure to cut again diagonally 2 inches apart in order to make diamond shaped.

Topping : (Measure and set aside).

> $\frac{1}{2}$ cup milk
> 1 egg, slightly beaten
> $\frac{1}{2}$ cup confectioners' sugar

Filling :

> 2 tablespoons butter
> $\frac{2}{3}$ cup walnuts, finely chopped
> $\frac{2}{3}$ cup granulated sugar
> 2 teaspoons orange rind, grated
> 2 teaspoons orange juice

Mix together (with a fork) butter, walnuts, granulated sugar, orange rind, and orange juice. When well mixed, place 1 teaspoon of the filling on each piece of diamond shaped pastry.

Moisten the edges of the filled pastry with the milk that was set aside; fold over the pastry edges and seal. Brush with the slightly beaten egg.

Place on baking sheet. Bake in preheated oven 425°F. 10 to 12 minutes. When baked, remove from oven, and, while still hot, roll each horn in confectioners' sugar.

Makes 3 dozen horns.

CHINESE ALMOND COOKIES

 $\frac{1}{2}$ cup butter
 $\frac{1}{2}$ cup granulated sugar
 2 eggs
 2 cups rice flour
 3 drops almond extract
 24 almonds, blanched

Cream together butter and sugar; add eggs and gradually work the rice flour into the mixture. Add almond extract; knead well. Chill dough for 30 minutes.

Form chilled dough into balls about 1 inch in diameter and flatten with palm of hand. Press 1 blanched almond into the center of each cookie. Bake in oven 350°F. about 25 minutes, or until straw-colored.

Makes about 2 dozen cookies.

21. quick cookies

QUICK COCONUT KISSES

2 cups shredded coconut
½ cup condensed milk
½ teaspoon salt

Mix together coconut, milk, and salt. Blend well.
Drop by teaspoonfuls onto greased baking sheet. Bake in preheated oven 350°F. 12 to 15 minutes.

Makes 1 dozen kisses.

COCONUT MERINGUE BARS

1 roll slice 'n bake cookies
1 egg white, unbeaten
3 tablespoons granulated sugar
¼ cup coconut

341

Slice cookies about $\frac{1}{4}$-inch thick; arrange in bottom of greased 9 x 9 x 2-inch pan. Bake in oven 375°F. 15 to 20 minutes.

While the cookies are baking, beat egg white until soft peaks form. Gradually add sugar to the beaten egg white; beat well after each addition. After all sugar has been added, continue to beat until the meringue stands in peaks; fold coconut into the meringue.

When cookies are done, remove from oven and, while still hot, spread with the meringue. Place meringue-covered cookies 4 to 5 inches below the broiling unit. Broil about 3 minutes, or until lightly browned. Cool and cut into bars. Dip knife in water as necessary.

Makes about 2 dozen bars.

DATE-FILLED BARS

1 roll slice 'n bake cookies
1 cup dates, finely chopped
1 teaspoon lemon rind, grated
1 teaspoon lemon juice
$\frac{1}{4}$ cup brown sugar, firmly packed
$\frac{1}{4}$ cup confectioners' sugar

Slice cookies about $\frac{1}{8}$-inch thick. Arrange half of the cookies in bottom of greased 8 x 8 x 2-inch pan. Combine dates, lemon rind, lemon juice, and brown sugar; mix well. Spoon the date mixture over cookies in the pan; top with remaining cookies.

Bake in oven 375°F. 20 to 25 minutes. When done, remove from oven; cool slightly before cutting into bars. Sprinkle with confectioners' sugar.

Makes about $1\frac{1}{2}$ dozen bars.

INSTANT CHOCOLATE FROSTED COOKIES

Bake icebox cookies as directed on package. Remove from oven when done and top each cookie with 4 or 5 semi-sweet chocolate pieces. When chocolate softens, spread to frost. Garnish with shredded coconut, peanuts, or other nuts.

For Chocolate Filled Cookies, slice cookies very thin; bake. Frost half of baked cookies; top with remaining cookies, sandwich-style.

Makes about 3 dozen cookies.

QUICK ROCKY ROAD BARS

Slice 1 roll of slice 'n bake cookies $\frac{1}{4}$-inch thick; arrange in an ungreased 8- or 9-inch square pan. Overlap the cookie slices as necessary, so cookies will bake together. Bake in oven 375°F. 15 to 20 minutes, or until golden brown.

While cookies are baking, prepare 1 package Creamy Fudge Frosting Mix according to package directions. Sprinkle 1 cup miniature marshmallows over hot baked cookies. Spread prepared frosting over melting marshmallows. Cool completely; cut into bars.

Makes about $1\frac{1}{2}$ dozen bars.

INSTANT WALNUT COOKIES

$\frac{1}{2}$ cup brown sugar
$\frac{1}{2}$ cup walnuts, chopped
$\frac{1}{4}$ cup butter
24 graham crackers

Place brown sugar, walnuts, and butter into top of the double boiler over hot water; stir constantly until ingredients melt. Place the graham crackers close together on a baking sheet.

Drop 1 small teaspoonful of the melted mixture into the center of each cracker and spread slightly. Bake in preheated oven 350°F. about 8 minutes. Remove from oven and cut crackers in halves while hot.

Makes 4 dozen cookies.

QUICK CANDY CANES

Slice 1 roll of sugar or butterscotch nut slice 'n bake cookies ⅛-inch thick. Roll each cookie slice on a pastry cloth or board to about the thickness of a pencil. Shape each into a cane on an ungreased baking sheet.

Bake in oven 375°F. 7 to 10 minutes. Cool 1 minute before removing to a rack. Cool. Frost cooled cookies with white icing, then stripe with red icing.

Makes about 3 dozen canes.

CANDY FILLED COOKIES

Slice icebox cookies very thin. Place half of slices on an ungreased baking sheet. Top each with a chocolate candy wafer (peppermint, rum, or other flavor) and cover with another slice. Bake in oven 375°F. 10 to 12 minutes. Cool 1 minute before removing from baking sheet.

Makes about 3 dozen cookies.

YUMMY GUMDROP SQUARES

1 roll slice 'n bake cookies
1 cup gumdrops, small and brightly colored
¼ cup confectioners' sugar

Line 8 x 8 x 2-inch pan with aluminum foil; leave edges long. Slice the roll of slice 'n bake cookies ⅛-inch thick and arrange about half of the slices in the foil-lined pan. Press the cookies until the bottom of the pan is covered completely. Sprinkle gumdrops over the dough-covered pan; press into the dough. Cover the gumdrops with the remaining cookie slices.

Bake in oven 375°F. 14 to 16 minutes. Remove from oven and sprinkle lightly with confectioners' sugar. Cool about 15 minutes before lifting foil and baked cookies from the pan; peel off foil. Cut into squares. Dip knife in water as necessary.

Makes about 1½ dozen squares.

PEPPERMINT BARS

Slice 1 roll of slice 'n bake cookies into ¼-inch slices; arrange in an ungreased 8- or 9-inch square pan. Overlap the slices as necessary for the cookies to bake together. Bake in oven 375°F. 15 to 20 minutes, or until golden brown. Sprinkle immediately with ¼ cup finely crushed peppermint candy. Cool completely; cut into bars.

Makes about 1½ dozen bars.

MINT-TOPPED COOKIES

Slice icebox cookies as directed on package; place on an ungreased baking sheet. Bake in oven 375°F. 7 to 8 minutes until very delicately browned. Remove from oven; top each cookie with pastel mint pattie. Bake 1 to 2 minutes longer. Cool 1 minute before removing from baking sheet.

For Mint Pattie Sandwiches, slice cookies very thin; bake 7 to 8 minutes. Top half of cookies with patties. Bake all cookies 1 to 2 minutes longer. Put cookies together sandwich-style.

Makes about 3 dozen cookies.

ICE CREAM COOKIE SANDWICHES

Thinly slice refrigerated icebox cookies or sugar cookies. Place 4 cookies together in a square on an ungreased baking sheet with sides touching. Press edges together to cover space in center, making 1 large cookie.

Bake in oven 375°F. 7 to 9 minutes until lightly browned. Cool 1 minute before removing to a cooling rack. Cool completely.

Slice brick of ice cream into $\frac{1}{2}$-inch slices. Place each slice between 2 cooled cookies. Freeze for at least 1 hour. Serve as sandwich, or as dessert with fudge or other topping. Garnish with nuts, coconut, or maraschino cherries.

LITTLE ANGEL COOKIES

Slice 1 roll of crunchy peanut or butterscotch nut slice 'n bake cookies into $\frac{1}{8}$-inch slices. It will take $1\frac{1}{4}$ slices for each angel. Cut a narrow strip from 2 sides of a cookie slice, leaving a triangular-shaped piece to form the body. Divide 1 slice into 4 pieces, using each for an angel's head, after rolling it into a ball.

Arrange cut slices on an ungreased baking sheet in the shape of an angel. Bake in oven 375°F. 7 to 10 minutes. When done, remove from baking sheet to a rack; cool. Decorate cooled angels with white icing, confectioners' sugar, or small candies.

Makes about 3 dozen cookies.

CHRISTMAS ANGELS

Slice 1 roll of sugar or toasted coconut slice 'n bake cookies into $\frac{1}{8}$-inch slices. For each angel, cut a narrow strip from 2 sides of a cookie slice, leaving a triangular-shaped piece to form the body. Place on an ungreased baking sheet. Use cut pieces at sides for wings. Make a small ball from $\frac{1}{4}$ of another slice for head.

Bake in oven 375°F. 7 to 10 minutes. When done, remove from oven and cool 1 minute on baking sheet before transferring to a rack. Cool. Decorate with white icing, confectioners' sugar, or small candies.

Makes about 3 dozen angels.

COOKIE CHRISTMAS TREES

Slice 1 roll of butterscotch nut or crunchy peanut slice 'n bake cookies into $\frac{1}{8}$-inch thick slices. Arrange 6 slices in tree shape and a half slice for the trunk pressing together slightly. Sprinkle with colored sugar or cake decorations before baking.*

Bake in oven 375°F. 7 to 12 minutes. Cool 1 minute; loosen with spatula and cool completely on baking sheet.

* Or, frost cooled baked cookies with icing and decorate.

Makes $\frac{1}{2}$ dozen cookies.

MINIATURE COOKIE WREATHS

Slice 1 roll of sugar or butterscotch nut slice 'n bake cookies into $\frac{1}{8}$-inch thick slices. It takes 1 slice for each wreath. Roll each slice on pastry cloth or board to about the thickness of a pencil; twirl through green colored granulated sugar.

Shape dough into a wreath on an ungreased baking sheet; overlap the ends slightly. Bake in oven 375°F. 7 to 10 minutes. Make bow with red cinnamon candies, if desired; or, decorate cooled wreaths with colored icing.

Makes about $3\frac{1}{2}$ dozen wreaths.

SNOWBALLS

1 angel food cake
Seven Minute frosting
$1\frac{1}{3}$ cups flaked coconut

With a fork or fingers, carefully separate angel food cake into balls about 2 inches in diameter. Dip each ball into the frosting; roll in coconut. The coconut can be tinted in various colors.

Makes 1 dozen snowballs.

FROSTY SNOWMAN COOKIES

Slice 1 roll of sugar or toasted coconut slice 'n bake cookies $\frac{1}{8}$-inch thick. It will take 10 slices for each snowman. Cut 2 slices in half for the arms and feet. Cut a square out of the center of another slice for the hat.

Arrange cookie slices on an ungreased baking sheet in the shape of a snowman. Bake in oven 375°F. 8 to 11 minutes. Spread cooled snowmen cookies with creamy vanilla frosting. Sprinkle with coconut. Use raisins or candies for buttons and faces.

Makes 4 snowmen.

COOKIE CUT-OUTS

Let 1 roll of sugar or toasted coconut slice 'n bake cookies stand at room temperature about 1 hour or until softened. Roll dough on floured surface to $\frac{1}{8}$-inch thickness. Cut into desired shapes using assorted cookie cutters.

Place the cut-outs on an ungreased baking sheet. Bake in oven 375°F. 7 to 10 minutes. Cool 1 minute before removing from baking sheets. Ice and decorate, if desired.

Makes about 3 dozen cookies.

QUICK COOKIE CUT-OUTS

Let 1 roll of slice 'n bake cookies (any flavor from the grocer's dairy case) stand at room temperature about 1 hour, or until softened. Roll dough on floured surface to $\frac{1}{8}$-inch thickness. Cut into fancy designs and traditional shapes, using a knife free-hand or using holiday cutters.

To make gay cookie bells, use a bell-shaped cutter and cluster 2 or 3 together on ungreased baking sheet; overlap the cookies slightly. Cut small dough triangles with a knife and arrange at top of bells for bow effect.

Bake any shape of cut-out cookies in oven 375°F. 7 to 10 minutes. Let cool 1 minute before removing to cooling rack. Decorate cooled cookies with icing and colored granulated sugar or tiny cake decorations.

The bell clusters can be decorated in all white and served at bridal showers.

Makes about 3 dozen cookies.

MOLDED COOKIES

Let roll of icebox cookies stand at room temperature about 1 hour until softened. Break off pieces of dough and mold into 1-inch balls. Place balls of dough on an ungreased baking sheet. Bake in oven 375°F. 10 to 13 minutes, or until golden brown. Cool 1 minute before removing baked cookies from baking sheet.

Makes about 2½ dozen cookies.

QUICK PRESS COOKIES

Let 1 roll of icebox cookies stand at room temperature until very soft. This should take about 1 hour. Press dough through cookie press onto a greased baking sheet. Larger press plates are advisable for nut-filled cookie dough. Chill the sheet of cookies several minutes before baking. Bake

Original Toll House Cookies (in jar), Chocolate Coconut Chews (on board), Cookie Lollipops, and Holiday Treats *(The Nestlé Co., Inc.)*

Merry Christmas Pattern Cookies *(Wheat Flour Institute)*

in oven 375°F. 7 to 10 minutes. When done, cool 1 minute before removing from baking sheet.

Makes about 3 dozen cookies.

ICEBOX COOKIE NUGGETS

Let 1 roll of icebox cookie dough stand at room temperature about 1 hour, or until softened. Break off pieces of dough and mold into $\frac{1}{2}$-inch balls. Place the balls of dough on an ungreased baking sheet. Bake in oven 375°F. 10 to 13 minutes, or until golden brown. Cool 1 minute before removing from baking sheets.

Makes about 2$\frac{1}{2}$ dozen cookies.

22. frostings and fillings

CONFECTIONERS' SUGAR FROSTING

$\frac{1}{4}$ cup butter or margarine
3 cups confectioners' sugar, sifted
2 tablespoons cream
1$\frac{1}{2}$ teaspoons vanilla

Place butter in top pan of double boiler; melt over boiling water. Blend sifted confectioners' sugar, cream, and vanilla; add to melted butter and mix well. Remove pan of frosting from double boiler; beat until of desired consistency.

Use to frost Ginger Stars, Eskimo Cookies, Thumbprint Cookies, Candied Fruit Bars, Yummy Frosted Bars, Cobana Bars, and other cookies and bars.

TINTED COCONUT

1 teaspoon milk or water
few drops food coloring
$3\frac{1}{2}$ ounces flaked coconut

Place milk or water into a bowl; add food coloring and mix well. Add coconut to the colored liquid and toss with a fork until coconut is tinted throughout.

If desired, instead of mixing the ingredients in a bowl, the coconut can be measured into a glass jar. Do not fill the jar more than half full of coconut. Dilute the food coloring with the liquid and sprinkle over the coconut. Cover the jar and shake vigorously until the coloring is distributed evenly.

MINT-GREEN COCONUT

$\frac{1}{2}$ teaspoon water
3 drops green food coloring
2 or 3 drops peppermint extract
$3\frac{1}{2}$ ounces flaked coconut

Dilute food coloring in the water. Sprinkle diluted food coloring and peppermint extract over coconut, which has been placed in a mixing bowl or glass jar. Tint coconut until coloring and flavoring are distributed evenly.

TOASTED COCONUT TOPPING

$\frac{3}{4}$ cup coconut
1 tablespoon granulated sugar
2 teaspoons butter, melted

Blend coconut, sugar, and melted butter. Mix thoroughly. This can be used to cover Toasted Coconut Brownies before baking.

LEMON ICING

$2\frac{1}{2}$ cups confectioners' sugar, sifted
1 tablespoon butter, soft
3 tablespoons bottled lemon juice
red or green food coloring

Blend together sifted confectioners' sugar, butter, and bottled lemon juice; mix until smooth. Add desired food coloring; blend. Spread icing on top of cooled Lemony Bon Bons or other cookies.

LEMON CREAM ICING

2 cups confectioners' sugar, sifted
2 teaspoons lemon juice
$1\frac{3}{4}$ teaspoons lemon rind, grated
3 tablespoons cream

Combine confectioners' sugar, lemon juice, grated lemon rind, and cream in a bowl; mix well. Add more cream, as necessary, to make icing of the right spreading consistency.

This recipe is perfect for Orange Date Sticks.

ORNAMENTAL ICING

1 cup confectioners' sugar, sifted
$\frac{1}{4}$ teaspoon salt
$\frac{1}{2}$ teaspoon vanilla
    cream
    red or green food coloring

Blend confectioners' sugar, salt, vanilla, and enough cream to make an icing that will hold its shape but can be pressed through a pastry tube. Add red or green food coloring, if desired.

Use to frost Christmas Lemon Cookies and other cookies.

ORANGE ICING

$1\frac{1}{2}$ cups confectioners' sugar, sifted
$2\frac{1}{2}$ tablespoons orange juice

Combine confectioners' sugar and orange juice. Blend to spreading consistency. Use to ice Orange Nut Bars and other bars.

ORANGE FROSTING FOR BARS

1 tablespoon margarine
1 cup confectioners' sugar, sifted
$\frac{1}{2}$ teaspoon orange rind, grated
1 tablespoon and 1 teaspoon orange juice

Cream margarine in mixing bowl until soft. Blend confectioners' sugar, orange rind, and orange juice into creamed margarine; beat until smooth and creamy.

Spread this frosting on baked Orange Date Skillet Bars or other freshly baked bars and cookies.

ORANGE FROSTING

    2 tablespoons butter
    $\frac{1}{4}$ cup frozen orange juice, defrosted
    $\frac{2}{3}$ cup condensed milk
    $3\frac{1}{2}$ cups confectioners' sugar, sifted
    3 tablespoons orange rind, grated

Cream butter. Blend together orange juice and milk. Mix $\frac{1}{4}$ cup of the liquid mixture into the creamed butter. Add sifted confectioners' sugar to the creamed mixture; blend thoroughly and add the remaining liquid mixture a little at a time. When all the liquid mixture has been blended into creamed mixture, beat the mixture about 5 minutes. Stir orange rind into the well-beaten mixture.

This frosting can be used to ice mince meat cookies or other freshly baked cookies.

HOLIDAY ORANGE ICING

    2 tablespoons butter or margarine
    1 tablespoon orange rind, grated
    $1\frac{1}{4}$ cups confectioners' sugar, sifted
    2 tablespoons orange juice

Cream together butter and orange rind. Add sifted confectioners' sugar and orange juice to creamed mixture; mix until smooth.

Spread icing over baked Holiday Florida Orange Bars before cutting into bars. This icing can be used on other freshly baked bars and cookies.

ORANGE SYRUP

$\frac{1}{2}$ cup orange juice
1 cup granulated sugar
1 tablespoon orange rind, grated

Combine orange juice, sugar, and rind in small saucepan. Stir ingredients over low heat until sugar dissolves; increase heat and boil rapidly for 5 minutes or until 230°F. is reached on candy thermometer.

Use to ice Orange Juice Gems.

BUTTER FROSTING

$\frac{1}{4}$ cup butter
2 cups confectioners' sugar, sifted
$\frac{1}{2}$ teaspoon vanilla
  few grains salt
2 to 3 tablespoons milk or cream

Cream butter and 1 cup of confectioners' sugar. Add vanilla, salt, and milk to creamed mixture; mix thoroughly. Blend the other cup confectioners' sugar into the mixture.

Use to frost Pecan Fingers, Eskimo Cookies, Spicy Coconut Bars, and other cookies.

This recipe makes $1\frac{1}{8}$ cups frosting.

BROWN BUTTER FROSTING

6 tablespoons butter
3 cups confectioners' sugar, sifted
1 teaspoon vanilla
¼ cup hot water

Brown butter in saucepan over low heat. Add sifted confectioners' sugar, vanilla, and hot water to browned butter; beat well.

Ice Butterscotch Dessert Cookies or other cookies with this frosting.

CREAMY BROWNED BUTTER ICING

3 tablespoons butter
1½ cups confectioners' sugar, sifted
3 tablespoons half and half

Heat butter until it is a light brown color. Let butter cool slightly. Stir sifted confectioners' sugar and half and half into cooled butter. Beat until smooth.

Use to frost Frosted Christmas Jewels, other bars and cookies.

GOLDEN BUTTER FROSTING

½ cup butter
3 cups confectioners' sugar, sifted
1 teaspoon vanilla
  hot water

Measure butter into a heavy saucepan; bring to a boil and let boil until lightly browned. This should take approximately 6 minutes. *Caution:* Do not burn. Stir sifted confectioners' sugar and vanilla into the browned butter. Blend hot water into the butter mixture until frosting is of a spreading consistency. When spreading the frosting, if it begins to spread unevenly, add more hot water.

Ice Stuffed Date Butter Cookies with this frosting.

BUTTERSCOTCH MERINGUE TOPPING

2 egg whites
1 cup brown sugar
1 cup nuts, chopped
1 teaspoon vanilla

Beat egg whites stiff. Gradually add brown sugar to beaten egg whites; beat thoroughly. Blend nuts and vanilla into egg white mixture. Spread mixture on top of Butterscotch Meringue Bars before baking the bars in an oven 350°F. 20 minutes. When the bars are done and cooled, cut into squares.

DE LUXE CHOCOLATE FROSTING

2 ounces sweet chocolate
1 one-ounce square unsweetened chocolate
3 tablespoons butter or margarine
$3\frac{1}{4}$ cups confectioners' sugar
5 tablespoons hot milk
$\frac{1}{2}$ teaspoon vanilla

Melt together sweet chocolate, unsweetened chocolate, and butter in a saucepan over low heat. Dissolve sugar in hot milk; pour into chocolate mixture and add vanilla. Beat mixture until thick enough to spread.

Use as an icing on cookies or Better-Than Brownies and other bars.

QUICK CHOCOLATE FROSTING

    2 one-ounce squares unsweetened chocolate
   14 or 15 ounces sweetened condensed milk
    1 tablespoon water
      dash of salt
    $\frac{1}{2}$ teaspoon vanilla

Melt chocolate in top of double boiler over hot water. Gradually blend milk into chocolate; mix well. Add water and salt to the chocolate mixture; blend thoroughly. Cook mixture 5 minutes over rapidly boiling water; stir constantly. Remove pan from heat; add vanilla. Cool.

This recipe can be used as a frosting for Chocolate Nut Squares.

CHOCOLATE FROSTING

    1 one-ounce square chocolate
    1 egg yolk, beaten
    1 tablespoon cream
      confectioners' sugar

Melt chocolate in saucepan over a low flame. Blend beaten

egg yolk and cream into melted chocolate. Add confectioners' sugar to attain spreading consistency.

Use to ice Frosted Chocolate Drop Cookies or other freshly baked cookies.

CHOCOLATE BUTTER FROSTING

1 one-ounce square baking chocolate
¼ cup butter
2 cups confectioners' sugar, sifted
½ teaspoon vanilla
few grains salt
2 to 3 tablespoons milk or cream

Melt chocolate in top of double boiler; set aside to cool. Cream together butter and 1 cup confectioners' sugar. Add vanilla, salt, and milk to creamed mixture; mix thoroughly. Blend remaining confectioners' sugar into the mixture. Add cooled chocolate to the frosting; mix thoroughly.

Use to frost Pecan Fingers and other cookies.

This recipe makes 1⅛ cups frosting.

CHOCOLATE CREAM FROSTING

½ cup evaporated milk
dash salt
1 cup semi-sweet chocolate morsels
1 teaspoon vanilla
1 cup confectioners' sugar, sifted

Combine evaporated milk and salt in a saucepan; place

over moderate heat and stir constantly until mixture *just* comes to boiling point. Remove from heat. Add semi-sweet chocolate morsels and vanilla to hot evaporated milk mixture; stir until smooth. Cool approximately 5 minutes. Gradually blend sifted confectioners' sugar into the chocolate mixture.

Use to frost Frosty Chocolate Squares and other bars.

CHOCOLATE GLAZE

    2 tablespoons butter
    2 one-ounce squares unsweetened chocolate
    3 tablespoons milk, hot
    1 cup confectioners' sugar
      dash salt

Place butter and chocolate in top of double boiler; heat over boiling water until melted. In a mixing bowl, combine hot milk, confectioners' sugar, and salt; add melted chocolate mixture and gradually blend.

While mixture is still warm, pour from a teaspoon as a glaze for Chocolate Tea Puffs.

JAVA COCOA ICING

    2 cups confectioners' sugar
    1½ tablespoons cocoa
    ¾ cup butter or margarine
    3 tablespoons cold coffee
    1 teaspoon vanilla

Mix together confectioners' sugar and cocoa; add butter and mix until smooth. Add coffee and vanilla to sugar mixture; blend thoroughly.

Use as frosting for Buttermilk Drop Cookies or other freshly baked cookies.

WALNUT KRISPIES' DECORATION

To decorate Walnut Krispies use colored sugar crystals and candies. Make tiny flowers, letters, faces, or whatever happens to be in season—such as Fourth of July or Halloween. If it is for a birthday party, shape the decorations into the age of the person being honored.

Chocolate shot and tiny triangles of contrasting dough also make delightful and tasty decorations for Walnut Krispies.

No matter what type of decorations are used on these cookies, be sure to sprinkle a few walnut halves or pieces over each cookie. These add to the flavor and looks of each cookie.

SEVEN MINUTE FROSTING

2 egg whites, unbeaten
$1\frac{1}{2}$ cups granulated sugar
dash of salt
5 tablespoons water
$1\frac{1}{2}$ teaspoons light corn syrup
1 teaspoon vanilla

Combine egg whites, sugar, salt, water, and corn syrup in top of double boiler; mix thoroughly.

Place pan of mixture over rapidly boiling water; beat constantly with rotary egg beater (or at high speed of electric mixer), and cook 7 minutes, or until frosting stands in peaks.

Remove from boiling water; add vanilla and beat until thick enough to spread.

For half recipe, use half of the ingredients and reduce cooking time to about 4 minutes.

ANGEL FLUFF FROSTING

4 cups confectioners' sugar, sifted
4 tablespoons butter, melted
2 egg whites
1 to 2 tablespoons light cream

Combine about 1 cup confectioners' sugar with the butter; mix thoroughly. Beat egg whites, 1 at a time, into butter mixture; mix well after each addition. Gradually add other 3 cups of confectioners' sugar to the butter mixture; cream until the desired consistency is attained.

Dip cookies first into the frosting, then into Tinted Coconut. Place the coconut-frosted cookies onto a cake rack and let set from 30 minutes to 1 hour.

This recipe makes 2 cups of frosting. The frosting can be stored in the refrigerator and used as needed. When needed, add cream to return the frosting to the desired consistency.

DECORATING FROSTING

4½ cups confectioners' sugar
½ cup butter or margarine, soft
¼ cup light cream or milk
1 teaspoon vanilla
¼ teaspoon wintergreen extract

Blend about 2 cups confectioners' sugar into butter or margarine. Add cream, vanilla, and wintergreen extract to the sugar mixture; mix thoroughly. Add enough of the remaining confectioners' sugar to make the frosting of the desired consistency. Spread on cookies or use for decorating.

For fancy cookies, use colored sugar, silver dragees, multicolored candies, chocolate shots, red cinnamon candies, currants, or raisins.

Use as frosting on Merry Christmas Pattern Cookies or other freshly baked cookies. This recipe makes about 2½ cups frosting.

HE-MAN FROSTING

1 tablespoon margarine
1½ one-ounce squares unsweetened chocolate
1½ cups confectioners' sugar, sifted
2 tablespoons milk

Melt margarine and chocolate together in a saucepan over low heat. Blend sifted confectioners' sugar and milk together in a small mixing bowl; add hot chocolate mixture and mix well. Let mixture stand a few minutes; stir occasionally until the mixture becomes of the right consistency to spread.

Use this frosting to ice Double Chocolate He-Man Cookies or other plain chocolate cookies.

VALENTINE DECORATION

There are 2 methods of decorating Valentine Cookies. Either method results in lovely, delicious cookies.

One method is to fill a pastry tube with white or colored confectioners' sugar Ornamental Icing. Decorate edges of the heart-shaped cookies with this mixture.

The other method is to brush a heart outline on each cookie with white corn syrup. On the syrup place small cinnamon candies.

APRICOT FILLING

1 pound dried apricots
1 cup granulated sugar
$\frac{1}{2}$ cup water
1 tablespoon lemon juice

Rinse, drain, and cook dried apricots. When apricots are cooked, combine with sugar, water, and lemon juice in a saucepan. Stir and cook all the ingredients until mixture becomes thick. Beat to blend. Cool mixture before spreading on dough.

Use this recipe as a filling for Fruit Fills.

APRICOT-NUT FILLING

$\frac{1}{3}$ cup flour, sifted
$\frac{1}{2}$ teaspoon baking powder
$\frac{1}{4}$ teaspoon salt
1 cup brown sugar, packed
2 eggs
$\frac{1}{2}$ teaspoon vanilla
$\frac{1}{2}$ cup nuts, chopped
$\frac{1}{2}$ cup apricots, cooked and chopped

Sift together sifted flour, baking powder, and salt. Gradually beat brown sugar into a bowl containing eggs. Add sifted dry ingredients to sugar mixture; mix well. Blend vanilla, nuts, and apricots into sugar mixture; beat until smooth.

Spread mixture over baked Luscious Apricot Bar layers. Bake in oven 350°F. 30 minutes, or until done. Cool in pan. When cool, cut into bars; roll in confectioners' sugar.

HONEY COCONUT FILLING

$\frac{1}{2}$ cup granulated sugar
$\frac{1}{3}$ cup honey
$\frac{1}{2}$ cup water
$\frac{1}{4}$ teaspoon salt
3 cups coconut
$\frac{1}{2}$ teaspoon vanilla
2 teaspoons butter

Measure sugar, honey, water, salt, and coconut into a saucepan; blend thoroughly. Place the saucepan over medium heat; cook mixture until coconut absorbs all the syrup. This should take about 10 minutes. Constantly stir the mixture to prevent scorching. When done, remove from heat; add vanilla and butter to the hot mixture and blend well.

Cool and use as a filling for Coconut Filled Honeys.

DATE FILLING

1 pound dates, pitted
1 cup granulated sugar
½ cup water
1 tablespoon lemon juice

Chop dates. Combine dates, sugar, water, and lemon juice in a saucepan. Stir and cook all the ingredients until mixture is thick; beat to blend. Cool before spreading on dough.

Use this as a filling for Fruit Fills.

MINCE MEAT FILLING

1 pound mince meat
1 cup granulated sugar
½ cup water
1 tablespoon lemon juice

Break mince meat into small pieces. Combine mince meat with sugar, water, and lemon juice in saucepan. Stir and cook all ingredients until mixture thickens. Beat to blend. Cool before spreading on dough.

Use this recipe as a filling for Fruit Fills.

PEACH FILLING

4 canned cling peach halves
¼ cup brown sugar, packed
⅛ teaspoon salt
1 tablespoon butter or margarine
½ teaspoon almond extract

Finely chop peach halves; add brown sugar and salt. Cook mixture in saucepan over low heat; stir constantly until brown sugar is melted and mixture is thickened slightly. Add butter and almond extract to mixture in saucepan; blend well. Cool.

Use as a filling for Peach Filled Cookies.

PRUNE FILLING

1 pound prunes, pitted
1 cup granulated sugar
½ cup water
1 tablespoon lemon juice

Rinse, drain, and cook prunes. When prunes are cooked, combine them with sugar, water, and lemon juice in a saucepan. Stir and cook all ingredients until mixture becomes thick. Beat to blend. Cool before spreading on dough.

Use this as a filling for Fruit Fills.

FRUIT FILLING

1 pound raisins
1 cup granulated sugar
$\frac{1}{2}$ cup water
1 tablespoon lemon juice

Rinse, drain, and chop raisins. Combine prepared raisins with sugar, water, and lemon juice in a saucepan. Stir and cook all ingredients until mixture thickens. Beat to blend. Cool before spreading on dough.

Use this as a filling for Fruit Fills.

RAISIN FILLING

$\frac{3}{4}$ cup seedless raisins
1 teaspoon orange rind, grated
$\frac{1}{2}$ cup orange juice
$\frac{1}{4}$ cup granulated sugar
$\frac{1}{4}$ cup walnuts, chopped

Rinse and drain raisins. Place drained raisins in saucepan. Add orange rind, orange juice, and sugar to drained raisins; boil slowly until thick. Cool. Stir walnuts into cooked mixture.

Use this filling to fill Raisin Filled Cookies or other plain dough cookies.

RAISIN BONANZA FILLING

1 cup light or dark raisins
$\frac{1}{4}$ cup brown sugar, packed

1 teaspoon cinnamon

2 tablespoons butter or margarine, melted

Combine raisins, brown sugar, cinnamon and melted butter in mixing bowl; blend thoroughly. Drop spoonful of filling into center of rolled square of Raisin Bonanzas.

RAISIN NUT FILLING

$\frac{1}{2}$ cup brown sugar, firmly packed

1 tablespoon butter

3 tablespoons water

$\frac{1}{2}$ cup walnuts, chopped and toasted

$\frac{1}{2}$ cup seeded raisins, chopped

1 to 2 tablespoons cream

Heat brown sugar, butter, and water in skillet; cook over medium heat until mixture forms a soft ball in cold water, or boil to 236°F. Remove skillet from heat; add nuts and raisins. Add cream to the mixture until it is of proper consistency to spread.

Use this filling between Chocolate Icebox Party Cookies to make Cookie Sandwiches.

MOCHA FILLING

2 tablespoons butter

dash salt

1 cup confectioners' sugar, sifted

1 egg white

$\frac{1}{2}$ cup confectioners' sugar, sifted

½ teaspoon vanilla
¾ teaspoon instant coffee
1 teaspoon cocoa

Cream butter. Gradually add salt and 1 cup sifted confectioners' sugar to creamed butter. Add egg white to creamed butter; blend. Add ½ cup sifted confectioners' sugar, vanilla, instant coffee, and cocoa; blend thoroughly. Beat well. Makes about 1 cup of filling.

Use as a filling for Santa's Brownies.

BUTTERSCOTCH FILLING

1 cup butterscotch morsels
1 tablespoon shortening
1 cup nuts, finely chopped
⅓ cup sweetened condensed milk
1 teaspoon vanilla
¼ teaspoon salt

Melt together butterscotch morsels and shortening in top of double boiler over hot (not boiling) water; remove from heat. Add chopped nuts, milk, vanilla, and salt to melted morsels. Stir until well blended.

Use as filling for Crunchy Butterscotch Fudge Bars.

COCOA WHIPPED CREAM FILLING

2 tablespoons cocoa
2 tablespoons granulated sugar
⅛ teaspoon salt
1 cup heavy cream

Mix together cocoa, sugar, and salt. Gradually add cream to the cocoa mixture; stir to keep mixture smooth. Chill 1 hour. After chilled, whip with rotary egg beater until stiff. This recipe makes 2 cups of topping.

Use as a filling for Chocolate Tea Puffs.

CHOCOLATE WALNUT CREAM FILLING

4 to 6 tablespoons granulated sugar
2 tablespoons flour
dash of salt
$\frac{3}{4}$ cup milk
1 one-ounce square unsweetened chocolate
1 tablespoon butter
1 teaspoon vanilla
$\frac{1}{2}$ cup cream, whipped
$\frac{1}{2}$ cup walnuts, chopped

Combine sugar, flour, and salt in top of double boiler; gradually add milk and stir until well blended. Add chocolate and cook over boiling water until thickened; stir constantly.

Continue cooking 5 minutes; stir occasionally. Blend butter and vanilla into mixture. Chill thoroughly. Fold whipped cream and walnuts into chilled mixture. Makes 2 cups of filling.

This filling can be used as a filling for Chocolate Tea Puffs.

MINT FILLING

3 tablespoons butter
1½ cups confectioners' sugar
3 tablespoons milk
4 to 5 drops mint flavoring
  green food coloring

Combine butter, confectioners' sugar, milk, mint flavoring, and food coloring in a large mixing bowl. Beat all ingredients until smooth and creamy.

Use as a filling between Coco-Mints.

SUGAR COOKIE FILLING

½ cup granulated sugar
½ teaspoon salt
1 tablespoon cornstarch
¼ cup cold water
½ cup raisins
1 cup dates, chopped
2 tablespoons lemon rind, grated
1 tablespoon lemon juice
½ cup nuts
  sugar cookie dough*

Combine sugar, salt, and cornstarch in saucepan. Gradually add water into sugar mixture; stir until smooth. Add raisins, dates, and lemon rind; cook to jam like consistency. Remove saucepan from heat; blend lemon juice and nuts into mixture. Cool.

Roll sugar cookie dough to ⅛-inch thickness. Cut with a 2-inch cutter.

Place 1 teaspoon filling in center of cut-out cookie dough. Cover each filled cookie with a plain cut-out cookie, sandwich style. Press edges to seal; sprinkle with granulated sugar.

Place on greased baking sheet. Bake in preheated oven 375° to 400°F. 10 to 12 minutes.

* Can use the recipe for Crisp Sugar Cookies or Mary's Sugar Cookies.

This recipe makes 1½ cups of filling.

WAFER FILLING

    2 tablespoons Pream
    2 tablespoons butter
    1½ cups confectioners' sugar
    1 tablespoon hot water
    1¼ teaspoons almond extract

Measure Pream, butter, confectioners' sugar, hot water, and almond extract into a mixing bowl. Thoroughly blend all ingredients. If desired, tint pink, green, or yellow.

Spread this filling between Rich Pream Wafers.

MERINGUE FILLING

    3 egg whites
    1 teaspoon vanilla
    ¾ cup granulated sugar

$\frac{1}{2}$ cup dry bread crumbs, finely broken
$\frac{1}{4}$ cup nuts, finely chopped, or $\frac{1}{4}$ cup candied fruit

Beat egg whites until they hold a stiff peak. Beat vanilla into egg whites. Gradually add sugar to egg white mixture; continue to beat until meringue is stiff and glossy. Mix crumbs and nuts (or $\frac{1}{4}$ cup candied fruit) together; fold into meringue. This recipe makes enough filling for about 6 dozen cookies.

Use to fill Flaky Meringue Cookies.

bibliography

Austin, Alma H., *The Romance of Candy,* Harper and Brothers, New York, 1938.

Berolzheimer, Ruth (Ed.), *Culinary Arts Institute Encyclopedic Cookbook,* Culinary Arts Institute, Chicago, 1949.

Black, H. C., "Edible Fats and Oils," *Collier's Encyclopedia,* V. 7, Collier & Son Corp., New York, 1956.

Bush, George L., "Sugar," *The World Book Encyclopedia,* V. 15, Field Enterprises Educational Corp., Chicago, 1958.

DeGros, J. H., *Holiday Candy and Cookie Book,* Arco Publishing Co., Inc., New York City, 1954.

Dudik, George F., "Food Industries," *Collier's Encyclopedia,* V. 8, Collier & Son Corp., New York, 1956.

Graubard, Mark, *Man's Food : Its Rhyme or Reason,* The Macmillan Co., New York, 1943.

Jacobs, Morris B., "Food Flavors," *Collier's Encyclopedia,* V. 8, Collier & Son Corp., New York, 1956.

377

Kirk, Dorothy (Ed.), *Woman's Home Companion Cook Book*, P. F. Collier & Son Corp., New York, 1951.

Laklan, Carli, and Frederick-Thomas, *Gifts from Your Kitchen*, M. Barrows & Co., Inc., New York, 1955.

Marsh, Dorothy B. (Ed.), *The Good Housekeeping Cook Book*, Stamford House, New York, 1949.

Rombauer, Irma S., and Becker, Marion Rombauer, *The Joy of Cooking*, The Bobbs-Merrill Co., Inc., Indianapolis, 1952.

Seranne, Anne, *The Complete Book of Home Baking*, Doubleday & Co., Inc., Garden City, 1950.

Snyder, Clara Gebhard, "Flour," *The World Book Encyclopedia*, V. 6, Field Enterprises Educational Corp., Chicago, 1958.

Somers, Lee A., "Sugar Beet," *The World Book Encyclopedia*, V. 15, Field Enterprises Educational Corp., Chicago, 1958.

Sumption, Lois Lintner, and Ashbrook, Marguerite Lintner, *Cookies and More Cookies*, The Manual Arts Press, Peoria, 1948.

Thone, Frank, "Sugar Cane," *The World Book Encyclopedia*, V. 15, Field Enterprises Educational Corp., Chicago, 1958.

Verrill, A. Hyatt, *Perfumes and Spices*, L. C. Co., Boston, 1940.

Von Loesecke, Larry W., *Outlines of Food Technology*, Reinhold Publishing Corp., New York, 1949.

BOOKLETS AND LEAFLETS

"The Accent's on Almonds," U.S. Department of Agriculture, San Francisco, 1959.

"Briefs on Butter," American Butter Institute, Chicago.

"Butter," National Dairy Council, Chicago, 1943.

The California Walnut, Diamond Walnut Growers, Inc., Stockton, 1959.

Chiquita Banana's Cookbook, United Fruit Co., New York, 1959.

"The Chocolate Lovers' Collection," The Nestlé Co., Inc., White Plains, 1959.

"Christmas Goodies Unlimited," Wheat Flour Institute, Chicago, 1958.

The Compleat Cordial Cookery and Cocktail Guide, H. Walker and Sons, Inc., Peoria, 1959.

"Cookie Jar Favorites, Butter Cookies," National Dairy Council, Chicago.

Cooking Adventures with Butter, American Dairy Association, Chicago.

Culinary Capers with ReaLemon Lemon Juice, ReaLemon-Puritan Co., Chicago, 1958.

Delicious New Raisin Recipes, Sun-Maid Growers of California, Kingsburg, 1964.

Food Freezing Facts, Edison Electric Institute, New York, 1954.

"Glorious Eating," The Wesson People, New Orleans.

Golden Book of Sour Cream Recipes, California Dairy Industry Advisory Board, Sacramento, 1956.

Haven, Nancy, "Christmas Foods Designed for Giving," Western Beet Sugar Producers, Inc., Los Angeles, 1957.

————, *Fashions in Frostings,* Western Beet Sugar Producers, Inc., Los Angeles, 1957.

————, "Sugar Tricks with Cookies," Western Beet Sugar Producers, Inc., Los Angeles.

————, *The Way of All Cookies,* Western Beet Sugar Producers, Inc., Los Angeles, 1958.

"Institute Ideas, April–May," Wheat Flour Institute, Chicago, 1958.

"Let's Be Raisin-Able and Create Some Taste Surprises," California Raisin Advisory Board, Fresno.

Logan, Martha, *Our Best Cooky Recipes*, Swift and Co., Chicago, 1955.

————, "Questions and Answers about Jewel Oil," Swift and Co., Chicago, 1955.

————, "Questions and Answers about Swift'ning Shortening," Swift and Co., Chicago, 1959.

————, "Questions and Answers about Swift's Jewel Shortening," Swift and Co., Chicago, 1955.

More Downright Delicious Sun-Maid Raisin Recipes, California Raisin Advisory Board, Fresno.

Morgan, Mary, "Back to School Lunch Box and Cookie Jar Suggestions," Food Basket, San Diego, 1960.

————, "Holiday Cakes, Cookies and Confections," Food Basket, San Diego, 1959.

"Morsels of Interest from the Nestlé's Test Kitchen," V. 12, No. 1; V. 13, No. 1; V. 13, No. 3; V. 14, No. 1, The Nestlé Co., Inc., White Plains, 1958, 1959, 1960, 1961, respectively.

Nestlé's Semi-Sweet Chocolate Kitchen Recipes, The Nestlé Co., Inc., White Plains, 1959.

"Plentiful Foods Monthly List," U.S. Department of Agriculture, San Francisco, November 1958, December 1958, November 1959, January 1960, July 1960; Dallas, January, 1959.

"The Story of Butter," American Butter Institute, Chicago.

To Your Taste . . . Butter, National Dairy Council, Chicago, 1954.

Year 'Round Recipes with ReaLemon, The ReaLemon Co., Chicago, 1965.

Young Ideas in Cooking, American Dairy Association, Chicago, 1959.

21 'None Such' Mince Meat Recipes, The Borden Co., New York, 1952.

index

383

Caramel-Chocolate-Coconut
Chews, 102
Caraway Seeds, 52, 82
Carbohydrates, 32
Cardamon Seed, 52
Carrot Cookies, 259
Carum carvi, 52
Cashews, 59
Cassia, 52–53
Cereal Macaroons, 329
Cherries, 57
Candied, 82
Chews
Caramel-Chocolate-Coconut,
102
Chocolate Coconut, 293
Date Honey, 283
Chewy Coconut Macaroons, 321
Chicken Fat, 37
Chinese Almond Cookies, 340
Chip Cookies
Chocolate (See Chocolate
Chip)
Devil's Food, 128
Honey, 148
Instant, 126
Chippers, Potato, 163
Chips Cookies, Scotch 'N, 156
Chocolate, 62–63
Bars, Pineapple, 290
Bon Bons, 243
Brownies, 299
Honey, 301
Chews
Caramel-Coconut, 102
Coconut, 293
Chip (See Chocolate Chip)
Clusters, Raisin, 123
Cookies
Drop, 117
Frosted, 118
Raisin, 122
Sugar, 121
Frosted, Instant, 343
He-Man, Double, 120
Marble, 224
Meringue, 121
Oatmeal, 134

Party
Coconut, 246
Icebox, 245
Sour Cream, 329
Sugar, 170
Crispies, 296
Coconut, 103
Criss Crosses, 191
Drops
Oat, 134
Raisin, 115
Flavoring, 57
Filling, Walnut Cream, 373
Frosting, 360
Butter, 361
Cream, 361
De Luxe, 359
Quick, 360
Glaze, 362
Melting, 63–64
Munchers, 119
Nuggets, 326
Puffs, 123
Tea, 326
Shots or Bits, 82
Snowballs, 190
Squares, 296
Frosty, 246
Fruit, 297
Nut, 298
Storing, 62–63
Substitute, 62
Yum Yums, 295
Chocolate Chip
Bars
Coconut, 293
Scotch, 294
Cookies, 124
Oatmeal, 125
Drops
Orange, 125
Orange, Milk, 244
Macaroons, 327
Meringues, 258
Choco-Walnut Drops, 127
Christmas
Angels, 347